LUNA

MY&TH
MYSTERY

Kathleen Cain

Johnson Books: Boulder

*This book is dedicated to the spirit and memory
of the late W. G. Gaffney
(professor emeritus, University of Nebraska-Lincoln),
who taught me how to question everything
I thought I knew (and still do).*

Cover and text design by Bob Schram

Front cover photograph courtesy of Gates Planetarium.

Back cover photograph by Scott Monahan. Near Tarbert, County Kerry, Ireland. The author is standing in the doorway of the ruins of the cabin her family was forced to abandon in 1847 during the Great Famine of Ireland.

Library of Congress Cataloging-in-Publication Data

Cain, Kathleen.
    Luna : myth & mystery / Kathleen Cain.
      p. cm.
    Includes bibliographical references and index.
    ISBN 1-55566-070-3
    1. Moon—Mythology. 2. Moon—Religious aspects. I. Title.
BL325.M56C35   1991
398'.362—dc20

91-40571
CIP

Printed in the United States of America by
Johnson Printing
A division of Johnson Publishing Company
1880 South 57th Court
Boulder, Colorado 80301

CONTENTS

◉ Pasiphae and the Minotaur

*T*o understand lunar mythology, which is almost always part of a larger astronomical mythology in any culture, it is helpful to read and think differently. One of the dangers of reading mythology has always been the tendency to do it literally. Why else would it be so frequently dismissed as fantastic, ridiculous, fabulous and silly, and come to have a meaning of simply being untrue, if we did not try to take it literally?

Freud and Jung helped us all see mythology differently. So did James Frazer. So have Mircea Eliade, Joseph Campbell, Esther Harding, Marion Woodman, and a host of others. They have moved us away from a literal interpretation that has bound us to a rigid way of examining mythology and led us toward the world of symbolic language. As successors of Descartes and the ages of Reason and the Enlightenment, we are probably lucky in some respects to even remember what metaphors and similes and symbolic language are, although beyond a textbook definition probably most of us have little opportunity to use the language in that fashion on a daily, practical level. That is not meant to sound condescending; it is simply the truth of our lives.

As an example of reading a myth in a different way, not reading it literally, let us examine one Greek myth differently for a moment, the story of Pasiphae. Who is Pasiphae, you ask. Let me try again. This is also the story of the minotaur, the bull-monster who was half human, half animal. Pasiphae was his mother. She is often overlooked, or simply blamed for what occurred.

I would like to read the myth of Pasiphae and the minotaur as a lunar myth. Are there grounds for doing so? Yes. James Frazer, among others, thought that the story of Pasiphae's mating with a bull and giving birth to the minotaur recounted a religious ritual in which human characters celebrated a "sacred marriage" between the sun and the moon. *The Encyclopedia of Religion* says that the story of Pasiphae is probably a moon myth, and springs from an area where bull worship was present.

First of all, here is the story in its basic form. Of course there are many versions, adaptations, and translations of this myth, as with any myth that has survived so long. What follows is a composite, the story at a general level rather than a scholarly one with all the attendant footnotes and explications (though they should not be ignored for the serious pursuer of mythology).

In Greece King Minos once ruled in Crete. He was married to Pasiphae, whose name meant "She Who Shines On All." Pasiphae became enamored of a bull that Minos owned, known as the Bull of Minos. It was no ordinary animal, but a beautiful white bull that had been a gift from Poseidon, the god of the sea. It was given with the understanding that Minos would in turn sacrifice it to Poseidon. But Minos became too fond of his gift, and refused. In one version, it was said that Poseidon enchanted Pasiphae so that she fell in love with the bull; in another she was not, but was disguised inside the skin of a white cow, in which form the bull mated with her. Pasiphae became pregnant and gave birth to the minotaur, a creature that was half human and half bull. His name was "Asterios." Asterios was banished to the labyrinth below the palace of Minos, where he was kept alone, deprived of either animal or human company. Every nine years, Minos demanded from the Athenians a tribute of seven young men and seven young women, to be sacrificed to Asterios. Eventually the minotaur was destroyed through the efforts of Ariadne and Theseus, but that is another story.

Scholars and mythographers have given this myth loving care and attention by studying it, though many have read it literally and dismissed it as an example of depraved Greek bestiality and let it go at that. Joseph Campbell redeemed Pasiphae's reputation by reading the myth in light of the role and responsibility of Minos, Pasiphae's husband and the king of Crete. But even in that telling, the focus was not on Pasiphae or her lunar qualities. There are plenty of clues within the story itself that suggest we should try reading it as a lunar myth.

Instead of reading this as the story of a human woman, let us try reading it as a story of the moon goddess, who represents the moon. We have good reason to do that. One of Pasiphae's nicknames, "She Who Shines on All," is also a nickname for the moon. So then, instead of a woman falling in love with a bull, we have the moon falling in love with her husband's finest bull. Where her husband is concerned, we should also keep in mind that in many cultures, the husband of the moon was quite often the sun.

Either under enchantment or acting on her own, Pasiphae is disguised inside the skin of a white cow. If this is the story of the moon, it still makes sense, because another way the moon was depicted (in Greek culture and in other cultures in the Mediterranean before and after the Greeks) was as a white cow. Europa and Io are two examples from within Greek culture. So now, instead of the bestiality we have imposed on Pasiphae with our literal interpretation, we have a more ordinary mating between the Celestial Cow (yet another name for the Moon) and a bull, often a figure seen among the stars, and also one that has lunar qualities.

But what of Asterios, Pashiphae's bull-child? A clue to his identity lies in his name as well. It means "starry one," perfect for the offspring of two celestial bodies. When he is brought to earth, perhaps through generations of storytelling, or the deterioration of religious ritual, which is the basis of much Greek mythology, he becomes the familiar half-human, half-animal monster, again a literal interpretation. He is like the moon calf that will emerge in later ages, thought to be the offspring of women who mated with the moon, ill-formed fetuses that rarely lived long. The son of the moon, he is banished to the underground labyrinth, to the dark world, hidden from view, much like the moon itself in its dark, mysterious phase, often associated with death and sometimes evil. Does he in fact represent the dark of the moon, much in the way that Hekate completes the symbolic triad of the moon in the company of Persephone and Demeter? Of such a grotesque nature, he is feared. Sacrifices are made to him. He devours human children. Again, if we try to read behind the obvious words a little, what we may have is the story of a ritual sacrifice made to the Greek deities, perhaps in honor or fear of the dark of the moon.

A C K N O W L E D G M E N T S

I would like to recognize the following people who have helped this book become a reality: Kim Long of *The American Forecaster* and *The Moon Book*, for his original idea, patience, kindness, practical advice, sense of humor, and for being the "Lamaze coach" for Luna's birth; Tom Auer and Marilyn Auer of *The Bloomsbury Review* and Pat Wagner of the *Open Network* for unflagging belief, often when I didn't believe myself; David Guerrero, who was a warrior for the Colorado Council on the Arts and Humanities' individual artists' program; the entire Cain clan—Helen and Jerome, Kellie, Dan, Kathy, Adam, and Sean (the younger), Sean, Dot, and Ahsha, Keenan, Peg, Dillon, and Elliot—for their enthusiasm and encouragement and for the sources, ideas, and information they helped track down; the editor Rebecca Herr, who has given generously of her time, advice, and knowledge, particularly of Mayan beliefs about the moon; Peg Murphy, who never let the supply of chocolate chip cookies or optimism get low; the late Lorenzo Cruz, for his generous sharing of knowledge about Aztec and Maya lunar beliefs and his loving friendship; Sean, Kim, and Sara O'Connor for friendship, good food, and normalcy; Mark Boyko, Moira Edwards, Maggie Manuele, Mary Casper, and so many other coworkers for constant encouragement and the ability to see beyond the immediate; Marilyn Auer, Mary Carhartt, Jean Fortier, and Kim Long for reading and commenting on the manuscript; my women's support group for their faith, hope, and love; Mike Montag for enthusiastically sharing his computer expertise and encouraging me to try new ideas which made the task easier; John Willenbecher and Alex Martin for their generosity; Laurens van der Post for good advice; Prem of Mysterium Visionary Music/Art in Boulder for help in compiling a list of "moon music" tapes; Dave Heineman of North Denver video for help in compiling a list of movies about the moon; Italian Bakery and Pastries of North Denver for keeping me supplied with loaves of moon bread; Night Noise and Enya for the best music to write a moon book by; and finally, Luna herself, who constantly peeked in through the window at different times of the night and day to see how things were going.

Acknowledgment is made for permission to reprint the following works:

"Autumn" by Jeanne Shannon, reprinted by permission of the author.

"Bomber's Moon: New York, 1944" by Betty Chancellor, reprinted by permission of the author.

"Circled by Moons" by Lois Hayna was first published in *Never Trust a Crow* (James Andrews & Co., Inc., 1990). Reprinted by permission of the author.

"The Crescent Moon" by Mei Yao Ch'en, translated by Kenneth Rexroth. Reprinted by permission of New Directions Publishing.

"Hymn to Selene" and "Selene and Endymion," translated by Gregory McNamee, reprinted by permission of the author.

"Lune Concrete" by Raymond Federman first appeared in *ADAM* (International Review) edited by Miron Grindea, Nos. 334-336, 1969, reprinted by permission of the author.

Mock Moon Cake recipe by Rhoda Yee, reprinted by permission of the author.

"The New Moon" from *Carmina Gadelica* by Alexander Carmichael reprinted by permission of the Scottish Acadmic Press Limited.

"Orbit" by Paul Dilsaver, reprinted by permission of the author.

"Sumi-e" drawings and three haiku poems by Ann Newell first appeared in *Moon Puddles* (Bread and Butter Press, 1991). Reprinted by permission of the author.

"Walking Off a Night of Drinking in Early Spring (for Joe Nigg)" by Joe Hutchison first appeared in *Crossing the River: Poets of the Western United States* (Permanent Press, 1987). Reprinted by permission of the author.

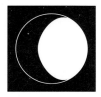

INTRODUCTION

*T*he original purpose of writing *Luna: Myth and Mystery* was to provide a mythological handmaiden for *The Moon Book* (Johnson Books, 1988) written by Kim Long. His is a sensible straightforward guide, meant to explore "the meaning of the methodical movements of the magnificent, mysterious moon and other interesting facts about the earth's nearest neighbor." *Luna* was, in fact, his idea. When suggestions arose as to who might be the person to write this book, *Luna* came to me.

I had been preparing the ground for longer than I knew. My own particular area of interest lies with Celtic mythology, literature, and folklore, to which I have devoted years of reading, study, and travel. I have followed with a hound's determination the work that the new scholarship on women continues to unravel about lunar wisdom. Likewise, I love following the trail of antiquarians and folklorists from other centuries and countries. Being an independent researcher with more than fifteen years' experience in the reference department of a college library provided the perfect background for one aspect of the work. My curiosity about how other worlds and other times relate to this one also served me well. *Luna* brought together all those curiosities and possibilities in one project.

Luna is more than slightly ambitious. Its aim is to examine how people throughout the world, at different times and places, have viewed the moon through mythology, folklore, legends, stories, poems, and customs. I have chosen to follow the definitions that Stith Thompson, who compiled the major motif-index for folklore, used. Mythology then is the account of the activities of deities. Legend denotes the history of a local or regional person, place, or object. Folklore encompasses the practices, beliefs, and customs followed by ordinary people, often based upon mythology and legend.

Myth and story, song and poem, folklore and custom are all ways that humans have recorded their fascination with the moon. Though these means of transmitting culture are sometimes viewed with skepticism, as Joseph Campbell has pointed out, mythology is not a denial of the truth, but rather a metaphor for it. The secret is in understanding what the metaphor is, and thus the truth behind the myth.

Luna: Myth and Mystery concentrates on the way people in different cultures all over the world have viewed the moon through their myths, legends, stories, folk traditions, poems, songs, and customs; and how those cultural elements may have been continued in current practice. In the modern, technological way of looking at the world, we tend to assume that all those old wives' tales and superstitions were something that belonged to a bygone era. In many cases we assume that they were either worthless or next to it. But, as a nurse who teaches, writes, and researches in the area of critical care medicine says, "wherever there are old wives' tales or folk customs about medicine, you'd better track them back, because something's there." She is right. Perhaps these beliefs should be called "wise tales," as many beliefs about the moon held by cultures in the past reflect an understanding of the moon and its importance in ways that can be helpful today.

Why a book on the mythology, legend, and folklore of the moon? For one thing, most major nonscientific works about the moon predate the Apollo Space Program. I was determined to have a context for the older material, but curious to see what might exist in our own time. For another, even contemporary lunar lore is scattered through the annals of anthropology, folklore, religion, and modern psychology. In both cases, the sources were rich ones from which to gather. Without them there would be no present book. For example, I found Mircea Eliade's chapter from *Patterns in Comparative Religion* entitled "The Moon and Its Mystique" to be a touchstone for the writing of *Luna*. I returned to it often for inspiration and clarification.

Exploring the ways that people in different cultures have viewed the moon shows how reverence, awe, and even fear played into the way they incorporated the natural world into their daily lives and rituals. Their attitudes and ideas developed from direct observation. The moon was as much a participant in their lives as other members of their families were, or their tribes, or their nations. It was more than an abstract object floating through the sky; more than a beautiful sight to be admired from the hilltop or the plain.

Precisely how people observed the moon is important, too. They did not all see the same thing when they looked up into the night sky. The physical view offers a frame of reference for mythological observation and provides clues to how people thought and how they viewed themselves in relation to their world and their universe. Understanding the vantage point is always necessary when considering the lunar myths, legends, and stories of any group of people. For example, Babylonian and Sumerian sky watchers followed an ecliptic or zodiac-based system. The ecliptic is an imaginary circle that traces the path the sun appears to follow through the sky. The zodiac, familiar to us from astrology, has been designed by the human imagination, too, a group of twelve constellations that resemble animals and mythical figures, through which the moon and sun and planets appear to move. Planetary movements through the zodiac were crucial to Chinese observation. Native Americans and ancient northern Europeans alike both used horizon points to mark lunar movements.

It is impossible to find a culture that does not have some fascination with the moon, that does not have some myth, legend, story, song, poem, or tradition that links the moon with human life. The mysterious moon has been watched by humans as it wandered through the sky before either writing or language existed.

In cultures throughout the world, special sites that helped mark or count the passage of the sun's movements were significant. Most scholars agree that as agriculture became more developed and more important to human existence, the awareness of solar cycles and activity became increasingly important, too. Being able to follow the seasons and learn when to plant and harvest became essential for survival. It seems clear that as agriculture developed, so did society; being able to establish a definite, reliable civil and social calendar became equally important. But without exception, following the lead of Robert Briffault's study of lunar calendars in *The Mothers*, scholars seem to agree that long before the solar days were marked and kept, humans looked to the movements of the moon to guide and regulate their lives.

For many of us the moon has become a symbol. It can still be found on the flags of fourteen nations. Its image has long appeared on coins. To this day it remains an emblem of romance, intrigue, mystery, and enchantment. But for ancient people it was more than that. It was tied to the reality of their daily lives. They believed that it caused the fertility of fields, of the earth, of animals and humans, that it influenced the weather. Its appearance or disappearance was believed to presage disaster or good fortune.

It was a guide for their lives. As the mythographer Mircea Eliade has proposed, it was by watching the moon that ancient people may have learned the first lessons of the cyclical nature of life. By paying attention to the moon they learned how to watch on earth for all that changes, all that dies and is reborn, all that comes and goes, ebbs and flows, and eventually comes back to itself. They learned the division and fluctuation of time, days and nights as well as the larger cycles of other heavenly bodies. They learned to predict the eclipses that frightened them. They learned to understand the motions of stars and planets, of the sun. They learned the association between the cycles of the moon and the cycles of women, between the journey of the moon and the tides of the ocean. As Eliade quotes from Eduard Seler, the moon may have been the first creation to be seen dying and then three days later rising from the dead. This image of death and resurrection is now most often associated with the Christian deity in the figure of Jesus, but the archetype predates Christianity or any of the other major religions.

The purpose of *Luna* is to try to gain a better understanding of how ancient peoples perceived the moon, without trying to label them according to whatever religious persuasions exist these hundreds and thousands of years later. Another purpose is to enjoy and even savor the delightful stories and tales the ancients created in order to understand and explain their own lives and the life of that mysterious and shining orb which, even though it went away, always came back to them.

We still watch the moon. We may not know as much about its
stories and lore as we once did, except for the obvious ones from
nursery rhymes and fairy tales. As urban dwellers we are less likely
to know even what phase the moon is in. Bright lights, big cities,
tall buildings, pollution, and busy lives force us to depend on calendars and watches instead of natural timepieces that hang in the sky.
But we do still watch the moon and talk about it. Something about
the moon still gets to us.

Simply understanding the moon through books and scientific
theories is not enough. Watching is important. Perhaps through
observation, both naked-eye and with the aid of telescopes and
other sophisticated mechanical methods, a renewed sense of awe
can bring a better understanding of how ancient people felt (and
how plenty of contemporary people still feel) by watching, night
after night, the moon above them, steady in its course. Ironically,
one of the most common modern ways to observe the moon is to
take a quick look at our moon watches to see what phase the moon

is in, rather than glancing up at the sky. In our own way, we have brought the Moon to Earth!

The number of creation myths involving the moon are as plentiful, illuminating, and ever-changing as the moon itself, and readers are encouraged to seek out others and share in the richness they provide about the development of the human mind and the human spirit.

With the "Green" movement in full bloom around us, with the danger of the greenhouse effect looming larger all the time, with the fearsome poisons we have created and used without fully knowing how they will affect all the life on Earth, perhaps a look at how our ancestors viewed the moon and their relationship to it can provide some guidance and direction in restoring understanding to our own lives. At the least, these traditions about the moon should be thought-provoking and entertaining. At the most, like Luna herself, perhaps they will allure, enchant, and guide.

While *Luna* is not a scholarly work, perhaps it can be a bridge to the work of scholars whose efforts have proved the deep and basic meanings the moon has had for human life. Though it was extremely important to me to make sure that *Luna* stood on solid scholarly ground, my aim is to allure, enchant, and guide general readers to a different view of the moon—one that provides an overview of human experience but has some context for modern life—and to have a little fun as well. I would consider it the highest compliment to know that something in *Luna* led a reader to pursue another source. Doubtless there are some sources, some myths or legends I have left out, some piece I do not know about yet. I would be the first to admit it, and to whine a little that the limitations of time and space begin to have their own lives in a publishing project. I would also be the first to ask for the source or the reference so I could include it next time.

THE MYSTERIOUS GUIDE

"Moonlight is the best restorer of antiquity."
–H.D. Thoreau

FOR A MOMENT, imagine yourself not as a dweller in the twentieth century, but as an inhabitant of a far distant time. Count backwards and let the centuries slip by—twenty, nineteen, eighteen, seventeen, sixteen, fifteen, fourteen, thirteen, twelve, eleven. Then make the familiar countdown heard so often during the space age as the test flights led one after another to the momentous occasion when humans aimed for the moon— but remember, these are centuries. Ten, nine, eight, seven, six, five, four, three, two, one. Keep going for another thousand years. Two thousand. Three. Four. Five. Six. Stop.

The world is much quieter now. The sound of thunder and the streaks of lightning and storm coming nearer will alarm you, as will any unexpected noise from the heavens or the earth. Tonight you have come to sit near the lake at Ishango in Africa. You have brought with you the bone of an animal you killed. You have been marking this bone yourself, keeping close at hand what you see in the sky. As the bright light of the sun steps down to the horizon, a smaller light emerges and begins to climb through the sky. You can make the same shape, first with your right hand, and then with your left, in half circle motions, and follow it as it comes and goes, marking its increase and then its decrease, until it disappears and leaves you in the darkness once again. You can make the same shape on the bone. Tonight you carve one mark. Tomorrow night you will carve another. For every night and day you can see the silver light emerge, you make a mark. Whether you are a man or a woman, you mark the bone for your own reasons. Maybe you are keeping track of a good time for the animals to come. Maybe you are keeping track of your own time and the moon's. Perhaps you are just curious.

Though you did not deliberately leave the bone behind for others to find, they did find it. Nearly eight thousand years later, a man named Alexander Marshack studied the markings you made in a different way. While working on a book about the Apollo Moon mission, Marshack was shown your piece of engraved bone from Lake Ishango in the African Congo. His scientific curiosity aroused, he abandoned the moon book project and spent the next several years examining thousands of bone and stone fragments that dated to the Paleolithic Age and beyond. Microscopic examinations led him to believe that the engravings were not whimsical scratches or artistic decorations, but were in fact notations made to mark the passage of the moon through the sky.

Humans have been innately curious about our surroundings at every period in history. And we have always taken some action to show our curiosity: to carve a piece of stone or bone, to tell a story or create a myth, to draw and paint and carve on cave walls, on hides and shells and stones, on whatever we could find to suit our purpose. We have observed and encountered and participated in our world since the beginning of time. One object that has held our fascination unceasingly is the moon. We are drawn to it the same way it is drawn to its orbit around the earth—always changing, yet always the same.

We do not know what myth or story the Ishango carver might have told about the moon, what folklore or custom was held fast in regard to the lunar orb. We do know that many moon myths survive in Africa. They have come down through oral traditions for thousands of years. No one is certain when spoken language first developed. Anthropologists and linguists still wrestle with the question. Some evidence indicates that the creature we call Australopithecus, who lived on earth nearly two million years ago, may have used gestures to communicate. Later on, Homo erectus, the upright human being, living some two to three hundred thousand years ago, may have been the first human communicator, perhaps the first storyteller to use words instead of signs to tell a tale. Some students of humanity, like the explorer Laurens van der Post, believe that tales of the Bushmen of Africa may take us back in storytelling, myth-making time, as far as we are likely to go. Even among some tribal peoples today the stories endure, sometimes taking new shape and form as they pass through the generations. Author Alex Haley found out about the durability of oral tradition when he went in search of his ancestral African roots and had to wait three days until the tribal historian and genealogist came to that part of the account which mentioned Haley's own people, since the story was told in histori-

cal, chronological order, the way it was developed and passed on.

Without meaning to imply that one grew from another, there is an interesting parallel that seems worth scrutinizing, between the view presented on the Ishango artifact (if we accept Marshack's suggestion that it is a lunar notation) and a lunar tale of the Bushmen described by Laurens van der Post. The creator god among the Bushmen was a praying mantis, called in the Bushman language *!kaggen*, who walked beneath the desert sky at night in the darkness. To help out the world and humanity, one night !kaggen took off his shoe and threw it up into the sky. By doing this he created the moon, which became known as "!kaggen's shoe." To the Bushmen the moon waxing and waning in its path became the sign of !kaggen's footprint walking across heaven. What better symbol to record the movement of the moon, whether in story or on a piece of stone or bone, than the god's footprints?

◐ *Different Views of the Moon*

From Africa, we move to another part of the world and another time, where ancient human eyes were also steadfastly intent upon the skies. This time, the night is clear among the hills and valleys of Mesopotamia, barely disturbed by a thin layer of clouds in the sky. Enheduanna waits. Perhaps the name of the daughter of King Sargon, perhaps a special title given to the priestess of the moon god, this word has been found on ancient monuments and records of Ur, a city dedicated to the moon god Nanna-Sin and restored after its destruction by a king named Nabonidus. A priest on a nearby hill, when he sees what he wants in the sky, records the observation, as the priests had done for hundreds of years previously during the time of the Akkadians, then the Chaldeans, the Sumerians, and the Babylonians. He sends a messenger to inform the king that all is well. The moon god Nanna-Sin, the god of wisdom and light, has appeared in his small crescent boat once again and started to make his way across the sky. The month can begin. The danger of the dark time and the fear that Nanna-Sin will not return can be put aside once more. The celebration can begin, by shouting and singing for joy, for the country has been released from the fear and the darkness once more.

The tradition of looking to the moon god Sin and watching his every movement in the sky was old by the time it reached the Sumerian people. It was prevalent among the Chaldeans, a much older people whose gods were local deities: each city had its own. George Smith, in describing the Chaldean version of Genesis (which predates the Biblical version), tells us that Sin was also called Acu and Agu from Akkadian times, names that meant the "Lord of Crowns" and the "Maker of Brightness." He was one of a pantheon of twelve gods, which included the goddess Belat, wife of Bel, and Ishtar (called Gingir in Akkadian and better known as Ishtar), both of whom were both much older than he. Smith offers a way to better understand the different names and aspects of the gods and goddesses that sometimes seem confusing as we begin to sift through the records of the past. The notion of many gods instead of one God is still foreign to many people. But it was the norm in the religious development of all cultures. In addition, as religion began to take on a state as opposed to a local character, local gods and goddesses became state deities. Both their stories and their identities became mixed. Thus, in one city the goddess Ishtar was found to be associated with Venus, the morning star; in another, with the evening star; in still another, she is the daughter of Sin, the moon god.

Likewise, the Sumerians had a far different view of god, heaven, and the moon than we do. In order to appreciate and understand their views, we must put aside our twentieth-century ways of understanding even basic astronomy,

religion, and culture, and use both our imagination and our empathy to understand the way these early people viewed their physical and spiritual surroundings. The adage "as above, so below," which comes to us from the religious and philosophical traditions of the Far East, can guide us toward understanding Sumerian cosmology. In addition to the other names mentioned above, the Sumerian moon god was also known as Nanna (sometimes Nannar) as well as Sin, which most scholars believe to be a word of Semitic origin. We can see the moon god's name in the name of Mt. Sinai, known long before the time of Moses as the "Mountain of the Moon" and, like the Sinai Desert, named for this lunar deity.

Nanna-Sin was not chief among the gods. In fact, he belonged to the second threesome of gods that represented the forces of nature. The other members of this triad included An-Ki, whose name has been deciphered as meaning "heaven-earth"; and Enlil, who assumed supremacy over the Sumerian pantheon, and whose name refers to breath, wind, air, and spirit. Nanna-Sin was prominent within this group, though, always described as the father of Inanna (known also as Ishtar, she personified the planet Venus before she became so closely associated with the moon that today she is unhesitatingly described as a lunar goddess) and of Shamash (Utu), the sun god. In family history, this gives us a clue to the early importance of lunar awareness—if Shamash the sun god is the son of the moon, then the moon is the older deity. Sin, who was perhaps the first "Man in the Moon," and Ishtar, who superseded him in the heavens, will be discussed in later chapters.

To ancient minds, the stories of Sumerian and Babylonian gods paralleled human existence. The comparison was obvious. Consider how Nanna-Sin came into existence. Samuel Noah Kramer, one of the foremost Assyro-Babylonian scholars, brought this story forward for modern readers. Following her mother's instructions, the beautiful goddess Ninlil went bathing in a stream where Enlil, the chief god, was bound to see her. Not only did he see her,

University Museum, University of Pennsylvania

Line drawing of seal impression. Seated goddess with crescent moon above her right hand with two figures presenting offerings.

he raped her. The other gods hated what Enlil had done and sent him to the underworld as punishment for the harm he had done. Ninlil, however, followed him. Her action upset Enlil, since it meant that their child, who they knew would be the moon god Sin, would be born in the darkness of the underworld when he was meant to illumine the night sky. And so here the moon is born in violence and darkness, two qualities that frequently accompany lunar stories wherever they are told. Based on this account, it is no wonder the Babylonians and Sumerians were fearful when the moon left them in darkness. Likewise, the story is a way of relating the moon's travels as observed by the naked eye, into and out of the darkness.

The cardinal rule of the underworld was that no one who entered could leave without providing a replacement; the offspring of a god and a goddess was no exception. Knowing this, Enlil disguised himself and once again impregnated Ninlil, this time producing three beings who served as replacements for the newborn moon god, Nanna-Sin, who then assumed his rightful place in the sky.

In discussing these astronomical tales, the physical vantage point from earth is important to keep in mind. Astronomy is the scientific and mathematical study of matter that exists beyond earth. It has the advantage of powerful equipment and advances in human thinking that have unfolded scientific theory and method, although many today feel we are out of balance in our approach, having become perhaps too scientific and too theoretical at the expense of some of our other equally important human qualities— such as intuition, compassion, and feeling—that might serve to balance the rationality, judgment, and logic of science.

But to return to the older moon watchers, how has the knowledge of

Mesopotamian representations of the moon and sun.

their observation been preserved? Or is it dead and gone, just as the moon is sometimes now dismissed as nothing more than a hunk of dead rock staring sightless from the sky? If our space-age exploration has given us new scientific and historic information about the moon, what about the knowledge and lore passed along to us through untold previous generations? This lore, as it turns out, is very much alive. Scattered through the annals of anthropology, history, religion, folklore, literature, art, and oral tradition, it is there for us to recover and savor as we go forward at this very moment, trying to understand our world a little better.

In the ancient world, the definition and purpose of astronomy were not the same as they are today. As James Cornell, a noted archaeo-astronomer, makes clear, in the ancient world the astronomical systems of the Babylonians and Egyptians, the megalith builders of western Europe, and the pyramid builders of Meso-america were all developed to predict the time of evil influences and to avoid them. The method of observation was with the naked eye. The process took a great deal of time and constant attention of a different sort than that currently demanded by research assisted by machines and equipment. Instead of mathematically predicting the new moon based on scientific knowledge of the lunar and earth orbits, the month began when the moon was actually sighted by those whose job was to watch for it. This created the possibility of error; one cloudy night could be enough to throw the observation off, something that would not happen in a mathematical system of observation. Practically speaking, being off a little was not much of a problem, and reality was simply adjusted to fit.

In China the observation system was based on the reference point of the pole star. In ancient Scotland and other places throughout the British Isles and megalithic Europe, such people as Alexander Thom and Gerald Hawkins have found that observations were made by using points on the horizon to keep track of the moon's movements. As Cornell mentions, a similar system has been found on the North American continent among some Native American observers. In Central and South America, however, we find cultures using the zenith, the

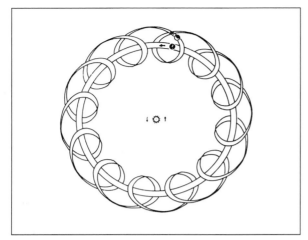

Fig. 1. One year

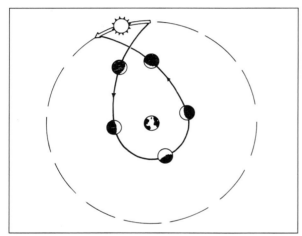

Fig. 2. One month.

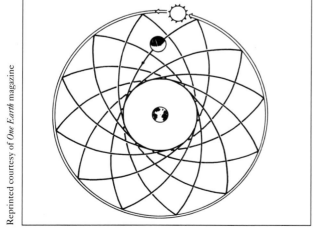

Fig. 3. Twelve months.

Orbits of the moon, earth, and sun.

imaginary point directly above a given location, as the frame of reference. In a more recent and different look at the moon, writer Ian Turnbull described the motions of Moon, Earth, and Sun in their monthly and annual patterns that almost describe mandala patterns instead of the circular, straight-line planes we have been used to seeing from school days onward (see illustrations). Turnbull depicts the moon in an elliptical orbit around the earth, a closer match with reality than the perfect circle the Greeks were so enchanted with, and which we absentmindedly continue to use. Though his illustrations of the ribbon-like weaving of the moon's movements around the earth are intended to be more esoteric than scientific, he proves the importance of understanding a different view, of seeing from a different angle. As the Apollo astronauts helped us all discover, how you see something can have a powerful effect on the way you proceed in the world.

The figures in such sources as Mayan codices and other written or printed records provide a clue that instruments used to observe the sky did exist. Pairs of crossed sticks are often shown in the scenes that identify astronomers. These would have been used as observational markers, as sighting sticks, a method still used in rudimentary sighting and surveying today. Conversely, in the Old World, quite often instruments are found but no structures remain. Galileo first observed the moon through a telescope in either 1609 or 1610.

Francis Graham, president of the American Lunar Society and editor of the society's quarterly publication *Selenology*, has discussed the possibility of another instrument used for ancient observation. Graham cites evidence from Pompeii that glass globes filled with water could have been used as an early form of magnifying glass. Placed over written text, the globe enlarges the printed words. In the 1800s a Harmonite community in Pennsylvania used such globes as lenses. Graham explored this idea, wondering if older cultures might have constructed a "telescope" by pairing and aligning globes to observe the moon and other planets and stars. He constructed such a device, and though he points out that such construction does not necessarily mean it was used for lunar observation in human history, it could have been so used. He also reiterates that no such device has been found, but feels that some of Plutarch's observations of the shadows of the moon were impossible without some visual aid beyond the naked eye. After all, consistent observation of the moon is not that difficult. It may only seem so to us (true astronomical observation aside) because observing the moon has become a pleasurable pastime rather than a necessity.

The search has not ended for the discovery or uncovering of possible astronomical instruments humans may have used in the past; or for their observational sites, either. Another apparently fine place for Old World viewing of the night sky was the rocky jagged landscape in northern Scotland, filled with notches and valleys that still provide good places to mark the rising and setting points of the moon. Did the ancients who lived here take advantage of these outcroppings and use them to gauge the moon's passage through the sky, and by doing so find a way to gauge the passage of their own lives? At least two people believed they did. Scotsmen Alexander Thom and his son Archie studied the megalithic sites of Scotland. Their observations and calculations led them to entertain the possibility that at Callanish, on the Isle of Lewis in the Outer Hebrides off the coast of Scotland, the people who dwelt there some five thousand years ago used the standing stones to measure and determine the moon's passage.

One important event that most likely captured the attention of the ancients in northern Scotland (and other observers in the northern latitudes, too) at the time of the midwinter rising would have been the "midnight moon," as spectacular as the better-known "midnight sun." At this time of year (winter in the northern hemisphere) the moon, rather than rising high in the sky and setting, would merely have brushed the horizon in its passing. Stories from even farther north, in Siberia, tell of an ominous man-in-the-moon figure who descended to earth. Given the physical movement of the moon at this time of year, the story seems a natural development, the moon peering like a great and powerful eye or presence on the horizon.

Even the Egyptians, whose name to us is still synonymous with "sun worship," in their earlier history looked to the moon. Inscriptions found on the temple of Dendera record the phases of the moon. Individual names for the thirty days of the month, a tradition of day naming found in many places throughout the world, are given there as well. These lists may be as old as the Eighteenth or Nineteenth dynasties, and there was evidence of them in Ptolemaic and Roman times. Among other names, the Egyptians also called the full moon "the eye of the moon." Briffault points out that they believed the rising of the Nile and the resulting fertility of the land were connected to the moon. As we shall see in Chapter Six, there were several older moon goddesses and gods lurking in the shadows cast by the later sun gods.

Lunar observation seems to have been significant at certain times of the year, just as solar observation eventually came to be. The midwinter rising of the full moon may have had as much significance as the winter

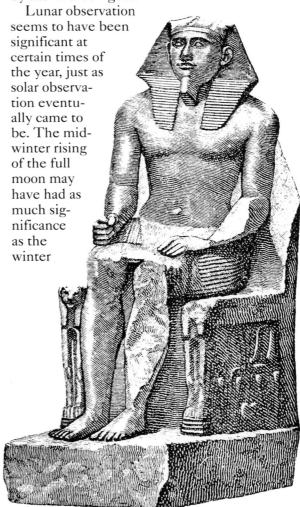

ᴡᴏRDS FOR THE MOON

Aah (Egypt)
Arma (Hittite); means "big, pregnant"
Aku (Akkadian)
Amawas (India); means "last day of the moon"
Auchimalgen (Chile)
Cabar (Saracen); means "The Great"
Citatli (Aztec)
Ganumi (British New Guinea); synonymous
  with nanamud, the word for menstrual blood
Gaus (Sanskrit); means cow
Gizis (Native American)
Gounja (Hottentot)
Khaldi (Armenian)
Mami (Sanskrit); means "I measure"
Mas (root word for English); means
  "to measure"
Men (Anatolia)
Men Ouranios (Anatolia); means
  "Lord of the Sky"
Menes (Latvia)
Menothryanas (Anatolia); means
  "Lord of the Moon"
Mens (Aryan)
Menu (Lithuania)
Metzli (Aztec)
Mh (Egypt)
Mityan (Australian); also name for a cat
Mona (Anglo-Saxon, Celtic, Teutonic)
Mwei (Africa)
Mwuetsi (Africa)
Nanibonsak (Abenaki)
Paravans (India); new moon and full moon
Pe (African Pygmy)
Sasanka (Sanskrit): means "having the
  marks of a hare"
Sasin or Sasanka (India); means, hare mark,
  or hare spot
Shing Moo (China); means Holy Mother,
  Perfect Intelligence
Soma (India); means healer and owner of
  women
Tetevinan (Mexico); Mother of God
Yarih (Canaan)

- *Among North American Algonquin tribes, the word for moon and water was the same.*

- *In Peru during pre-Columbian times, the same word was used for moon, sea, and woman.*

solstice would come to have. At midwinter the lunar disc reaches its farthest point north in the sky. The moon's position would have certainly been observed. How can we say that? Well, we know attention was directed to celestial activities at that time of year—as evidenced by some of the great sites, such as New Grange in Ireland or Stonehenge in England. For example, astronomer Gerald Hawkins proposed new ideas about Stonehenge after completing computerized calculations on alignments there. He believes the site to be associated with the midwinter solstice and midwinter moonrise, one of fourteen possible lunar alignments. The accounts of Babylonian, Sumerian, and Egyptian observers indicate that there were continuing efforts to observe and interpret the movements in the sky during all times of the year in those cultures as well.

As observation of the winter solstice would have revealed the regularity of the sun's apparent movements through the sky, Evan Hadingham noted that constant observation of the midwinter moonrise would have revealed another predictable time period. The Saros Cycle repeats every 18 years and 11 days and eight hours. The Saros Cycle represents the amount of time it takes the Moon, Sun, and Earth to return to the same positions relative to each other. It was a simple (though time consuming), Old-World method of predicting eclipses. The Babylonians knew about it. So did other older cultures. Though modern people might believe this cycle too long and complicated for less technically developed people to understand, perhaps that is only because such observation is no longer deemed necessary. But for people who believed the activities of sky beings, eclipses in particular, determined the outcome of events on earth, it was critical to constantly watch, record, and report all celestial events.

Another long-term lunar cycle (which is easily confused with the Saros Cycle) is the Metonic Cycle, named for the Greek astronomer Meton, who observed it in the fourth century B.C.E. It consists of 235 lunar months, or nineteen years. At the completion of a Metonic Cycle, the phases of the moon occur on the same day of the solar year. Older sources say it was not an idea widely accepted by the Greeks, but newer scholarship questions this assumption; a gear assembly discovered by sponge divers in 1900 near the Greek island of Antikythera, and which dates to 87 B.C.E., may have been used to measure the Metonic Cycle. *The Encyclopedia of Religions* mentions evidence of the cycle's use in other places throughout the Old World. Druidic lore refers to this cycle of time, and the number nineteen was important to the Druids.

Confirming the knowledge of the Saros Cycle in another way, folklorists recorded early in the twentieth century that farmers in southwestern Ireland used the word *Duibhre* to indicate the time every eighteen or nineteen years that the moon does not rise above the nearby mountains. Contemporary researchers Hawkins and Cornell believe that the Metonic Cycle may have been observed or predicted at Stonehenge, an idea based on the computer calculations made by Hawkins. It may have been mentioned much earlier, however, by the classical writer Diodorus Siculus, who described how the "Hyperboreans" had a special "temple to Apollo" in the northern climes, a place that the god was known to visit every nineteen years. Though Apollo's reputation as a sun god endures, much research indicates (as with the Egyptian sun gods) an earlier lunar lineage for this lord of light. Diodorus connected moon worship with this famous temple, which many suspect describes Stonehenge. Interpreting "visit" in a metaphorical way, the meaning might just as clearly refer to the reappearance of the moon in its same phase once again after a long time.

While the scholar Aubrey Burl believed that such sites as Callanish may have been used to observe the path of the extremes of the moon's orbit in the sky, following the Metonic Cycle, there is other evidence that megalithic sites in northern Scotland may have been used not as lunar observatories, but as ceremonial sites or shrines. The nature of the sites themselves provided scholars with a natural clue. The locations seem too small for true astronomical observation, and the view from inside the chambers too limited. What does seem likely is that people gathered at these sites to celebrate special risings and settings of the moon, and that the moon was an important part of their spiritual beliefs. What leads scholars to this idea is often the alignment of sites to the moon's position in the sky at certain times, which is easy enough to determine, after all. Archaeologists have found that more than eighty sites studied in Scotland reveal a striking pattern. Recumbent stones—large stones that lie flat on the ground—are almost always present, most often oriented between the south and southwest points on a compass. Standing stones at a site are usually arranged in a way that shows a gradual increase in the height of each stone as it nears the recumbent, an arrangement which might indicate they were used for measuring. Fragments of bone (most notably the skulls of infants) as well as white quartz and pieces of pottery and jewelry have been found at the sites, though they are not strictly burial sites. These remnants and fragments could seem to indicate a ritual purpose for the sites rather than use as a lunar observatory, although observation of the moon may have been part of such rituals.

It is impossible to know for certain what the ancient inhabitants of Scotland believed about the moon. Starting with what is known and using it to help unravel what is unknown can help to retrieve and understand the past, however. Genealogists use such a technique, starting with as little information as a name or a date, using the smallest source to lead back to a record, another source, more information. Several people have provided a window to the past when it comes to lunar beliefs among the Scots and consideration of the remnants that have survived the development of contemporary society. Among them is Alexander Carmichael, who collected songs, poems, stories, and folklore among Scottish Highlanders and islanders during the late nineteenth and early twentieth centuries. He published the results in two collections known as the *Silva Gadelica* and the *Carmina Gadelica*. These works and others like them provide insight into the lunar beliefs of the past. Some of the customs about the moon that have survived from the areas surrounding Callanish and other sites in Scotland may be remnants from quite ancient times.

While Alexander Thom argued that megalithic Scottish sites at Kintraw, Clava, and Callanish could have served as lunar observatories, other evidence points to the possibility that they were lunar shrines and ceremonial locations. For instance, Thom reported that in a burial cairn (a deliberately built mound of stones) at Kintraw, a false doorway or gateway seems to be aligned to the moonrise. This may reflect a Celtic belief that the dead watched the path of the moon through the sky, an idea parallel to the suggestion that the rays of the winter solstice sunlight brought rebirth or regeneration inside the burial chamber at New Grange in Ireland, a site also used by the Celts. As late as the nineteenth century, folklorists found that the sites Thom studied were described by resi-

dents of the area as "moon temples" and were still used in connection with folk customs regarding love, birth, and marriage. Scottish Highlanders during this same time period were given to greeting the moon with a curtsey, a bow, by turning coins in the pocket, by wishing, and by saying a few words out loud. Not far away in physical distance, though separated by the ages it took to get the stories written down, the Welsh mythical cycle known as *The Mabinogion* mentions an interesting gateway. In the story, Prince Pwyll and his followers enter a gateway through the door of a cairn, which turns out to be the passageway to the Celtic Otherworld. Though *The Mabinogion* is Welsh and not Scottish, the two traditions share a common Celtic heritage. Both shared many similar lunar traditions as well.

Until the 1950s a religious tradition survived in Roman Catholic Ireland, perhaps from an older Celtic practice, of burying unbaptized infants outside the consecrated ground of the church. This ground was often given the name "killeen" (from *cilin* and probably related to *ceallanach*, which refers specifically to a graveyard for unbaptized children). Translated literally the word means "a little church or churchyard," easily identified by the pieces of white quartz that surrounded it. Likewise, some of the more notable sites such as New Grange are elaborately described in even older texts for the way they glittered and shone because of the white quartz used in their construction. Scholars have wondered if white quartz was somehow associated with the moon, or with moonstone, and thus with the attempt to reflect the light of the moon near the dead, or to work some magic or power, a notion similar to the Greek one of "drawing down the moon" that appears nearly 2,400 years later in history.

The interest in investigating possible ancient lunar and other astronomical sites in Ireland has increased in the last few years, spurred by the discovery of the entrance of a ray of sunlight into the sixty-foot chamber of the megalithic tumulus grave at New Grange, only near the midwinter solstice. Anthropologists, archaeologists, astronomers, and archaeoastronomers from within and outside Ireland have studied many possible sites, including Lough Crew in

County Meath and Knowth near New Grange.

A legend exists about Prince Tuathal (ca. 106 C.E.), whose name is found in many places in Ireland, and who is supposed to have built the temple to the goddess Fleachta at Meath, described as a temple to the moon. Likewise, near a site described as *Slieve na Grian* (the Hill of the Sun) is one called *Slieve na Man* (the Hill of the Moon) in Tipperary. A later incarnation of a much older lunar deity seems to be St. Luan, also known Molua, Euan, Lugidus, Lugad, Moling, and Lugadius—*luan* is an Irish word for Monday, and also means a halo, possibly of the kind that surrounds the moon. Many researchers, like Ronald Hicks, writing in a 1985 issue of *Archaeoastronomy*, have also turned to Irish mythology as a guide, where much information about the lunar beliefs can be gleaned from stories read with a discerning eye and heart. In a more inclusive kind of research, Hicks works from the perspective of the archaeoastronomer, but recognizes the value of sources from the literary and folk traditions and uses them as a measuring tool as valuable as any telescope or sky map.

At a slightly later date, in a world that had its own ancient history and tradition, but would come to be known as the "New World," people were also watching the skies. To say that the Mayan culture flourished in ancient Mexico about 1,700 years ago is true in one sense and not in another. Older scholars have explained that most likely the roots of Mayan culture extend three thousand years back to the Olmec culture. Anthropologist Dennis Tedlock, whose conscientious and first-hand approach produced a new translation of the fifteenth-century Maya book of wisdom known as *The Popol Vuh*, points out (as do the Maya themselves) that among the Quiche Maya of Guatemala, the ancient culture is rich and alive. Many of the old time-keeping methods, including lunar ones, are still in use. Among the Maya, a sky-watching people, there are many astronomical myths and beliefs. A long tradition of naked-eye observation of the moon exists in Mesoamerica, as evidenced by the eclipse tables recorded in the Dresden Codex as well as the prominence of a sophisticated lunar calendar in the Maya hieroglyphic inscriptions. The moon figures in Maya

ℒUNAR PLACE NAMES

Asheroth-Qarnaim—a city named after two moon goddesses; means "Astarte of the Two Horns."

Cave of the moon, shrine at Macchu Picchu, Peru

Crescent City, California

Crescent Lake, Washington

Diana's Mirror—the name of a lake near the moon goddess Diana's sacred grove at Nemi in Italy

Half Moon Bay, California

Island of the Moon (Coati Island), Bolivia

Island of the Moon in Lake Titicaca, Peru

Ladakh Kashmir, India, is known as the "Land of the Broken Moon"

Laguna de Luna, Argentina

Luna (town), Philippines

Luna (town), Spain

Luna County, New Mexico

Luna Island, New York

Lune River, England

Luni, Italy (ancient Etruria)

Luneville, France

Mirror of the Moon—a lake sacred to the Amazon Indians

Moon Island (or Moon; Mukhu, Russia), Baltic Sea

Moon Lake, Mississippi

Moon Stone Beach, New Jersey

The moonshell—a name once given to the Platte River by tribes of the Great Plains

Mount Sinai—The Mountain of the Moon

Mountains of the Moon (Mt. Rwenzori), Africa

Palace of the Moon—China

Pyramid of the Moon—Mexico

Sinai Desert—The Desert of the Moon

Sinim—The Land of the Moon (ancient Palestine)

mythological belief, and in local legend and folklore. Even to this day, the moon is valued as the regulator of important life events by the descendants of the Maya.

The study of the Maya has undergone many changes during the last hundred years. The first people outside Maya culture who had an important opportunity to study it were the same people who contributed to its destruction. Long before the conquest of ancient Mexico by the Spanish, the Maya, in a manner similar to the Egyptians, recorded their own history and culture in hieroglyphic inscriptions on stelae and other public monuments, as well as in books known as codices, which were made of a paper-like material from tree bark and folded in screen-like sheets, accordion-style. One name that remains infamously attached to the destruction of the codices is that of Bishop Diego de Landa, a Spanish priest. Only four of these codices have survived. One of the most famous, known as the Dresden Codex, records an eclipse table, among other things. The lives of ancient peoples were inseparable from the lives of their deities. As in other cultures, Mesopotamian or Babylonian or Egyptian, the Maya also regulated certain great festivals and religious activities according to the movements and positions of the heavenly bodies.

Ironically, Bishop Landa became the source later scholars turned to in order to understand Maya culture, and particularly in deciphering the glyphs the Maya used to tell their history. Though his work is filled with cultural bias and prejudice, it has helped modern scholars gain a more sensitive understanding of the Mayas. It is rare, even now, that indigenous people, particularly those invaded by outside cultures, can escape being viewed as rare or exotic. Though modern scholars attempt not to proceed that way, the Mayas came under the cultural scrutiny of nineteenth- and early twentieth-century scholars such as J. Eric Thompson and Sylvanus Morley. Valuable as Thompson's work was, he and Morley created the misleading picture that the Mayas were obsessed with time. One element Thompson used as proof of this obsession was that the Mayas used a complex calendrical system of distinct but overlapping cycles of time. The Maya case is particularly instructive because it shows the hazards of making interpretations based on partial understanding. To his credit, Thompson was able to see and admit the errors of his perception when they were pointed out to him.

Yet the system of cycles, once understood, is elegant and simple at the same time. Though some have come to describe the calendars kept by the Maya and the Aztec as "sacred," with a meaning that implies they are mystical or even mysterious beyond understanding, there are plenty who feel this description is misleading. Another misconception about the Mayas is that they "worshipped" the moon and the stars. It is easy at this remove to confuse the careful astronomical observation of another culture as worship.

With the advances in science and astronomy, particularly from naked-eye observation to the powerful views into the cosmos we are privy to via satellite and interplanetary probe, we have learned to worship the heavenly bodies in a different way. In a time when scientific belief has achieved the ardor of religious faith, it does not seem unfair to say we "worship" the stars or the moon by studying them intensely through mathematics, physics, astronomy, archaeoastronomy, and other branches of science. One of the results of the environmental movement of the last twenty years is a new kind of respect for the earth and the universe, a respect that borders on reverence, and some might even say, worship. And proponents of New Age ideas and beliefs are more open about consciously respecting the forces of the heavenly bodies in a worshipful way. And yet the mechanistic ways of observation and study are daily providing an awareness of the importance of taking care of the earth on a practical and individual level. They can also help us begin to recognize and repair the damage that has been caused, some of it irreparable within the lifespan of anyone now alive. Some cultures never lost such an awareness. Perhaps through their older ways they can teach another way to proceed.

Living during a time when there is no need to watch the moon with the naked eye night after night, year after year, decade after decade, makes such diligent and constant observation hard to imagine. Yet from the records of the

Babylonians, Egyptians, Mayas, and others, it is quite clear that these cultures engaged in regular and long-range observation of the moon. For an updated technological comparison, consider our own monitoring of the universe through the hundreds of satellites launched into space; or of the Mariner and Voyager missions. Astronomers and scientists, both professional and amateur, maintain direct and constant observation of the moon, as the list of organizations in the Appendix indicates. But their purpose is different than that of the ancient people who may have recorded the first nightly observations by carving them on a piece of bone or stone nearly eight thousand years ago.

There are still plenty of ordinary watchers, too, as programs at planetariums across the country attest to. The U.S. Naval Observatory has an ongoing program to encourage amateur astronomers to watch for the earliest crescent moon. Both amateur and professional astronomers watch the moon for both enjoyment and the furthering of science. For example, the Gates Planetarium in Denver, Colorado, features a "Shoot the Moon" party several times a year for photographers in search of a picture-perfect moon.

◐ *The Moon and Creation*

The Chaldeans, thought for so long to be the first astronomers, considered the celestial bodies to be writing in the sky. In fact, one translation of the word Chaldean is "moon worshipper." Babylonian myth portrayed the twelve animal signs of the zodiac as the retinue of the goddess of all life, Tiamat. Spend a few nights watching the sky and instead of seeing jumbles of stars with the moon passing through, imagine for a moment that those shapes have spirits and lives and stories of their own, that they represent the power of creation. Believing even for a moment as the ancients did, that the stars and moon came into existence through the power of a master creator, and that by honoring the creation you honored the creator, the sense of worship and awe that the Chaldeans felt is within reach.

One of the best ways to discover how different cultures viewed the moon is to consider their creation myths. Here is one that will be familiar to many readers.

> *And God said, "Let there be lights in the firmament of the heaven to divide the day from the night; and let them be for signs, and for seasons, and for days, and for years" . . . And God made two great lights; the greater light to rule the day, and the lesser light to rule the night . . . And God set them in the firmament of heaven to give light upon the earth. And to rule over the day and night, and to divide the light from the darkness."*

By and large, Western culture looks to this passage of Genesis from the Bible with a great deal of authority in citing the creation of the moon, the "lesser light." What has been forgotten, except by scholars and students who take their history as seriously as they do their religion, is that the Genesis story contained in the Bible is taken from the Chaldean version of creation. A pre-Christian, pre-Hebraic, pre-Buddhist people, they are like many cultures cited by Briffault and other noted writers who looked to the natural elements as a source of wonder, awe, and reverence. The Chaldeans apparently were able to predict eclipses. They also understood the Saros Cycle. In this account of creation, the moon is cast in the sun's shadow, mentioned only as the "lesser light," and not even named specifically. Even by this distant time, a lunar consciousness is already an old element of civilization.

The ark represented as a crescent moon.

The myths of certain cultures speak of a time before there was a moon. Both Arab and Hindu traditions refer to people who lived on a moonless earth. The Greeks also refer to pre-lunar earth dwellers. The now-extinct Chibcha Indians of Colombia and the Altaic people of Siberia also had traditions of a moonless time. The temptation for speculation is hard to resist: were these beliefs so old that they spoke to an astronomical reality of a time before the moon was created? It would seem not, considering that lunar samples gathered by the Apollo missions established that, at approximately 4.5 billion years, the moon is older than the earth. Perhaps the stories of a moonless time stretch back by way of logical extension into the darkness of unilluminated human consciousness. As a counterbalance to having no moon at all, some cultures described multiple moons in their mythologies. And, as we shall discover much later, there have been many scientific theories about the moon throughout history that often sound more like mythology than mythology does!

One interesting theme about the creation of the moon occurs in the notion of the "world egg," or the "cosmic egg." According to this idea, which appears in many early creation myths, the universe was visualized as an egg that cracked open. When it did, the earth and the moon were hatched. Metaphorically speaking, this makes for an interesting comparison with a scientific theory of lunar creation made popular by Sir George Darwin that the moon was once part of the earth, and that it emerged from the floor of the Pacific Ocean. This theory was popular from its introduction in 1880 but was put to rest when the Apollo 11 astronauts were able to bring samples of moon rock back to earth. Analysis of the samples established that the moon may be the earth's sister, since for all practical cosmic and geological purposes, the earth and moon were created at about the same time. The astronauts' samples proved that moon and earth materials are different, but not so different as to exclude the possibility that they were formed around the same time—time, cosmically speaking, being considered close when the matter of a million or so years is under consideration.

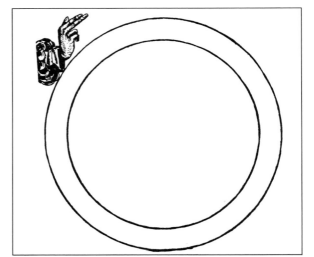

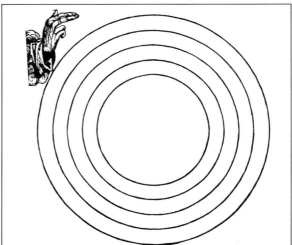

Pictorial representation of creation.

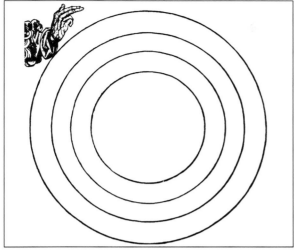

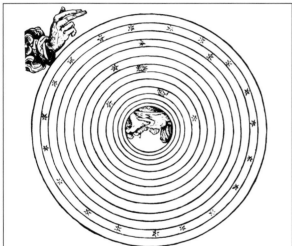

The creation cycle of Finland tells how the moon hatched from an egg. For thousands of years a woman named Ilmatar floated on the face of the ocean. Once a bird landed on her knee and laid seven eggs (which happens to parallel the number of the Sun, the Moon, and the five most visible planets). According to the tradition, it was out of these eggs that the world was created. From the white of one of them, the moon and stars emerged.

A creation tradition from Japanese mythology embodies the female and male principles as the source of life in the universe. The Chinese principles of Yin and Yang are better known than the Japanese In and Yo, but they share a parallel meaning. In one Japanese creation story retold by F. Hadland Davis, the male principle of In existed in the figure of the god Izanagi. The female principle Yo existed in the person of the goddess Izanami. In the early life of the universe, these two brought forth mountains, rivers, and vegetation upon the earth. They also became the parents of the famous sun goddess Amaterasu; the second child of Izanagi and Izanami was Tsuki-yumi, the moon god. Eventually the siblings quarreled, and as Amaterasu was the more powerful, she angrily decided to distance herself from her brother so she would not have to see him.

Another version of the same tradition that may be older claims that Izanagi, when he washed his left eye created Amaterasu, the sun goddess; when he washed his right eye, he created Tsu Yomi, the moon goddess. In later times Tsuki-Yomi underwent a transformation that we can come to expect from cultures as they experienced civil, social, political, and religious changes: she becomes a god.

Though the stories are not necessarily related, the mention of eyes brings to mind the name of one of the Egyptian moon gods, Horus. One of the nicknames for the moon was "the Left Eye of Horus." The right eye was the sun. This kind of information provides some fascinating clues to the ways the ancient Egyptians thought and related to their world.

Many creation stories claim that the moon came from the earth. Several scientific theories have emerged about the moon's origin that parallel this idea. One more prevalent today is that the moon was made up of other elements in the solar system that were "captured" by the earth's gravity. In contrast to this idea, among the Boshongo people of Africa was a creature named Bumba who vomited up the sun and the moon and the stars, and all of creation.

Melville J. Herskovits collected stories among the people of Dahomey (now Benin) about Mawu, the moon, who was the mother of the gods and the mother of humankind. Mawu has many characteristics. She appears as one, as two, as male and female, an all-encompassing presence and spirit of life. When she created the world, she traveled on the back of the serpent rainbow. Wherever they stayed, mountains were created. It soon became obvious to Mawu that she had created too much, that the earth was too big and too heavy. She commanded the serpent to coil itself around the inside of the earth. He obeyed, and much like the magnetic forces that we describe scientifically in the earth today, there he rests. Sometimes he moves uneasily. When he does, earthquakes occur. He is the serpent who keeps his tail in his mouth, known elsewhere as *ouroboros*, in order to maintain balance. It is said that when he swallows his tail, the world will end.

One of the most beautiful of all the creation myths that involve the moon was collected by Leo Frobenius in what was formerly southern Rhodesia. Frobenius called the story "The Moon and His Wives." The first man made by Maori the creator was called Mwuetsi, the moon. Mwuetsi, who first lived at the bottom of a lake, desired to go to earth. So Maori allowed it. But the earth was then cold and without life of any kind. It did not take long for Mwuetsi to grow lonesome, so Maori allowed Mwuetsi to have Massassi, the evening star, as his wife for two years. Massassi brought fire with her, and Mwuetsi owned a horn full of special oil called

ngona oil. When they lay down to sleep, Mwuetsi jumped across the fire that separated them and smeared a little of this oil on her belly. The next morning, Massassi's body nearly split open with creation—she gave birth to all the trees and plants and grasses of the earth. This creation generated more of the same. The trees caused it to rain. Lakes were created and fish lived in them. From all the plants came fruits and plenty to eat.

And so they lived for two years, until it was time for Massassi to return. Once again Mwuetsi grew lonely, and once again Maori allowed him to have a wife, this time named Morongo, the evening star. She also was allowed to stay for two years. This time, when they lay down to sleep, however, it was Morongo who invited Mwuetsi to jump across the fire. Unlike Massassi, she was not willing to settle for a little of that ngona oil to be smeared on her belly, but invited Mwuetsi to cover her loins and his own with the oil, and then to join with her in a different way. He accepted the invitation. The next morning, Morongo too, gave birth—to chickens and sheep and goats. Mwuetsi loved joining with Morongo in this way, and they continued to do so for three nights. Each morning Morongo gave birth to eland and goats, and then to boys and girls, who by the next day were grown.

Mwuetsi wanted to sleep with Morongo again, in spite of a warning from Maori not to, for fear of death. They ignored him, and next morning Morongo gave birth to many animals, to leopards and lions, snakes and scorpions. When Mwuetsi persisted, Morongo told him that since all the daughters were grown, he should mate with them. He did, and thus became the leader of many people. Morongo, in the meantime, mated with a snake. Mwuetsi eventually returned and wanted to sleep with

Morongo yet again. When he did, the snake, lying beneath the bed, bit him. He grew very ill, and as he did, the earth around him sickened, too. The rains stopped. The plants did not grow. The animals perished. His children grew concerned and gathered together to decide what to do. They consulted an oracle, which declared that Mwuetsi must die. The children strangled him, buried him with Morongo, and chose another king to rule them.

The tendency to interpret this story through our own cultural filters will immediately raise the question why anyone would think a story filled with incest and patricide is beautiful. Yet the Bible, considered by some to be not only the most beautiful but the most holy book ever written, is filled with such stories. Secondly, this retelling is only a summary. The myth should be read for itself to be fully appreciated. The description of the creation from the woman-morning star is lush and stunning, and the idea of the things of earth bursting forth from her in full life is a look at evolution in triple-time. The story is beautiful in its complication and intricacy. It tells the story of the creation of the moon and the earth as well as the foundation of kingship and human development early in the world. It would be hard to miss the connections between the tale of Adam and Eve and the Serpent in Genesis, or the connections between the ailing king and the ailing land that would be made famous so much later in history in the Arthurian tales. For the different view and perception, and yet for the many constant motifs, this tale is beautiful in its distinction.

While Briffault found that many cultures considered the moon to be the creator-father of humans and all life, as well as the ruler of death and resurrection, a story from Guatemala tells how the moon was once a beautiful woman who lived on earth. She was so beautiful that her father kept her hidden from all men, and especially from the sun, who had heard of her great beauty and hoped to marry her.

One day when the sun was not so bright (during a time of eclipse, perhaps) she stepped out into the shadow. Seeing how truly beautiful she was, the sun slid down on one of his rays and took her up to the sky, where the two were actually happy together. The moon's father was

MOON MUSIC

Allegheny Moon
Au Clair du Lune
Blue Pacific Moonlight
By the Light of the Silvery Moon
Carolina Moon
Desert Moon
Dreamy Hawaiian Moon
Florida, The Moon and You
Harlem Moon
In the Chapel in the Moonlight
Indiana Moon
Lazy Lou'siana Moon
Lonesome in the Moonlight
Der Mond (The Moon) (opera by Karl Orff)
The Moon and I
Moon of Alabama (aka The Alabama Song)
The Moon of Manakoora
Moon Over Bourbon Street (Sting)
Moon Over Miami
Moon Song
Moonlight Becomes You
Moonlight Cocktail
Moonlight Serenade
Moonlight Sonata
Moonlight, Starlight
Moonlight, Sunlight
Moonrise on the Lowlands
Moonshine
'Neath the South Sea Moon
Roll Along Prairie Moon
Shine on Harvest Moon
Song About the Moon (Paul Simon)
Swanee River Moon
Sweet Hawaiian Moonlight
Two Silhouettes in the Moonlight
Underneath the Harlem Moon
Underneath the Russian Moon
Wabash Moon
(Ooh) What a Little Moonlight Can Do
When the Moon Comes Over Kentucky

displeased. He was beside himself at the loss of his daughter, and decided to hire a man to build an enormous dart gun, the biggest one in the world, to shoot the sun. When the time came, however, the sun tricked the father by putting red pepper in the gun. This caused the father to sneeze so hard that his daughter fell out of the sun's arms and landed in the ocean, where she broke into a thousand pieces.

The scattered pieces cried so pitifully to be reunited with the sun that the fish, hearing the pleas, obliged. They gathered up the pieces and then wove themselves together in a ladder that stretched up toward the sun. They became the Milky Way. The daughter became the moon. Even to this day, she follows the sun across the sky, and at times she almost catches up with him.

The Popol Vuh, the sacred book of the Quiche Maya of highland Guatemala, recorded a creation myth in which the moon goddess takes part. She argues with a god named Lizard House and participates in the creation of humans. Her suggestion is to make humans from trees, but they cannot speak or walk properly and so are destroyed by the chief god. When the moon goddess and Lizard House are sent to earth, they mistreat the human spirits. For her punishment, the chief god puts the moon goddess in the sky, and tells her that trees will cover her face as she goes across the heavens.

A different sort of creation myth, the Aztec myth of the creation of the new race of people, after a long migration, involves the moon. One of the thirteen chiefs of the Aztecs, named Kuauhtloketzin, traveled along in a huge canoe one full moon night with four elders of the tribe. They moved through the canals of the lakes in the Valley of Mexico, arriving at Texcoco, the largest lake, and stopped. Kuauhtloketzin told the elders that he had dreamt that the war god Huitzilopochtli, son of the giver and taker of all life Coatlicue (herself a moon goddess) and brother to another moon goddess, Coyolxauhqui, had spoken in a dream. Huitzilopochtli instructed Kuauhtlokatzin to look down deep to the bottom of the lake where he could see a vision that the people had not been born yet, that they were still in the womb of their creator mother, and to notice especially that the moon had descended and been converted into the umbilical cord of the mother. The people were to notice that the moon had inscribed the word *Metzxiko* on the bottom of the lake. The derivation of this word is interesting: *metz* means moon and *xik* means navel, like the navel of a tomato (consider the lunar crater Tycho, when viewed at full moon, which looks much like the navel of either an orange or a tomato). In Metzxiko lies the origin of the word Mexico. These people always called themselves the "Cosmic Race," and it was said that that night as the tribe slept, starlight turned into stardust and floated down and

Pyramid of the Moon at Teotihuacan, Mexico.

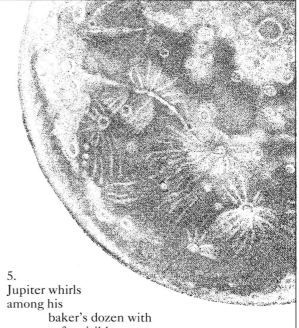

CIRCLED BY MOONS
by Lois Hayna

*M*oons orbit my life,
their dark sides facing me.
In sudden-silver moments one
or another gleams at zenith; two
grace first dusk, or I glimpse faint crescents
when least expecting light.

2.
Earth's one moon, maddening
seeds and seas, is moon enough.
Her ice-fire lures familiars, stirs
vast air-tides. Seeds
burst, embryos
tug to birthing, and the brain
tears at reason's umbilical cord.

3.
Jupiter juggles thirteen moons
under, above, around his mazy
path. We count them, name, and
spy on them until we know
Io, Ganymede, Callisto as we do our
neighbors.
Of their rending force on Jupiter
we sense nothing.

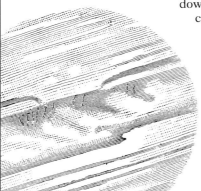

4.
Moon holds Earth captive
with slender mercies. Low tides suck away
        what high tides batter
          down. Continental
           crusts
             bulge and split
              as Moon
               seduces
               Earth's
               molten
               core.

5.
Jupiter whirls
among his
      baker's dozen with
        far-visible
          lightnings; displays spectacular aurora
          borealis, to protest as he can
          their thirteen forces threatening
          his deep-freeze entity.

6.
    Who appointed me
      planet to this spin of satellites?
   What is this wary
brood of moons that will not be
counted, known
or measured?

7.
Invisible, unfendable as Furies
they warp my hard-won orbit, crack
my core between their warring wills,
their wild
eccentric gravities.

impregnated all the maidens of the tribe with those who would become the new people.

The moon figures prominently among the creation myths of Native Americans. As Abenaki poet, storyteller, writer, and publisher Joseph Bruchac has said, probably at least one or more moon myths per Native nation could be found. The moon figures significantly in the Iroquois creation story. One fascinating myth recounted by Percy Bullchild, as he heard it from the Blackfeet tribal elders, tells not of a lovely inspiring figure, but of a maleficent moon, who betrays her husband and seeks revenge on him and their children.

According to this tradition, the moon was brought into being by the first source of all life, the Creator Sun, who took her as his first bride. Together they had seven sons who made up the Big Dipper. Before he brought the moon into existence, however, Creator Sun had first given life to the snakes. Quickly there grew to be too many of them, and since they refused to stop reproducing so fast, Creator Sun destroyed them all, except for one small female who was about to bear young. One of the snake descendants seeks revenge on Creator Sun for his earlier destruction of the snake people. Snakeman, as he is called, assumes human form and seduces the moon. Eventually Creator Sun discovers the betrayal, kills the Snakeman, and with his seven sons, runs from the moon.

She chases her husband and sons, with the aim of destroying them the way they destroyed the Snakeman. Creator Sun had given her special powers when he created her, however, and arms the sons against her. He gives each one a powerful tool to use against her: a bladder filled with water that would turn into a rainstorm and another that would become an ocean; a beautiful bird that would turn into thunder, lightning, and rain; a bladder of air that would turn into a powerful windstorm; a stick that would turn into a thick forest; a rock that would turn into

mountains; and a special power to use the fingers to draw a line in the dirt that would open into a canyon. In spite of all these obstacles, moon persists in her chase until, separated by an ocean from her husband and sons, she watches as they ascend into the sky. Through the power of sweetgrass incense and prayer, she, too, is lifted into the sky and resumes her chase. At that point, Creator Sun, worn out by the relentless pursuit, divides night from day to give himself and the boys a rest. The division also creates four days where moon is hidden altogether. And yet the chase endures; should it ever end, says Blackfeet tradition, so will life itself.

Anthropologist A.L. Kroeber and others recorded a creation story among the California Indians that described Wiyot, the last-born among several deities from whom humans sprang. Like other moon gods, Wiyot was wise. He gave humans law and art. He taught them how to make baskets. He was personified in the oak tree, whose seeds provided food for humans and animals. When Wiyot left the earth and rose into the sky, he was the moon. The people greeted his arrival and prayed that he would not grow smaller.

There are many more creation myths about the moon all around the world, too many to include here. These few have been chosen for their variety and interest, and to provide an overview of the different ways that people have depicted in mythology the creation of the natural world and the creation and lives of deities. From astronomical myth to astronomical truth, cultures of the world have let the moon be their guide to wisdom and understanding—more often about themselves than each other perhaps, but certainly about themselves and the way they stood in relation to their world. Now it is time to turn to an even closer examination of what the ancients saw when they looked as deeply as they could into the surface of the moon, and then far past it to what the mind's eye could also see.

CHAPTER NOTES
Page numbers are in parentheses at the end of each citation.

Marshack, Alexander. *The Roots of Civilization: The Cognitive Beginnings of Man's First Art, Symbol and Notation*. McGraw-Hill. New York. 1972. (8)

van der Post, Laurens. *A Mantis Carol*. Island Press. Washington, D.C. 1975. (9)

Smith, George. *The Chaldean Account of Genesis*, new edition revised and corrected by A. H. Sayce. Scribner's. New York. 1880. (10)

Kramer, Samuel Noah. *The Sumerians: Their History, Culture, and Character*. University of Chicago Press. Chicago. 1963. (10)

Cornell, James. *The First Stargazers: An Introduction to the Origins of Astronomy*. Charles Scribner's Sons. New York. 1961. (11, 15)

Turnbull, Ian. "The Sun and Moon Are the Same Size." 8 (3):16-18, Autumn 1988. (10) (See also illustrations in this chapter.) (12)

Francis Graham explored the possibility of the use of water globes for a "telescope" in his article "A Hypothetical Ancient Telescope," published in *Selenology* (no date listed). (12)

Thom, Alexander. *Megalithic Lunar Observatories*. Clarendon Press. Oxford. 1971. (12, 13, 16)

Briffault, Robert. *The Mothers*. Abrdg. Gordon Rattray Taylor. George Allen & Unwin Ltd. London. 1927. (13, 19, 23)

Hadingham, Evan. *Early Man and the Cosmos*. Walker and Company. New York. 1984. (14)

The Encyclopedia of Religion. Mircea Eliade, editor. Macmillan. New York. 1987. (15)

Some of Alexander Carmichael's collection was reprinted separately in *Celtic Invocations* (Vineyard Books: Noroton, Connecticut. 1972, o.p.). (15)

Information on theories of the Celtic afterlife was obtained during a tour of the New Grange tumulus grave in Ireland, tape-recorded on September 28, 1984. (16)

Walton, Evangeline. *The Prince of Annwn/The First Branch of the Mabinogion*. Ballantine Books. New York. 1974. (16)

Though detailed in other research, the discovery by Irish archaeologist Michael J. O'Kelly of the sunlight entering the passage grave at New Grange on the winter solstice is discussed in *Early Ireland/An Introduction to Irish Prehistory* (Cambridge University Press: Cambridge, 1989). (16)

In *The Stars and the Stones* (Thames and Hudson: London, 1983) Martin Brennan quotes from an Irish antiquarian who described these Sun and Moon sites in 1811. (17)

Hicks, Ronald. "Astronomical Traditions of Ancient Ireland and Britain." *Archaeoastronomy* VIII (1–4): 70–79. (17)

Tedlock, Dennis, tr. *The Popol Vuh*. Simon and Schuster. New York. 1985. (17)

Much of the information on the Maya time-keeping methods was provided in an interview with Rebecca Herr on November 10, 1990. (17, 18)

Thompson, J. Eric S. *Maya Hieroglyphic Writing*. University of Oklahoma Press. Norman. 1971. (18)

Cruz, Lorenzo. Interview on the Aztec and Maya calendar, conducted January 16, 1991. (18)

This passage from Genesis is taken from *The Oxford Annotated Bible with the Apocrypha*. Revised Standard Version. Herbert G. May and Bruce M. Metzger, editors. Oxford University Press. 1965. (19)

Davis, F. Hadland. *Myths and Legends of Japan*. Farrar & Rhinehart. New York. n.d. (21)

The complete story of "Mwuetsi and His Wives" can be found in Leo Frobenius' *African Genesis* (Stackpole Sons: New York, 1937). (22)

This retelling is based on a version by Dorothy Sharp Carter. *The Enchanted Orchard*. Harcourt, Brace, Jovanovich. New York. 1971. (23–24)

This portion of the creation story of the Aztec race was told by Maria Del Carmen Nieva Lopez in *Mexikayotl/Esencia del Mexicano* (Editorial Orion: Tenochtitlan, Mexico, 1969) and translated by Lorenzo Cruz. (24)

Information about the moon myths of Native Americans was provided in correspondence from Joseph Bruchac, September 22, 1990. (26)

Bullchild, Percy. *The Sun Came Down: The History of the World as My Blackfeet Elders Told It*. Harper and Row. San Francisco. 1985. (26)

WHO GOES THERE ?

✴

Inhabitants Of the Moon

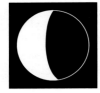

"Beautiful! Beautiful! Magnificent desolation."
–Edwin Aldrin,
second man on the moon

Opposite page: Untitled, by John Willenbecher, from the collection of Naomi Miller.
(Photograph courtesy of Naomi Miller and John Willenbecher)

IMAGINE A LAND where nothing happens. If you were to look up into the black sky above, you would notice stars shining there. They would shine constantly, all day, and long into the cosmic night. The sky would always keep its nighttime and never gain the hard marbled blue of a Colorado sky or the soft opalescence of an Irish one. No clouds would gather to obscure the view or to send rain, sleet, hail, or snow showering down onto this planet. Neither would they pass by to allow a balmy day, or one where the temperature was either too hot or too cold.

There would be no storms here of any kind. From a flat plain, the view to the horizon would never be obstructed, never change, because there would be no air, no atmosphere. No wind could stir this world up. No summer breeze or freezing arctic wind, no tornado or hurricane, no Chinook or El Niño would find its way across the surface of this planet. But since there would be no atmosphere, there would also be no erosion. Only the arrival of a meteor could disturb this land.

The lack of an atmosphere also means there is no color. This is the true land of total contrast. The shadows are pitch black, the light blindingly white. The subtle blues and greens of Earth are missing here. No desert golds or reds light its surface. No blue or purple haze sets the mountains shimmering. No fog lifts off to reveal the landscape. No seasonal changes set this world aflame with reds or yellows, or gentle it with the green foliage of spring one leaf at a time.

This is the same moon that unnamed prehistoric generations watched—the same planet that Moses must have looked up at, or Cleopatra, or anyone on earth, even your own untold generations. Though this sounds like a mythological world, it is the true world of the moon. It is a place where a day lasts a month, where the surface is covered with a fine powdery dust that would cling if you were to walk through it. Though it is a world that has inspired (some even say been the cause of) much life on earth, it is the ultimately still and quiet place. A good place for meditation. And vacuum-packing. And doing anything that requires a sterile environment, or doing heavy work, because its gravity is one-sixth that of the dense and heavy earth. It is one of the great anomalies of the universe, one of the great ironies of nature. From all appearances on Earth, it has been viewed as one of the liveliest members of creation, always moving, always changing, never even keeping the same appearance for long. Yet in reality it is breathless, airless, still.

Since there is no air, of course there is no oxygen. And nothing that needs oxygen to survive lives here—not animals or plants or human beings. Without water, there are no fish or water dwellers of any kind—no whales, dolphin, salmon, minnows. Also, there is no sound. You could pick up a rock from the surface and toss it and not hear it land. You could shout unhindered into the vacuum and not be able to hear your own voice. This is a world where nothing happens except for the slight tremor of a moonquake—once detectable through equipment left behind by earthlings (though that equipment has now also been stilled), or the crash of a meteor onto the surface, disturbing the perpetual calm by building craters or sending the surface dust scattering into rays that can be seen nearly a quarter of a million miles away.

And yet this land where virtually nothing happens has been filled with inhabitants—human, animal, mineral, vegetable, and combinations thereof—since the beginning of recorded human history. Human beings have always looked to the moon and seen something or someone looking back. The inaccessibility of the moon, coupled with its importance to human life for such a long time in history, has made it an ideal place to speculate about, the perfect place to populate with mysterious creatures or more ordinary residents. Who has not looked up from the earth and wondered aloud to others or silently who or what might live on the moon? Who did not once stare from the back yard or the roof, the mountaintop or field, and wonder about Lunarians, Selenites, or other possible moon dwellers?

An obvious place to let the imagination explore was around the mysterious regions of the Moon's spots. Since they are so clearly visible from earth, human fancy set to work early, determining just who or what they were. Through the benefit of science we know that the spots

on the moon are actually dark, flat, level plains known as *marias*. Marias is the plural form of the Latin word *mare*, which means sea. The man who gave them that name, a Jesuit priest named Riccioli, had his own notions about who or what inhabited the moon. Like Galileo before him, observing the moon through a telescope, he believed that the dark spots were seas. Thus it was that the Apollo 11 crew, landing in the Mare Tranquilitatis, the Sea of Tranquility, still wondered if the dark spots might be at all moist, though science doubted it.

Many scientific works about the moon today are slightly self-conscious and apologetic for the romantic notions that once governed the naming of the marias, but the older names do reflect, in addition to romance, a sense of wonder and imagination, and are much more interesting than simply assigning them a number or a letter. Riccioli also began the tradition of naming features on the moon, such as craters, for prominent deceased scientists, especially those who made contributions to the study of astronomy. This tradition is still continued by the International Astronomical Union.

◉ *Human Inhabitants*

Though everyone may know about the Man in the Moon, everyone may not know there is also a Woman in the Moon. Her story is quite old and enchanting in its many varieties. One of her oldest manifestations comes from Chinese mythology. A vestige of her memory still lives on in the midautumn Chinese moon festival celebrated in many places throughout the world wherever people from China and the other Far Eastern countries reside.

The celebration in Hong Kong is especially marked each year, as we shall discuss in Chapter 6. So, too, is one in Japan. This festival occurs on the fifteenth day of the eighth month of the Chinese lunar calendar (not August 15 according to the Gregorian solar calendar), and it is the time that special mooncakes made just for the occasion can be found in Chinese and Vietnamese bakeries.

The name of the woman in the moon comes to us in many different ways as Chang-O, Chang-Ho, Chang-E, and Cheng-O. Chang-O lived by herself in a jade palace on the moon, but was said to visit the earth each year on her birthday, the fifteenth day of the eighth month in the lunar year.

How she got to the moon in the first place is well worth knowing. She was the sister of a water god who caused terrible floods on the earth. A skilled archer was sent to stop the water god from sending floods, and when he saw Chang-O standing next to her brother, he was struck with her beauty at once, and so was careful not to harm her in any way. She eventually agreed to marry him, and they lived peaceably for a time until the archer received a special gift for all his efforts in keeping the people of the earth from destruction.

The gift was quite unusual and demanded great care. It was the pill of immortality that would, when taken, transport the archer to heaven. The goddess who had given it to him warned him that he was not to take it until he had properly prepared himself, and to hide it until he was ready. He hid it in the house he shared with his wife. One day when he was away, Chang-O accidentally saw it shining out from its secret corner. Drawn by its beauty and strangeness, she swallowed the pill and found herself quickly taken up to the moon. Some people say that she was transformed into a three-legged toad when she got to the moon. Others say that the toad is her companion.

At first the archer was angry with his wife, but he soon realized that he was responsible for the disaster and felt badly that she was separated from him because he loved her and he missed her. He built her a beautiful white jade palace on the moon where she would be comfortable and happy, living as she did with yet another animal companion and familiar fertility symbol, the hare in the moon, whose task was to grind the pill of immortality beneath a cinnamon tree. The archer visited his wife each month. In her happiness she grew full and round. When he left she grew thin and pale, and so it went.

Each year, on her birthday, the fifteenth day of the eighth month, and the day that some people still believe the moon shines brighter than at any other time of the year, she was able to visit the earth. The people celebrated her re-

turn. They decorated their tables and put the picture of the moon hare on them, along with the special mooncakes, full of fruits and nuts, honey and melon and sesame seeds, and sometimes a special tasty Chinese sausage. They set out bowls of apples and peaches and grapes, her special fruits, and sought her blessing on their lives. They hung bright lanterns everywhere, as they still do in Hong Kong. Though people still remember the hare in the moon and the mooncakes, sometimes they forget Chang-O.

A Japanese counterpart to Chang-O was called by one storyteller the Lady Kugasa. How she came to earth remains a mystery, but she was a moon maiden who was rescued as a small helpless child by a woodcutter and raised as his daughter. She grew up to be a beautiful young woman, and in spite of the love of many suitors, she was not able to live among the people of the earth. She was reclaimed by her own Moonfolk, who gave her the elixir of life to cleanse

Italian astronomer and physicist Galileo Galilei, 1564-1642.

her and a feathered robe to transport her back with them to live in her own land.

Other mythical women also lived in the moon. A haunting tale collected in both Wales and Lincolnshire during this century and retold by Ellen Pugh and others is entitled "The Buried Moon." The motif it reveals tells of a rare occurrence in western Europe of the Lady in the Moon. She descended to earth in an odd place in Wales, on the moorland near Mount Plynlymon. This particular place had an evil reputation for the dangerous and wicked spirits that lived in and around it. The Lady of the Moon decided to see for herself just what went on in this place, but as she stepped through the dangerous bog the spirits pulled her down beneath the ground and held her prisoner. On the night she was captured, a lone traveler heard the commotion and saw a sudden bright light but had no idea what had happened. Much later, as people who lived near the moor realized the terror of living without moonlight, the traveler consulted a wise woman and was able to understand that the commotion he had heard and the light he had seen was the moon being captured and buried. Following the old woman's warnings to guard themselves against the evil spirits by putting stones in their mouths and remaining silent, and carrying hazel sticks for protection (a wood well known in the British Isles from ancient times for its use against such spirits), the people walked into the moor. Following the old woman's precise directions, they approached a spot near a certain tree where a small shaft of light shone up from the ground, and rescued the Lady in the Moon, allowing her to return to the sky. It has been said that she shines brighter on that moor than anywhere else in Wales.

Many other peoples also saw the figure of a woman or a girl in the moon. Among the Maidu of North America the spots represented a girl holding a pail. In *The Mythology of All Races,* Louis H. Gray records a similar tale the Yakuts of Siberia had about the spots on the moon that sounds somewhat like the story of Jack and Jill, without Jack. A young orphan girl went out to fetch water in the moonlight. The moon felt sorry for her, and took her unto itself, where she can still be seen. The Buriats of Siberia had a similar tale, except that the girl, in her fear of being taken into heaven, grabbed a willow bush whose shadow is still cast against the moon.

Several couples have come, by way of folk imagination, to reside on the moon. The most famous is the nursery-rhyme pair, Jack and Jill. The scholar J.S. Baring-Gould has given this rhyme an elegant heritage in Scandinavian myth. Two children, Hiuki and Bil, were sent to the moon from a well on earth—no one says why, but then this is a legend. Like the buckets of water, their story was carried through many generations and transformed. It is easy enough to see how their names could have changed from "Hiuki" to "Hiuk" to Jack, and from Bil to Jill. Their affiliation with the moon is even stronger. According to Baring-Gould, "Hiuki" is a form of the verb *jukka,* which means to increase and "Bil" means to dissolve. Their names reflect the waxing and waning of the moon, and the buckets of water refer to the rain believed to accompany the changes of the moon.

A well-known story in many tribal cultures throughout the world that explains the spots on the moon's face also serves as a warning against incest. Harley and a number of others have recorded some of these older stories. Both an Algonquin and an Eskimo version tell how the sun, the moon's brother, once loved her dearly. He was good to her for a long time, but eventually he grew cruel and abused her. She fled from him, but before she did he burned one side of her face. He continued to chase her through the sky. As she fled, she turned her burned face toward Earth. In Greenland a similar tale exists, except that the sun is female and the moon male. Among the versions in Brazil, it is the sister who falls in love and has her face burned for her offense. In a contemporary study, John Bierhorst reports that in Greater Brazil, which he describes as the region in which the Tupian languages are spoken, incest stories of Moon and his sister are more widespread than in other areas of South America. In one tale that follows the familiar motif, and also explains the spots, Moon secretly visits his sister at night. Curious to know who he is, she smears his face with black dye. He cannot wash it off, and so is revealed, but not before Moon discovers she is pregnant. She goes off into the

ORBIT

by Paul Dilsaver

There is a man in the Moon

buried deep at its core
he sits in a cockpit
surrounded by buttons and gages
monitors and wheels

for ice ages now
he has kept his planet
from crashing into ours
but just barely

his neck's grown stiff as steel
his arms rigid with arthritis
still he strains to steer
against gravity

crankier each century
he cusses and spits at his machine
gears grind coarsely as he grits teeth
leaning on a rust-locked lever

if he knew on Earth
he was a symbol of romance
and subject of song lyrics
he would kill us today

Man in the Moon. (Reprinted by permission of Kim Long.)

forest alone, where she stays with Opossum. In some versions of the story she becomes pregnant a second time, but in others she gives birth to the culture hero, Son of the Moon.

Other sibling relationships extend to the story of the moon's spots. From Mozambique comes a tale that tells how the sun splashed the moon with mud, to get even with the moon, who stole some of the sun's bright feathers of light. But, not to be outdone, the moon gets even with the sun once in a while by splashing him back, causing him to show spots on his face as well. This story neatly explains both the moon's spots and the solar eclipse. According to the Luiya of Kenya, the sun and moon were two brothers who, in a display of sibling rivalry, had a wrestling contest in which the sun pushed the moon down into the mud.

A tale from New Guinea, in another version of the "buried moon" theme, tells how an old woman hid the moon in a pitcher of water, and how some young boys discovered it and set it free. The moon's spots are their hand prints, left from trying to hold on to it and keep it from rising back into the sky. Another version of this same story was collected by the late Laurens Hillhouse in *Man in Essence*, a book of folk tales from Irian Jaya in Indonesia. His is much richer, and tells the story of a certain farmer who suddenly notices, at full moon, that his crops have been pilfered. He suspects the moon, and asks a friend to hide in a tree and watch what happens. Sure enough, it is the moon who steals from the fields, helping herself to the abundant harvest. The farmer then asks his wife and her friends to capture the moon. His wife succeeds, and hides the moon in an earthenware jar. Their grandson and his friends later discover the hiding place, and as the moon returns to the sky, they shoot at it and wound it with their arrows. The angry moon declares that whenever it rises red and stays red, death will come to the farmer's family, and that likewise all the women will be visited by the monthly "moon sickness." As this story shows, the dweller in the moon is not always a kind and helpful creature.

Harley described a pair of creatures called "Moon Folk" in the folklore of Denmark. They were evil and harmful. The woman lured humans to her by playing beautiful harp music.

She killed those who came too close. The man took his victims by breathing on them. His foul breath caused illness. These creatures may have been one way of describing the damp air of the marshes and the foreboding winds that blew across them, making beautiful sounds perhaps, but dangerous. Similar characters can be seen in the Fairy Queen and Fairy King of *A Midsummer Night's Dream*.

Like the brothers of the Kenyan tales mentioned earlier, many men have been known to inhabit the moon. The notion of the Man in the Moon is particularly strong in European folk tradition, though it is far older than that, and dates to ancient Sumeria and Babylonia in the figure of the moon god Sin. His great temple was located at Ur, a city known to have been specially dedicated to him. Another of his special centers was at Harran in the south. His name is also given as Si-in, En-zu (and conversely Zu-en, then Su-en and Sin), as well as An and Anu. Anu was one of the names for the new moon. Inscriptions reveal that he was a god of light and wisdom. He was called the father of the goddess Ishtar and the first-born son of Bel, one of the oldest Babylonian gods. In Babylonian mythology, as the father of the sun he was created first. One of his nicknames is the "Father of All." His tasks were three-fold: to make the night beautiful, to make the day known, and to regulate the calendar. He was a helper to mankind, bringing fertility and growth, and MacKenzie notes that he presided over the third month of the Babylonian calendar. He is the earliest model for the man in the moon we know so far. He was often depicted as an old man with a beard sailing across heaven in his small boat, the crescent moon, the perfect representation for the god growing stronger and stronger. His beard was said to be the color of lapis lazuli, like the color of moonlight.

As Sin is the oldest man in the moon discovered so far, Ishtar is the oldest woman. We have to keep in mind, however, that Ishtar was already old by the time she was recognized by that name, around 3000 B.C.E., since she is a later incarnation of an older mother goddess that emerged from the Semitic cultures and is perhaps even older than the moon god Sin. We will talk about Ishtar and the worship of the

SEAS OF THE MOON

The Sea of Anguish (Mare Anguis)
The Australian Sea (Mare Australe)
The Sea of Crisis (Mare Crisium)
The Sea of Fertility (Mare Fecunditatis)
The Sea of Cold (Mare Frigoris)
Humboldt's Sea (Mare Humboldtianum)
The Sea of Humours (Mare Humorum)
The Sea of Showers (Mare Imbrium)
The Sea of Margins (Mare Marginis)
The Sea of Nectar (Mare Nectaris)
The Sea of Clouds (Mare Nubium)
The Oriental Sea, the Eastern Sea (Mare Orientale)
The Sea of Serenity (Mare Serenitatis)
Smyth's Sea (Mare Smythii)
The Sea of Spumans (Mare Spumans)
The Sea of Tranquility (Mare Tranquilitatis)
The Sea of Vapors (Mare Vaporum)

mother goddess at length in Chapter Six, but here let us at least get to know her a little. Her symbol, which also later represented Aphrodite, is recognized today as the universal symbol for women. Its use proves the durability of symbols, mythic as well as practical, considering its frequent use during the last twenty years as a totem of what has been called the "Women's Movement." Also associated with Isis, Ishtar was considered a moon goddess in spite of the fact that her name refers to Venus, the morning and the evening star. Certainly her close association with the moon would accord her this honor; in Babylonian mythology she was called the "daughter of the moon" or the "daughter of Sin" and ruled over the sixth month. Her temple was at Erech. The description of her descent to Hades, recently and beautifully retold by Samuel Noah Kramer and Diane Wolkstein in *Inanna: Queen of Heaven and Earth*, can also be read as the story of the waxing and waning of the moon. As a goddess of fertility, she presided over childbirth. More importantly for her own time as well as our own, she was the goddess of both love and war, a symbolic duality that should not be lost in today's current events, coming to be born as she did in the region currently known as the Middle East.

It is easy to see how humans would have described a father-daughter relationship between Sin and Ishtar for a couple of different reasons. The naked-eye method of observation reveals its own story. Venus-Ishtar, traveling in company with the moon, though smaller, could clearly be described as the child or "daughter." As the culture shifted, Venus-Ishtar assumed greater significance, and eclipsed her father by becoming associated with the moon completely. Using human relationships to describe celestial ones is a practical way to approach the universe and was used in many cultures.

An eastern European tale from Lithuania, noted by Jablow and Withers, explains how day and night came to be divided, in terms we could describe today as a battle for joint custody. When time first began, the sun and moon were husband and wife. They lived happily and peacefully with their daughter, the earth. As time went on, they grew weary of one another, the sun dissatisfied because the moon was too

cold, the moon unhappy because the sun was too hot. They decided to part company, but argued over who their daughter should live with. They could not decide, so they approached the thunder (a more powerful god) and asked him to judge. In a decision that equalled the wisdom of Solomon, thunder suggested that the sun care for earth during the day, and that the moon take care of her at night. And so they do.

In the nearby Baltic region, as *The Encyclopedia of Religion* records, a kinship story was used to explain the position of the moon and sun in the sky, as well as their mythical union and their gender. The sun (feminine) and the moon (masculine) were married, but he left her for the morning star (here comes Venus again, in another role this time). The chief of the gods, the storm god, was angered by this, and beat the moon god and not only bruised him but made him smaller. The moon thus never appears close together in the sky with his wife.

Harley tells of another husband-wife relationship, also not a happy one, found in a story from Colombia. There, an old man named Bochica was married to a woman named Huy-

Aphrodite

thaca. Bochica taught the people how to plant and sow and build and take care of themselves. Huythaca caused the river to swell and the water to carry away the work and the lives of the people. To punish her for this, Bochica made her the moon. He stopped the flood and gave the people the calendar of the solar year. In addition to explaining the movements and actions of the Sun and Moon, this myth may also describe the change from a lunar to a solar calendar.

The Mythology of All Races describes a Mongolian myth that describes the sun and moon as sisters, a sibling relationship not found all that often. Although the sun told the moon to walk about the earth during the daytime, the moon was too shy, and so chose the night.

These are just a few of the numerous lunar gods and goddesses thought to dwell in or actually representing the moon in cultures that developed between the Mesopotamian time and contemporary cultures. There are several sources and stories closer to the current era. One tale from Germany portrays not just the face of a man in the moon, as the spots can be imagined when viewed a certain way, but a full-grown man standing up. This man, so the story goes, went out to cut wood on a Sunday, still widely observed as a day of rest, the Christian Sabbath. When challenged about his activity (in some versions by an angel, in others by another person), the man responded that he would cut wood on any day of the week he pleased. For his refusal to honor the social constraints of the day of rest, he was transported to the moon, where he was made to stand with his bundle of sticks in his arms forever after. In Holland and Germany, where this tale was well known, the character is eventually seen carrying a bundle of thorns or a thornbush, and is accompanied by a dog. Shakespeare obviously knew of this tradition. In *A Midsummer Night's Dream*, the mechanical device known as Moonshine declares: "All I have to say is to tell you that the lantern is the moon; I the man in the moon; this thornbush my thorn-bush; and this dog my dog."

In commenting upon popular myths of the Middle Ages, J.S. Baring-Gould mentioned an earlier Biblical story that shares similarities with the Germanic tradition (though we should not

● According to an alchemical work, Ms. Harley 6482 in the British Library, the moon even has its own angel in residence. Described as "the seventh Olympic spirit" known as "Phul," this creature is associated with the metal silver, with water, healing, and long life.

● A German scientist named Schroeter thought the mountains of the moon were works of art rather than natural formations. Another named Gruithuisen thought the lunarians had constructed large fortifications on the moon.

● In his second lunar voyage, the Greek satirist Lucian encountered "horse vultures," also known as Hippogypians, on the moon.

● The philosopher Swedenborg had no doubt that Earth's moon (as well as those of Jupiter and Saturn) were inhabited by spirits and angels.

● An old man in the moon in China, named Yue-lao, was a friend to lovers, and determined who would marry. Showing the mystical influence of the moon over humans, he would tie the lovers' destiny together with a silken cord.

But yet another Chinese man in the moon was not so friendly or helpful. Before he went to live in the moon, he was the neighbor of a man who was so kind and thoughtful that when he found a bird with a broken wing he took the bird home and cared for it until it was healed. When it was, he released it. In gratitude, the bird dropped a magical seed in the man's hand, and told him to plant it. He did. It grew a large and beautiful vine, full of luscious fruits.

The jealous neighbor had heard this whole story, and thinking he might also be rewarded with a special seed, went into the woods and found a bird and broke its wing. He cared for the bird and freed it when it healed.

As with his neighbor, the bird rewarded the man with a seed and told him to plant it. He did. But instead of growing along the ground, this vine began to grow straight up into the sky. The greedy man, unable to resist knowing what was up there for him, climbed up the vine. When he reached the moon, the vine disappeared, leaving him stranded.

assume that one necessarily grew out of the other). In this story Moses met a man who was gathering wood on the Sabbath, a forbidden activity on the day of rest. Rather than toss the offender up to the moon, Moses had a solution that was just but not merciful: he ordered that the transgressor be stoned. In other European versions of this story a man or a woman (and sometimes a man and a woman) were put upon the moon for having stolen their neighbor's wood—or cabbages or sheep or some other valuable item—or for having violated the Sabbath by working, cutting wood, or making butter. For their behavior they were thrown up to the moon where their shadows could be seen within the dark spots.

There are some solitary moon dwellers, too. A counterpart to the stories of the young girls mentioned earlier might be a tale from the Haida Indians of Canada. According to a legend among them, the moon god Roong grew lonely and captured an earth man to keep him company. From time to time this man escaped and spilled a bucket of water, which created rain on earth. Though this is a unique explanation of both figures in the moon, it is interesting to compare it with the Jack and Jill story. Another exile from China, Wa Kang, was sent to the moon where his job was to cut down a cassia tree, a variety of cinnamon tree that was found there, and used to make the elixir of life. Wa Kang's work was as perpetual as the changes in the moon, for as soon as he finished chopping down the tree, another one sprang up in its place.

Though the Man in the Moon is often portrayed as a jolly soul, in an Estonian folk tale told by Selve Maas he appears as a more sinister figure, a devil named Vanapagan. When the creator of the universe, Vanaisa, first made the world, he made only the sun to shine during the day. The night was completely dark, which pleased Vanapagan and his followers, who needed darkness to do their work of entrapping souls. The blacksmith who created the moon out of silver and set it burning with a bright light from within was careful not to make it brighter than the sun, but still it burned all night long. Vanapagan was displeased about this, and set out to darken the moon. He and

his followers set out to climb to the moon with a bucket of tar to paint the face of the moon. Their first effort did not succeed, and the second was only slightly successful. Finally Vanapagan himself climbed up to the moon, carrying a brush made from the branches of a linden tree. He struck at the moon again and again, darkening one whole side of it. But before he could finish the job, Vanaisa surprised him and punished him for trying to darken the beautiful new creation. For his punishment, Vanapagan was bound to stay forever on the moon, where he can still be seen, upside down in a bucket of tar when the moon is full, still holding the brush in his hands.

If Vanapagan is not a figure widely recognized by everyone, there have been plenty of prominent men in the moon. An older Jewish tradition claimed that the face of Jacob looked down from the moon. A later story claimed that Judas was there, exiled for the betrayal of his master. Plutarch described the messenger of the gods, Hermes, sitting in the moon. At one time the Greeks believed that Pan, the god of nature, kissed the moon and left the spots as impressions.

◉ *Animals in the Moon*

Humans and gods were not the only inhabitants of the lunar regions. Many cultures have traditions about animals dwelling in the moon. As Harley noted, over time people have seen in the moon's spots the figure of a lion, a bear, a fox, a cat—even small cattle and a dog. As mentioned above, the Chinese goddess Chang-O was accompanied by the moon hare, whose perpetual job was to grind the elixir of immortality, also called the pill of immortality and the pill of life. This moon hare sat beneath a cinnamon tree to perform the task.

Although many Asian countries have a tradition of seeing a hare in the moon, it is particularly strong in China. The Rev. Timothy Harley recorded many of these older traditions in *Moon Lore*. In a tale that survives in several versions, the traveling Buddha loses his way in the woods. He is found by a hare, who offers to guide him. Buddha says that he is only a poor and hungry man and that he cannot repay the favor. The hare responds by offering himself as a sacrificial meal to the Buddha and jumps quickly into the fire. Buddha shows his gratitude by rescuing the hare just as quickly and throwing him into the sky, up to the moon, where he can be seen even now. In another version, a god named Sakkria travels into the country to visit a monkey, a coot, a fox, and a hare who have all sworn to become hermits and not kill any living thing. As Sakkria meets each of them he asks them to provide food for him. They do, except for the hare, who eats only grass, hardly suitable for a god. Instead, the hare offers itself for sacrifice, but just before the animal jumps into the fire, the god extinguishes the fire and takes the hare and throws it into the sky, up to the moon, as a mark of honor for its willingness to sacrifice itself. In a third version from Tartary, the god Sakyamuni dwells in the body of a hare and sacrifices himself for the good of a starving creature. He, too, is rewarded by being placed in the moon.

The Chinese tradition of the hare in the moon is not unique. Cultures of Japan, Tibet, and the Mongols of Central Asia, and many Native American tribes of the Southwest United States and Central and South America shared the belief that a hare lived in the moon. As studies by Briffault and dozens of others have revealed, the hare is also a major figure in African folklore, where he is often seen in the role of the moon's messenger. In many of the stories, his job, at the earliest part of creation, is to take a message from the moon to human beings, telling them they will have immortal life while the moon will die. He gets the message mixed up, and tells the humans they will die and that the moon will live forever, which is what happens. His misstatement earns him the well-known split lip of the hare in some versions. In others, he is tossed up to the moon as punishment.

According to an old story of the Tezcucans, who were related to the Aztecs, at the time of creation the sun and moon were equally bright. The gods did not view this as a good sign, and so took a hare and flung it at the moon, thus dimming the moon and leaving the shadow of the hare on it. The elusive mystery writer B. Traven related an Aztec creation myth about

the moon that involved a rabbit. At a time when the gods of evil had defeated the good gods in a battle for the universe, darkness spread over the world and the sun was hidden from human beings. This caused great anguish on Earth until a brave young man, with the help of the feathered serpent Quetzalcoatl, traveled among the stars to gather bits of each of them to make a new sun and restore light to the people. Many years later, this same man's wife dreamt about a sun that shone at night but was not as hot or bright as the daytime sun. Her young son, lonely for his father and wishing to help, traveled among the same stars to gather even smaller pieces of them to make the night sun or the moon. He carried with him two shields which he placed, one in front of the other, to make the moon grow smaller and larger by turn. He was aided in his great journey and task by a brave and courageous rabbit whom he eventually carried on his shield, where he can be seen even today.

Associations between hares and rabbits and the moon were viewed in other ways, too. One of the dark Greek goddess Hekate's aspects was a hare. She was honored as such at her most important centers of worship. In the Vedas, the sacred Hindu writings, a woman's beauty was said to come from the moon; eating the moon-hare increased it. Hare was not eaten by the ancient Britons and Briffault claims it was a sacred food for Irish kings, while Robert Graves records that in the late nine-

teenth century peasants in County Kerry said that to eat a hare was "to eat one's grandmother." Trevelyan records a Welsh custom that may parallel the Irish one, given the close physical and linguistic connections between the two cultures, namely that people would not eat a hare for fear it might be a witch. In Wales the patron saint of hares was Saint Melangell, known also as Melancella; her legend declares that she was an Irish princess. The behavior of the "March Hare" during spring mating was believed to be directly related to the moon. The Mad Hatter's tea party scene in *Alice in Wonderland* brought those traits to life in a fictional character that will never be forgotten.

Another creature from China said to accompany Chang-O to the moon was a three-legged moon toad. In one version of this story, which sounds like a compound of legends mentioned previously, while still on Earth the toad, like Chang-O, swallowed pills that caused visions and went to the moon. By coughing, the toad, named Heng-O, spit up a pill that turned into a rabbit; thus, the shape of the rabbit explains the shadows on the moon. Bound to its immortal task, the rabbit is still there, making the ingredients of the pill, with the help of an old man who cares for an acacia tree that also grows there.

As with most animals, the toad, like the hare and the rabbit, all have special reasons for being linked with the moon. In many cultures the

moon was believed to be responsible for water and moisture on the earth. The toad, able to hide in the moist, damp, dark and emerge like the moon, seemed a natural lunar creature when observed regularly. We must look more closely at the development of different cultures to appreciate some of these connections. In our own society, where animals are likely to either be pets, hunted for sport, or packaged neatly in sterile containers for food, it is hard sometimes to remember the role they have played (and still play in many cultures) in the daily lives of humans. For thousands of years, humans have shared the world with animals. As explorers and travelers have revealed, there are still a few places in Africa where the animals have no fear of humans. Extend that situation back a few thousand years and expand it to include many cultures in the world, and we can see a very different relationship between humans and animals. Even in hunting societies like those of some Native American groups in the nineteenth century, for example, the relationship between animals and humans was far different than it is today in this country. There was a recognition of the interdependence between humans and animals that does not exist in the same way anymore. For thousands of years and in many places around the world today, this view is still very much alive. In cultures in which the people observed more closely the life and behavior of everything around them, the associations between animals and the moon were common. It is not surprising, then, that we should find the habits of so many animals compared with the moon.

As if it were not enough to have the moon crowded with hares, rabbits, chameleons, and toads, during the seventeenth century, an Englishman

40

oracles. The tree of the sun told Alexander he would not return home. The tree of the moon told him the place of his death. According to the Funk and Wagnalls *Standard Dictionary of Folklore, Mythology and Legend*, Marco Polo later described these same trees. To other Greeks, the dark spots on the moon were filled with forests where the moon goddess Diana hunted.

Japanese folk belief held that the ornamental katsura tree grew on the moon. As the moon becomes full and its color changes, viewers said the katsura tree was turning red or yellow. The Admiralty Islanders saw their own familiar coconut-palm trees in the shadows of the moon. Malaysian Islanders saw a banyan tree with an old man crouched beneath it. Other traditions described groves of trees that grew on the moon, thus creating huge shadows, as well as a special laurel tree. And, if forests could grow on the moon, then grass would be no surprise; Mircea Eliade reports such an ancient Iranian belief. Not far away, a Greek named Philolaus, who lived at the time of Socrates, was fully convinced that the earth was like the moon because of all the plants and animals that, though fifteen times larger than those on earth, covered the lunar orb.

Many other stories, legends, and myths abound as to why the moon has its spots. An unusual tale from Algeria, mentioned by Jablow and Withers though originally collected by L. Frobenius and translated from the German, tells of the first tears on earth. A lonely orphan

reported having seen a live elephant on the moon. About one hundred years later, the report of other animals emerged. In September 1835, Richard Alton Locke published a story in the *New York Sun* that the astronomer Sir John Herschel had, with his gigantic telescope, seen sheep, oxen, and flying men in the moon. Locke had intended the story as a spoof, but in a response similar to the one that the radio broadcast of H.G. Wells' "The War of the Worlds," would receive nearly a century later, readers took the written word seriously. The use of the word "hoax" here has to be interpreted. Alton intended it as a kind of satire, and was really poking fun at those who believed there were such creatures on the moon. The reader response took the event in an entirely different direction. Readers took the printed word seriously, causing a minor scandal and much explaining on the part of the editor.

It is odd that none of these reports mentioned the animals wandering among trees, since so many cultures held that trees of all sorts grew on the moon. The Assyrians recognized a special moon tree that has been found on cylinder seals. The Babylonians had a similar image that depicted the moon god Nanna-Sin as a tree trunk with huge branches, an early version of the "world tree" that would become central to many other mythologies. Alexander the Great told Aristotle about two fabulous trees in India; one was the tree of the sun and the other was the tree of the moon. They were

boy wandered the earth, unloved and disregarded by everyone he met. He was filled with great sorrow, but he could not cry, as tears did not yet exist. The moon saw all that was happening with the child, and took pity on him. The moon came to earth one night and urged the child to cry, and to let the tears fall on him rather than on the earth, since that was the place where people also grew their food. The child did as the moon urged. He was not only greatly relieved by this, but he received the moon's blessing in return, and all who saw the boy from then on loved and cared for him. The moon returned to the sky, where the marks of the boy's tears may still be seen. Other tales similar to this, in which the moon takes pity on orphan children and helps them in some way, exist among the Eskimo and in western Europe. There are too many of these tales explaining the moon's inhabitants and the moon's spots to be able to include them all here, but the hope is that these selections provide some general insight to the variety and types of stories that have been collected and saved, many of which are still told.

Though the lunar landings of the Apollo space program have proven that the moon cannot support life as we know it, that there are no fantastic beings or even ordinary creatures, and no lush groves of trees or out-of-this-world plants, that the true lunar dwellers are dust and stone—this knowledge does not stop us from looking up at night and describing to our babies and young children or our friends what we see there. It did not stop a Navajo grandmother from telling her young grandson only a few years ago (he is now a college freshman) that the old moon got its spots because it came down close to Earth and teased Coyote too much, until Coyote could bear it no more. When the moon got close enough, Coyote leaped up and scratched the moon with his claws, leaving permanent marks. Though we know what the lunar astronauts found when they landed on the moon, since nearly one-fifth of us watched while they explored, the scientific knowledge that we hold does not prevent us, whether we admit it or not, from looking up and catching sometimes that fleeting glimpse of the Lady in the Moon, or the Man in the Moon, or the hare beneath the cinnamon tree, or the trees themselves, waving in our imaginations as they have all done for thousands of years. Without imagination, we would probably never have gotten to know the reality. There is still plenty of room for both in our lives.

CHAPTER NOTES
Page numbers are in parentheses at the end of each citation.

Frances Carpenter describes the celebration of Chang-O's return to Earth in *Tales of a Chinese Grandmother*. Doubleday, Doran & Company: New York, 1937. (31–32)

Pugh, Ellen. *More Tales from the Welsh Hills*. Dodd, Mead & Company. New York. 1971. (33)

Harley, Rev. Timothy. *Moon Lore*. Swan Sonnenschein, Le Bas & Lowrey. London. 1885. Reissued by Singing Tree Press. Detroit. 1969. (33, 34, 36, 38)

Hillhouse, Laurens. *Man in Essence*. Hillhouse Publications. Los Altos, California. 1990. (34)

Mackenzie, Donald A. *Myths of Babylonia and Assyria*. Bresham Publishing Company. London, 193?. (35)

Jablow, Alta and Carl Withers. *The Man in the Moon/Sky Tales from Many Lands*. Holt, Rinehart and Winston. New York. 1969. (36)

Maas, Selve. *The Moon Painters and Other Estonian Folk Tales*. Viking Press. New York. 1971. (38)

Briffault, Robert. *The Mothers*. Abridged edition. Gordon Rattray Taylor. George Allen & Unwin Ltd. London. 1927. (39)

Graves, Robert. *The White Goddess*. Farrar, Straus and Giroux. New York. 1948. (39)

Trevelyan, Marie. *Folk-lore and Folk-stories of Wales*. Norwood Editions. Darby, Pennsylvania. 1973. (40)

Eliade, Mircea. "The Moon and Its Mystique" in *Patterns in Comparative Religion*. Sheed & Ward. London and New York. 1958. (41)

The story of how Coyote scratched the Moon's face was told to me by Eric Rowland, whose grandmother told it to him. (42)

C H A P T E R　3

THE INCONSTANT MOON

"Soon as the evening shades prevail
The Moon takes up the wondrous tale,
And nightly to the listening earth
Repeats the story of her birth."
–Joseph Addison

ONE OF THE most beautiful ways of describing the waxing and waning of the moon comes to us from Greek mythology, though it has more ancient roots in Egypt and Sumeria in the accounts of the goddesses Isis and Inanna. There are other myths from other cultures that are equally as important as the Greek story in providing an understanding of both the prominent deities and the phases of the moon. Yet this particular myth captures the essence and meaning of the phases of the moon in a way that conveys the depth of feeling and attention with which older cultures viewed their natural environment.

On a fine beautiful day, Persephone, playing with her friends at the far end of a meadow, noticed a particularly beautiful flower, perhaps a daffodil or a jonquil, a poppy or a rose. When she reached for it, the earth opened up and swallowed her. It happened so quickly, even her friends did not know what had taken place. They ran to tell Persephone's mother Demeter, who was grief-stricken and then furious at the loss of her only child. She began searching everywhere for her daughter, but without luck. As she traveled over the earth she grew heavy with her sorrow, particularly since no one could tell her what had happened.

There were two who knew, however: Helios and Hekate—the Sun, and the dark of the Moon. Hekate, patroness of the dark and moonless night, who still watched when no one else was looking, saw and heard everything. She told Demeter that Hades, the Lord of the Underworld, the God of Shades, had plucked the bright beauty of her daughter in the same way Persephone bent to pluck the bright beauty of the flower. He had taken her to the Underworld, where she dwelt with him in darkness, and where he intended to keep her forever.

Demeter, in the meantime, resolved to take her troubles to the high court on Mount Olympus, to Zeus, the father of the gods. Zeus found himself in a double-bind, however. Though Persephone was his daughter, Hades was his son. Zeus refused to help Demeter, who then took matters into her own hands. As the goddess of the crops and the harvest and the fertility of the land, she blighted the earth and refused to help humans, upon whose worship the gods depended, until she received some help herself. Eventually Persephone spent part of each year on earth with Demeter and the rest of her time in the Underworld. This is the part of the myth that is more familiar. It explains, as only a myth can, in the metaphorical images of a story, the change of seasons. When Persephone returns from the underground, with her arrives spring and the flowering and blooming of the earth. The land is reborn as she emerges out of the darkness. Together with her mother, Demeter, honored as the goddess of the harvest, she flourishes through the summer and autumn. When she returns underground, taking the light with her, the green world turns dry and shrivels and grows cold, losing its life until she returns in the next cycle of growing. Persephone is daughter, maiden, spring, light, and the spirit of life in its continuous cycle of rebirth.

On one level, this story could be read as the eventual separation that must come to mothers and daughters. It has also come to represent, in the study of western civilization, a story that explains why the seasons change. There is more. The names of the mother and daughter in this story are Demeter and Persephone. Their names are important. Demeter combines the meanings of "mother" in meter, and the word delta, the triangle, used in many cultures as a symbol for woman. The word Persephone (who is also known as Kore, the maiden) has no certain etymology. Several scholars think she may represent a pre-Greek goddess of the underworld, similar to Ereshkigal, the grieving sister of Inanna in the Sumerian myth, and possibly another name for Hekate. In the Greek myth, Persephone or Kore represents the maiden-daughter of Demeter who is abducted by Pluto (or Hades, as he is also known) and taken to the Underworld.

There is more to this story than a lovely explanation of the seasonal changes. To the ancient Greeks and to those before them, Demeter and Persephone and Hekate were not just three goddesses whose exploits made a good story to pass along the generations. There is evidence that suggests that these three figures also represented the different aspects of the moon.

Whenever we hear stories of goddesses or gods who travel in threes, we should lean in a little closer, because what we may be hearing is an old story of the moon. How do we know this? We must thank the scores of scholars, who through their careful detailed work studying the history of words and religion and culture, pieced together new information about ancient times. This scholarship has shown that the Greeks had separate names for the different phases of the moon. Today, we speak formally of four phases of the moon: first quarter, full moon, third quarter, and new moon. Another way to describe the phases is by shape: new, waxing crescent, gibbous, full, and waning crescent. Some sources combine shape and phase in describing the positions of the moon: new, waxing crescent, first quarter, waxing gibbous, full, waning gibbous, last quarter, and waning crescent. Most people are less formal than that and simply say the moon is either new or dark, a crescent, full, or . . . as one three-year old girl describes it, "my friend the broken m-o-o-o-o-n!"

To an ancient Greek looking up at the same moon, though, if the view might have been the same, the sense was entirely different. It was not simply one moon going through changes. Each phase was distinct enough to have its own unique aspect, its own personality. The crescent moon was called Persephone, the young maiden emerging out of the dark, growing into womanhood. As she grew rounder and fuller, her name changed to Demeter, the fertile mother. The comparison could hardly be missed, then or now, between a pregnant woman and the rounding moon. And as the moon grew slender again, shrinking even as old women shrink when they age, she was called Hekate, the crone, the witch, goddess of the darkness, the one who could see everything below her as she traveled above the earth, unseen in the daylight, darker even than the night itself, but watching nonetheless all the time. The Greeks also used the names of other goddesses to describe the different phases: Artemis, like Persephone, has been called the maiden and the crescent; Aphrodite and Pasiphae have both been identified with the full moon.

Learning or relearning the way ancient people viewed their world may not cause a radical change in our society, but it may help, in a time when the dangers of not taking the world and the environment personally enough have become not only obvious but ominous, to stop and watch Persephone or Demeter or Hekate, who are still traveling through the sky. This more attentive approach to the natural world is still important and available, without trying to turn back the clock or without wishing on a star (or a moon) for what some wistfully think might have been better times. Learning to see the moon differently may help reshape a personal, even a world view. Seeing the earth from the outpost of the moon certainly did.

The Greeks were not the only ones who saw the moon, and other heavenly bodies, too, in different aspects. Simple naked-eye observation of the moon in its different phases led many cultures to give distinct names to the deities that represented those phases. According to Thorkild Jacobsen, the moon god Nanna-Sin, who was worshipped by the Sumerians and the Babylonians, had three aspects. As Nanna he represented the full moon; as Su-en, another version of his name Sin, he represented the crescent. And as As-in-babbar he was the "new light."

The astronomer Sir Norman Lockyer gave evidence of this differentiated view as it applied to other heavenly bodies. In his studies of Egyptian astronomy, for example, he was convinced that the Egyptians had one name for the morning star and another for the evening star, though both are the same planet, Venus. This was true for other stars and constellations. In societies where the belief in many deities dominates the religious and spiritual thinking of the people, this would not seem at all unusual. Likewise, in societies where the belief in only one deity persists, we are likely to find the moon, the stars, and the planets with only one name and one aspect—for example, an early notion of Selene representing a generalized notion of fertility. Polytheism and monotheism are more than spiritual beliefs. Each encompasses and determines a way of looking at all of existence.

◑ *Phases of the Moon*

From two to twenty-eight phases of the moon have been recognized and described by human observers. The two most obvious divisions were a period of light and dark, divisions which influenced the cosmogony and mythology of the East, and can be studied particularly well in India and among other Indo-European peoples. The lunar deities reflect this division. The figure of Kali clearly shows an attention to the dark side, as does the figure of the Black Virgin, whom we shall examine at length in Chapter 5. The Celts left evidence of such a reckoning in the Coligny Calendar. The oldest written record of the Celts found so far, the calendar has been dated to the late first century B.C.E. The Maori of New Zealand divided the month according to two phases of light and dark described by Webster as "moon growing" and "moon lessening." It was not unusual for these two distinct times to have their own names and features like those discussed above. Much of the symbology of light and dark can be traced to these two distinct periods of the moon's waxing and waning.

As the story of Demeter and Persephone indicated, many cultures recognized three distinct phases of the moon's passage and named or considered them accordingly: waxing, full, and waning. This is in contrast with the notion of four phases of the moon most often recognized today. Perhaps this difference has to do with the obvious comparisons people could see in the human life cycle. Webster reported that the Karaja tribe of Brazil recognized a fifth phase, which they counted between new and full. There is still much discussion and study of the ritual cycle of thirteen days kept in ancient Mexico among the Quiche Maya. While some scholars have found connections between this count and the lunar year of thirteen months, others have found in it a recognition of thirteen phases of the moon's waxing and waning. Webster noted the Quiche use of Aztec words from the Nahuatl language: *mextozoliztli* referred to the "moon's waking" and *mecochiliztli* meant the "moon's sleep."

Dividing the moon's journey across the sky into twenty-seven or twenty-eight phases seems

Old crescent moon.
(Photograph courtesy of
Lick Observatory.)

like a natural one. In naked-eye observation, this is what one sees as the moon completes a cycle. In some instances, phase is not the most precise word to describe what was being considered. For example, as contemporary archaeo-astronomers Brecher and Feirtag and others have pointed out, a similarity exists between the lunar zodiac system used by the Maya, the Chinese, and the East Indians. Additionally, the Babylonians and Egyptians had a similar way of keeping track of the moon's sojourn. In each system the moon was seen to pass through twenty-eight positions in its course through the sky. These were called "moon stations" or "lunar mansions" and describe the stars or star groups that the moon seems to pass through in its orbit around the earth. The Anglo-Irish poet William Butler Yeats developed his own mythological system based on the twenty-eight positions of the moon and published his ideas in *A Vision*. In Indian mythology the twenty-eight stations are described as daughters of a sky god who marry the moon. These stations or mansions became significant in early cultures that studied the stars and determined the effect of their passage on human events, which became known as the study of astrology. Because these cultures looked to the heavens for guidance in their lives, they came to attach certain meaning and importance to the phases of the moon.

In our own time, astrology has become so much a part of popular culture that the phrase "What's your sign?" made its way from an opening line used to break the ice to become a satiric slogan for comedians. The argument about the validity of astrology continues, and is far too complex to consider here, but the history of astrology and its relationship to the moon is important.

Today, millions rush to the page of the newspaper that contains the daily horoscope to see what is in store, but charting the future was not always addressed to individuals. In its early stages, as we know from studies about the Chaldean, Sumerian, and Babylonian cultures, astrology was not personal but social. It revealed what effect the planets and stars would have on state affairs: the best time to conduct ceremonies and rituals of all sorts, whether agricultural, civil, or royal; the time to avoid certain activities, such as war, or to begin new endeavors, such as war. Particularly in the Babylonian system, for instance, the lunar eclipse was generally viewed as a bad omen. Reflecting the concern with the larger issue of the country's welfare rather than that of individuals, the face of the moon was divided into four sections representing the different countries: Akkad/Babylonia (south), Assyria (north), Elam (east), Amurru (west). The direction in which the shadow moved across the moon determined which country the ill or good fortune would befall.

Though there is plenty of evidence of the use of augury, divination, oracle, and prophecy in Greece, since the study of astronomy was not tied to religion, it became freed from the confines of astrology and took an entirely different direction. One result was the development of a mathematical system that became nearly an art form. Among other things, this led to a fascination with the idea of the perfect circle, a model still used in many texts and reference books to illustrate the orbit of the moon around the earth, an orbit which is in fact elliptical.

The zodiac, a band of constellations through which the sun, moon, and planets are seen to pass, has existed since Babylonian times. The word zodiac means "a circle of animals," and is the path through the twelve major constellations that include the imaginative figures of a goat, a half-animal archer, a scorpion, a lion, a crab, a bull, a ram, and fish. The Chinese and Egyptians also had zodiacal systems. Determining individual astrological patterns has to do with the relative position of the sun, moon, planets, and stars (all viewed from the pre-Copernican position of the earth as the center of the universe) at the time of a person's birth. Contemporary naturalist and journalist Francis Wylie describes a poet, Manilius, as the first astrologer mentioned during the time of the conquest of Alexander the Great. An Egyptian astrologer helped Julius Caesar adjust the calendar.

What has the moon to do with all this? In astrological metaphor, the moon symbolizes personality, the physical body, matter, the mother, and the cycle of earth life, as well as the psychic or hidden side of life, the mysterious, the intuitive, and, like the tides it controls, the fluctuating side of human nature. Anne Kent Rush notes that it has a special influence on women and babies, as it regulates the menstrual cycle and rules the night. It also rules Cancer, the fourth sign of the zodiac. As the famous "Moon Man" of the almanacs reveals, astrologically the moon is seen to hold sway over the emotions, as well as the brain, stomach, bowels, left eye (for men), and right eye (for women). Eliade points out that among the Mediterranean peoples the moon influences the left eye, the sun the right. In Egypt the moon was known as "the left eye of Horus."

In addition to the new moon, the other phases of the moon also marked and presaged good or ill fortune. Relying on observations with the naked eye meant that calculations were often inaccurate. As Jastrow points out, the moon might thus appear to be delayed or come too early, which in turn could be a bad omen. The arrival of the new moon was a particular cause for celebration. It not only meant that the month could begin, but that the moon god Nanna-Sin had returned from the dark. The dark of the moon was feared, as indicated by inscriptions begging the moon god not to hide his face.

The works of the classical writers inform us that, as in many other cultures clustered around the Mediterranean, the day when the new moon was visible began the lunar month and was officially celebrated by the Greeks. This day is mentioned in the *Odyssey*. Though business as normal was conducted on this day, certain activities were suspended, similar to the observance of the sabbath day in other areas. Like other special days, the time of the first appearance of the new moon had its own name, which meant just that: *Noumenia*. two gods most often associated with the new moon were the sun god Apollo, who possesses some characteristics that are markedly lunar, and Hera, who seems to have succeeded an older moon goddess. Among the Greeks, the time of the new moon was more significant than that of full moon, which was known as the *Dichomenia*. In assigning other names to the moon, the Greek poet Hesiod's name has been attached to a listing of lunar days which describe the kind of activity good for each particular time. Interestingly, some days are described as "mothers,"

CHINESE MOON STATIONS

*L*ike the Babylonians and the East Indians, the Chinese described twenty-eight "moon stations" or constellations that the moon seemed to move through. One scholar suggested that the use of these stations extended to 17,000 B.C.E. The heavens were divided into four quarters, each ruled by an animal. The moon proceeded through configurations in each. Each station also had qualities assigned to it, such as can be found in the I-Ching.

Eastern Quarter: *Spring (Azure Dragon)*
The Horn (Chiao), four stars near Virgo's skirt
The Neck (Kang), four stars near Virgo's feet
The Bottom (Ti), four stars in lower part of Libra
The Room (Fang), four stars in Scorpio's head
The Heart (Hsin), three stars in Scorpio's heart
The Tail (Wei), nine stars in Scorpio's tail
The Sieve (Chi), four stars in Sagittarius' head

Southern Quarter: *Summer (Phoenix)*
The Well (Ching), eight stars in the feet and
    knees of Gemini
The Imp (Kuei), four stars in Cancer
The Willow (Liu), eight stars in Hydra
The Star (Hsing), seven stars in Hydra's heart
The Bow (Chang), five stars in Hydra's coils
The Wing (I), twenty-two stars in Crater and
    Hydra's third coil
The Crossbar (Chen), four stars in Corvus

Western Quarter: *Autumn (The White Tiger)*
Astride (as in someone walking) (Kuei), sixteen
    stars in Andromeda
A Mound (Lou), three stars in Aries' head
The Stomach (Wei), three brightest stars of
    Musca Borealis
Pleiades (Mao), seven stars of the Pleiades
The End (Pi), six stars in Hyades and Taurus
To Bristle (Tzu), three stars at the top of Orion
To Mix (Shen), seven stars in Orion's shoulder
    and legs

Northern Quarter: *Winter (Tortoise)*
The Ladle (Tou), six stars in Sagittarius'
    shoulder and bow
The Ox (Niu), six stars in rear of Sagittarius
The Girl (Nu), four stars in Aquarius' left hand
Emptiness (Hsu), two stars at Aquarius' left
    shoulder and Equleus' forehead
Danger (Wei), three stars at Aquarius' shoulder
    and Pegasus' head
The House (Shih), two stars in Pegasus' leg
The Wall (Pi), two stars in Pegasus' Wing and
    Andromeda's head

51

The Zodiac. The Northern Hemisphere by Albrecht Dürer.

some as "stepmothers." The difference between the two is unclear.

The time of the new moon was and is still generally considered by moon watchers everywhere to be good for beginnings. According to much folklore, this is a good time to marry, to start building or move into a new house, to cut your hair, pare your nails, count your money, and gather herbs and dew. Estonians, Finns, and Yakuts preferred to celebrate marriage at new moon, in the belief that as the moon grows

52

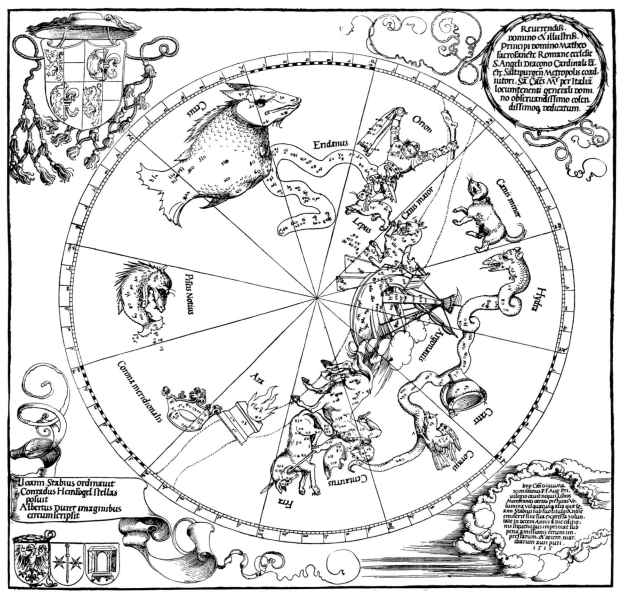

The Zodiac. The Southern Hemisphere by Albrecht Dürer.

full so would their wedded lives. This notion was popular and powerful enough that the laws of the Catholic Church eventually dictated that phases of the moon in general, not just the new moon, should have no bearing on the dates set for weddings or other special ceremonies.

It was often believed that whatever you were doing at the time of the new moon, you would be doing all month long. In parts of India, however, just the opposite was true. There the new moon was not a good time for new beginnings.

THE NEW MOON

*T*his little prayer is said by old men and women in the islands of Barra. When they first see the new moon they make their obeisance to it as to a great chief. The women curtsey gracefully and the men bow low, raising their bonnets reverently. The bow of the men is peculiar, partaking somewhat of the curtsey of the women, the left knee being bent and the right drawn forward towards the middle of the left leg in a curious but not inelegant manner.

The fragment of moon-worship is now a matter of custom rather than of belief, although it exists over the whole British Isles.

In Cornwall the people nod to the new moon and turn silver in their pockets. In Edinburgh cultured men and women turn the rings on their fingers and make their wishes. A young English lady told the writer that she had always been in the habit of bowing to the new moon, till she had been bribed out of it by her father, a clergyman, putting money in her pocket lest her lunar worship should compromise him with his bishop. She naively confessed, however, that among the free mountains of Lock Etive she reverted to the good customs of her fathers, from which she derived great satisfaction!

In name of the Holy Spirit of grace,
In name of the Father of the City of Peace,
In name of Jesus who took death off us,
Oh! in name of the Three who shield us in every
*   need,*
If well thou has found us to-night,
Seven times better mayest thou leave us without
*   harm,*
Thou bright white Moon of the seasons,
Bright white Moon of the seasons.

And, contrary to most contemporary astrological belief, Webster records that John Aubrey, a seventeenth-century Englishman, declared that astrologically the new moon was not a good time to start new endeavors; nor did he think the full moon much better; and he further discouraged such undertakings during an eclipse! In a belief that is not culturally connected but parallels Aubrey's in an interesting way, the Badaga of southeastern India thought children born at either new moon or the three days preceding and including the full moon would lead unlucky lives.

◉ *The New Moon*

New moon was celebrated as a religious or spiritual occasion in many older cultures. The ancient Hebrews celebrated the arrival of the new moon, and the Kabbalists even had a special blessing for the new moon:

Blessed is thy Former, Blessed is thy Maker,
Blessed is thy Possessor, Blessed is thy Creator

Tribal peoples such as the Andaman Islanders of India, the Buriat of Asia, the Mandingo of western Africa, and the Tatars of Mongolia paid special attention to the new moon as a time to undertake new tasks. Even journeys were postponed until the phase of the moon was in keeping with the starting time. Other tribal groups in eastern Europe also paid special attention to the new moon. Caesar noted that the Germans believed they would lose the fight if they undertook a battle during the period before the new moon. The Zulu tribe of Africa held the same belief. The Germans also held other beliefs about the effect of moonlight, and believed that work undertaken by moonlight, such as spinning, sewing, and hanging clothes out to dry, was dangerous and full of ill luck. Among the Scottish Highlanders, too, good fortune came with the new moon and no important work was done in the waxing phase. Briffault commented that among the Ibo of Nigeria a special celebration of the new moon was called "Women's Day." For the Bushmen of the Kalahari Desert, the time of the new moon was a cause for special celebration, since it marked a time of restoration.

In certain places, the way in which a person observed the new moon upon its arrival in the sky determined luck or ill fortune. There is a tradition in contemporary Ireland that it is bad luck to view a new moon through glass, referring more specifically to windows, as eyeglasses do not count. An older piece of wisdom in both Ireland and Wales claims it is bad luck to view the new moon through the branches of a tree. To bring good luck in viewing the new moon, an English custom was to observe it through a silk handkerchief that had never been washed. Many European traditions claim that to see the new moon first over your right shoulder or directly before you means good luck, but to see it over your left or behind you is bad luck. Marie Trevelyan, a folklore collector in Wales, related the beliefs that new moon was the best time to gather both dew and herbs for healing, and that fine weather followed a clear bright three-day-old moon. Additionally, holding a sixpence up to the moon guaranteed financial security, but one should never turn one's back on the new moon while wishing. On a more somber note, she recounted the belief that death in the family at the time of new moon meant that three more deaths would follow.

Where wishes were concerned, a widespread belief among many European cultures, and one that still holds among many people today, was that to tell wishes made on the new moon meant they would not come true; an antidote to this was to kiss the person next to you when you saw the new moon, and then they would come true. Although the full moon is mentioned more often in connection with romance than the new moon, an old English custom in Berkshire was for young women to go out into the fields to view the new moon, repeating as they went:

New moon, new moon, I hail thee!
By all the virtue in thy body.
Grant this night that I may see
He who my true love is to be.

In cultures from South America to western Europe, young girls often looked to the moon to foretell the future of their married lives. In various kinds of divinations, young women sought to know who and when they would marry, as well as the turn of fortune they might enjoy in wedded life. Briffault recorded a song that young French women sang to the moon: "Lune, lune, belle lune, faites me voir en mon dormant le mari quie j'aurai de mon vivant." Translated, it means, "Moon, moon, beautiful moon, in my sleep let me see the husband I will have in my life." Webster echoed a similar and more direct sentiment expressed by young girls in Paraguay who wanted husbands: "Moon, moon, I want to get married." Medieval French wedding tapestries depicted moon symbolism.

From Wales comes the story of St. Dwnywen, who may represent a Christianized version of an older moon deity. Her story is a variation on the familiar theme of unrequited love. She was in love with a Welsh prince, and he with her, but her

father prevented the match. Her lover became bitter, and turned his bitterness towards her. This distressed her so much that she fled to a quiet wood and lived a hermit's life. In a dream, an angel appeared to her and gave her a drink that fulfilled her desires. In the dream the angel offered the same potion to Dwnywen's beloved, but it turned him to ice. The angel then granted Dwnywen three wishes.

Her first wish was that her lover be turned back from ice into human form, a wish that only true love could inspire. The second wish was for all lovers, that they either attain the object of their desire or be freed from the spell of love. The third wish was that lovers would never wish to marry, a wish that had brought Dwnywen only pain.

Dwnywen's symbols were the crescent moon, a magic girdle, and, like the Roman moon goddess Diana, the bow of destiny. On her last visit to earth, the Hag of the Night (another frequent figure in moon myths and epithet for the moon) seized Dwnywen's bow, turned it to stone, and put it in a cave in Glamorgan. To find out if they would be married

within the year, lovers would seek to toss a stone over the arch of the bow; if they succeeded on the first toss, the answer was yes. Dwnywen's feast day was celebrated in April in South Wales because it was believed that was the month she had last visited earth. This sounds a bit like Persephone in her maiden aspect of the new moon, who leaves the bright spring flowers to bloom in her footsteps. In North Wales, at the church of Llandwwynwen in Anglesey, a Druidic center, her festival was celebrated in January.

Though new moon lore is generally filled with proclamations of an auspicious time, not all cultures held that to be true. A new moon on certain days of the week was viewed as unlucky in some places. In France that day was Saturday; in northern Italy, Wednesday. An old saying from Norfolk in England takes the ill omen one step further in declaring:

Saturday's new and Sunday's full
Never was good, and never wull.

Peoples all over the earth have greeted the new moon in many ways, with far more than a passing nod of the head. Some recognized its reappearance in the sky with shouts of joy. Others openly expressed fear or disdain. Some clapped their hands; others went so far as to jump three times in the air or declare a special day of celebration. Some threw stones and spears and burning sticks at it; others offered it their prayers or some item of devotion.

Plato wrote that nurses taught Greek children to bow to the new moon. During later times, and up until the nineteenth century in the British Isles, in the Highlands of Scotland, it was an ordinary custom for men and women to bow or curtsey to the new moon. Though the Koran says: "Bend not in adoration to the sun or moon," the nineteenth-century antiquarian Timothy Harley claimed that as late as the nineteenth century Muslims were known to clap their hands and say a prayer upon seeing the new moon. The Caribs of South America simply said, "Behold the moon!"

It is difficult to find some culture where the moon has not been greeted at some phase of its rising or travels through the sky. Among the most ancient mythological proclamations found in Babylonian and Assyrian culture is a fragment recorded by Morris Jastrow. After defeating Tiamat, the goddess of chaos, the then-reigning god Marduk restored order and addressed the moon:

> *At the beginning of the month in rising over the*
> *land*
> *Thou wilt show a horn for a period of six days.*
> *On the seventh day the crown will be divided (?)*
> *On the fourteenth day thou shalt stand opposite, it*
> *being the half (of the month).*
> *When the sun-god in the foundation of heaven (is*
> *opposite thee).*

Greetings to the new moon were once frequent in Africa. Some people greeted the moon by singing, clapping, and crying out: "So may I renew my life as you are renewed." This sense of renewal was important along the Gold Coast, too, where people once said to the new moon "I saw you before you saw me," and blew ashes at it; without this greeting, it was thought that the person would grow weak as the moon swelled to fullness. In many traditional cultures mothers held their children up to the moon as a kind of blessing on the child: as the moon grew, so would the child.

According to Briffault, Cameroon mothers held their newborns up to the moon and said "This is your grandfather." Likewise, the South African Kaffirs, in showing their infants to the moon proclaimed, "See, your child is growing." The Hottentots of southern Africa had a practical greeting for the new moon: "I salute you; you are welcome. Grant us fodder for our cattle and milk in abundance."

Anne Kent Rush recorded a Gypsy greeting that expressed the same sense of restoration and renewal found in other places: "The new moon has come out—may she be lucky for us—She has found us penniless—May she leave us with good fortune—and with good health, and more." Farther north and west, in eastern and western Europe, different peoples had similar greetings. A favorite rhyme among Europeans, one still spoken by Irish children, is:

> *I see the moon and the moon sees me*
> *God bless the moon and God bless me.*

The Celts, ancestors of the modern Irish, Welsh, Cornish, Breton, and Scots, observed a lunar calendar, even beginning their year in the dark. Perhaps a remnant of this kind of observation, a beautiful, haunting, and anonymous invocation to the new moon lingers on from the Gaelic:

> *Welcome, precious stone of the night,*
> *Delight of the skies, precious stone of the night,*
> *Child reared by the sun, precious stone of the night,*
> *Mother of the stars, precious stone of the night,*
> *Welcome, precious stone of the night.*

Not far away in England, it was once thought irreverent to point at the moon, or to discuss it. In Yugoslavia, charms to the moon were used to help treat illness. One had to coax the moon into helping, to begin by greeting Luna as "pretty little moon."

There also existed greetings to the moon during its other phases—full, waxing, and during eclipse. Of special concern to human culture before science was what caused the phases of the moon. Though the phases could be clearly witnessed on earth, they were not fully understood. Humans turned to mythology, legend, and story to explain what they saw. Today's store of wisdom is richer for the imagination and powerful creativity that different cultures have left in the heritage these stories provide. In looking beyond the obvious and literal interpretations, it seems clear that these ancient people knew far more than they are often given credit for having known.

◉ *The Waning Moon*

The waning of the moon generally caused our early human ancestors a great deal of consternation. During the time when constant migration was a way of life, the moon was a source of light for traveling. Its dark phase prohibited many activities. The idea of monsters or animals or sickness or evil causing the phases of the moon, particularly as it went into decline, figures early and endures throughout human history. While such notions may seem childish or foolish at this remove, remember that in most cases the people whose stories we are discussing could not reach over and switch on a light to dispel the darkness. They did not have "control" over their world and could not change their landscape or their environment as we do today. True, the human technology required to create the pyramids of Egypt or ancient Mexico is testimony to the human ability to create and change the natural environment, but in gazing at the moon ancient people were in the role of bystanders, watchers in a way that those of us who have witnessed the Apollo lunar landings and now read about suggestions to mine and even live on the moon, are not. Monsters and evil and illness were familiar to ancient humans from their own lives and would have seemed a natural explanation. In latter-day Scotland, beliefs about the waning moon abounded, as Alexander Carmichael discovered among the Highlanders: never begin any new business, marry, or slaughter animals when the moon is waning. Older people once invoked the moon's blessing when the monthly cycle was complete. Caretakers of the royal forests in France were once under written rules to cut oak trees only at the waning of the moon and then only if the wind blew from the north.

The Burmese once believed the phases of the moon were caused by a dog swallowing the moon. The Yakuts of Siberia attributed the waning of the moon to its being eaten by wolves and bears. This theme is found the world over. The Bakairi tribe of Brazil believed that the moon declined each month because it was swallowed by animals. An Assiniboin tale explained that moles ate the moon each month, and were punished for this behavior by being sent to the prairies. Other animals whose mythological eating habits included the moon are the crow, eagle, hawk, and owl.

A Kutchin Indian tale from Canada, recorded by Jablow and Withers, tells how several animals were responsible for the moon's phases. Originally, Bear stole the moon and kept it in a bag so he could sleep undisturbed. But other animals wanted moonlight, so Fox and Raven plotted to get the moon back from Bear. They went about it like this: they went to visit Bear, and Raven began to tell a story that went on and on and on. Bear became so drowsy that he fell asleep. When he did Fox and Raven grabbed the bag and released the moon into the sky. Bear woke up, but he was too late. Though he called to the moon to return, it sailed into the sky, sometimes giving light and sometimes disappearing from view.

Another tale that explains the phases of the moon comes from the Chukchi people of Siberia and was told for children by Jeanette Winter. The story begins with the full moon, seen as a man who came to earth. He sought out a young girl whose task was to keep watch over her father's reindeer herd all by herself, isolated from her village and its people. The moon man had seen her many times as she kept her lonely vigil, and heard the lovely music she made on the flute she played to keep herself company.

The moon man came to earth in search of her, determined to have her for himself and take her back to the sky with him. But a wise old reindeer stag who looked out for the girl saw the moon man coming, and hid the girl by changing her into a lamp. Though the moon man searched everywhere in her tent, a thing the full moon could do easily, he could not find where the girl had gone. As he left the tent, she changed back into her human form and called out to him, taunting him. He turned back toward the tent again, only to find it empty except for a blanket, a bed, and a lamp.

As he tried to find her, he grew pale and thin. At last he was weak and thin enough for the girl to tie him up with a rope. He begged to be let go, growing even thinner as he did. At first she refused, because of the cruelty of his search for her. Finally she agreed to let him go, but only

THE CRESCENT MOON

The crescent moon shines
Over the corner of my house.
My neighbor's dogs howl.
The family is in trouble.
In the middle of the night
Spirits fly about and strange creatures stir.
A murmur runs over the high grass
Although no wind blows.

—Mei Yao Ch'en (translated by Kenneth Rexroth)

New crescent moon.
(Photograph courtesy of
Lick Observatory.)

59

after he promised to stay in the sky and not return to earth to bother her. He kept his promise, and there he remains in the sky, shining brightly and spreading his light over all.

One group of animals that has had a special link to the moon throughout history is horned animals—bulls, goats, deer, oxen, cattle. The similarity in shape between their horns and the moon was noticed early. Likewise, the growth of the horns, and their shedding and replacement gave them another common feature with the moon.

The moon has often been depicted as both a cow and a bull. The well-known Egyptian goddess Hathor was pictured as a white cow. The "Bull of Heaven" was a name given to the moon, as it appeared to be shepherding the cows, or stars, across the night sky. Scholars such as R.F. Willetts observed that as cultures developed and cows became identified with the moon, the bull became a solar symbol. In a more earthly discussion, Paul Katzeff recorded the observations of an East Indian researcher who noticed that buffalo cows mated during the dark of the moon. Perhaps the ancient connections between cattle and the moon had to do with similar observations.

In Greek mythology the goddess Io is a white cow. Zeus seduced her in the form of a bull. Like the moon, Io is often seen changing color from black to white. Europa, whose name means "broad-faced," was another cow goddess associated with the moon. Another famous Greek cow goddess is Pasiphae, whose name is an epithet of the moon, "She Who Shines on All." The Minoan culture from which Pasiphae emerges had other associations between the bull and the moon. Pasiphae is the mother of the minotaur, fathered by the bull of Minos and named Asterios, "the starry one." James Frazer, among others, thought that the story of Pasiphae's mating with a bull and giving birth to the minotaur recounted a religious ritual in which human characters celebrated a "sacred marriage" between the sun and the moon. *The Encyclopedia of Religion* says that the story of Pasiphae is probably a moon myth, and springs from an area where bull worship was present. Pliny described a "moon-calf," a shapeless, non-human creature born to a woman believed to have been impregnated by the moon (could he have been describing a premature stillbirth?). The minotaur's name, Asterios, means "Starry One." Perhaps Asterios was among the first mooncalves. Even the powerful Hera, wife of Zeus, had more humble origins as a cow goddess. Io was one of her priestesses. Willetts' investigations also suggest that the story of Io and Zeus may have been a ritual "sacred marriage" between the lunar cow and the solar bull.

Since the moon was often seen to grow ill or weak or even die as it went through its phases, a lunar sympathy was engendered on earth among humans, where the phases of the moon were thought to influence illness. Many of the diseases mentioned reflect this sympathy; swelling or decreasing, for example, or rashes, or other observable marks an illness might cause. At one time or another, the influence of the moon has been held responsible for apoplexy (rupture of a blood vessel), vertigo (dizziness), lunacy (mental illness), scrofula (a kind of tuberculosis that causes swelling of the lymph glands and neck), tuberculosis, palsy, cholic, dropsy (an abnormal accumulation of fluid), and smallpox. Harley adds jaundice, paralysis, fatigue, colds, convulsions, and epilepsy to the list of ailments that have been attributed to the moon in times past. Ulcers, measles, unexplained blotches on the face, cataracts, and even blindness and dysentery were also moon maladies. Katzeff describes a once-prominent theory that epilepsy was caused by too much water on the brain, a result of the moon's influence over water in the body, similar to its observable effect on the tides.

Just as the beliefs existed that the moon was the cause of illness, so too could its influence help effect a cure. Harley recounts an older English cure for whooping cough. A sick child was taken outside to look at the new moon while a special formula was repeated, one that would encourage the moon to increase and the disease to decrease. Anne Kent Rush describes a Japanese cure for someone who was upset which seems reasonable and practical in today's stressful, anxiety-ridden world: go out into the moonlight, bow three times, then calm yourself with meditation—when the meditation is complete and the cure effected, bow low three times in thanks. With the popular acceptance meditation has gained in cultures outside those of the East, where it has been a part of daily living for millennia, this suggestion seems worthwhile.

◐ The Moon and the Natural World

The belief in the moon's rule over nature, over the green world of plants, fruits, vegetables, and other growing things is unparalleled, having vast influence in the world's cultures. Even today, this belief not only lingers but is put into practice by the habits of gardeners and farmers using methods that range from the Stone Age to the New Age and most ages in between. The moon was early associated with the fertility of all plants and vegetation in traditional cultures. Willets, Harding, and others mention that this association was extended to women, who were the first farmers, the ones who gathered and tended the crops and learned to use the roots, leaves, stems, and fruits of plants for food as well as medicine.

From the most ancient times, a belief existed that moonlight had an effect on plants and vegetation that was as important as the effect of the sun. In fact, Eliade mentions an Iranian belief that plants grew by the warmth of the moon, a notion that held in more than one hot dry climate. If this seems silly, there are some scientists who thought the first idea was worth exploring experimentally. Moonlight, after all, is

light. Even the most simple observation reveals that living creatures respond to it. A study conducted by H. Munro Fox demonstrated that plants respond to moonlight, that the stomata of certain plants actually open in the moonlight.

In another study, a Kansas agricultural researcher found that the leaves of certain trees in the Philippines opened on warm moonlit nights. A third study conducted by Frank A. Brown, Jr. and Carol S. Chow revealed that pinto beans absorb water faster at each lunar quarter.

By their names, moonflower and moonvine bear a special tribute to Luna. Over time and through cultures, many flowers have been specially given over to the moon. Some flowers of the moon that we might expect include the lotus, the lily, and the poppy. Another name for the thousand-petalled lotus was "the place of the hidden moon."

The lily was a special moon symbol in Minoan culture, where, as Willetts found, the goddess was depicted in a field of lilies or with lilies at her feet. Two of Aphrodite's sacred plants were the lily and the myrtle. The poppy was a special symbol of the moon because of its sleep and dream-inducing qualities. According to Pliny, poppy seeds were used to stop menstruation, also ruled by the moon. The rose also has a special affiliation with the moon, given its unfolding, hidden nature, in perfect summer sympathy with the earth's sister satellite. In Greece roses were sacred to the moon. Even today, the roses and poppies that were carved into the shrine to Demeter and Persephone remain side by side at Eleusis. Lunaria bears in its name a Latin variation of Luna. Considered an old-fashioned garden plant (many of which are quickly coming back into fashion), today it is more commonly known as the "money plant" for its ever-so-slight resemblance to silver coins, but the earlier connection was with the moon. Its leaves, pearly and opalescent when dried, reveal the connection at once. Moonwort is another less common name for lunaria.

Many fruits are also associated with the moon. One of the earliest was the pomegranate. It was the seed of a pomegranate which Hades put into Persephone's mouth, thus binding her to the Underworld because she had tasted its food. Others, such as apples, oranges, peaches,

melons, and cherries, have been considered moon fruits because of a link that can be traced to the belief in sympathetic magic: the round shape and the belief that the moon, like the seeds themselves, caused fertility.

Herbs, whether used in magic (black and white) or healing, were associated with the moon and its phases. Like so many others, the moon goddess of Minoan culture was linked to the magic use of herbs. Trevelyan reports a Welsh tradition, well known from other classical writers to have been a continental practice as well, of the Druids collecting vervain, an herb used in making a love potion, at the rising of Sirius, the Dog-Star, only in the dark of the moon. As with many herbs, it was believed that

in order to have any effect, they had to be picked in accordance with a phase of the moon, to be in sympathy with the lunar rhythms. We will talk more about dark-moon practices and beliefs in Chapter 5.

Many more trees on earth had special lunar associations. The palm tree was once said to be ruled by the moon, and that at each rising of the moon a new twig sprouted. In India the sacred soma was said to be picked in the moonlight and washed in milk and water.

The willow, oak, murex, and myrtle were likewise special to the moon. Mistletoe was important in Druidic ceremonies, particularly that found on the oak trees, a rare occurrence even today, according to a study reported by Paul Katzeff and conducted in Great Britain. Many accounts tell how the Druids ritually gathered the mistletoe, cut with a special golden sickle and dropped onto a white cloth. Some say the sickle represented the sun because of its color; others claim that the sickle shape resembled the crescent moon. Sap-bearing trees, for their affinity with the waxing and waning phases, were also thought to be ruled by the moon. An aged tree in the churchyard at Nevern in Wales, called the "bleeding yew tree" because of the reddish-colored sap that still oozes from its side, was said to have been once associated with the moon goddess.

In addition to having plants particularly associated with the moon, agricultural tradition is full of references to the moon's part in helping human beings learn to plant, sow, and reap their harvests. Many cultures find a heroic figure in the moon, one who they claim taught them the fine art of agriculture or gave them the knowledge of planting. This is a very interesting point to consider if you think of the moon "teaching" by the way its light passes over the earth, revealing in its path the secrets of growing, of planting, of time. Even today, there exist notions of the moon as the one who guides and teaches us when and how to plant.

If you do not believe that, pick up a copy of the *Old Farmers Almanac* (or any almanac for that matter, though the OFA is a perennial favorite). Llewellyn's annual *Moon Sign Book and Lunar Planting Guide* provide even more detail. There can be found the directions for

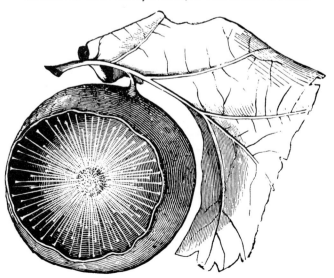

MOON GARDENS

*T*hough she may not have been the first, the Bloomsbury writer Vita Sackville-West was probably the most well-known person to recommend and plant an all-white garden. The garden still thrives today at her home in Sissinghurst Castle, Kent. In fact, it is open to the public, and a recent upscale travel magazine suggested it should not be missed during the final week of the Wimbledon international tennis tournament. While Sackville-West did not specifically name hers as a "moon garden," it is frequently mentioned as a model for today's gardeners, who are planting moon gardens. The flowers, herbs, and shrubs recommended for such a planting usually contain silver, white, pale green, pale blue, and lavender plants that offer both a beautiful sight and scent to the observer on moonlit nights. The concept is popular enough to prompt local nurseries to offer classes to their customers in planting moon gardens, and for one company to prepackage a moon garden with a variety of plants ready for the soil (see Moon Products section).

Some of the selections Sackville-West made for her white garden included different artemisias, grey santolina, white Regae lilies, delphiniums, eremurus, foxgloves, gypsophila, tree peonies, and campanulas. She also included giant Arabian thistles, sea buckthorns, white climbing roses, Japanese anemones, and white dahlias.

Some Moonflowers:
  Carolina Moonseed (*Cocculus carolinum*)
  Cosmos (Moonlight)
  Lady of the Night (*Brassavola nodosa*)
  Moon Daisy (*Chrysanthemum ulignosum*)
  Moon Fern (*Botrychium*)
  Moonflower (*Calonyction aculetum*)
  Moonlight Broom (*Scoparius*)
  Moonseed (*Menospermaceae*)
  Moonshine yarrow (*Achillea*)
  Moonstone (*Pachyphytum oviferum*)
  Moonvine (*Botrychium* and *Lunaria*)
  Moonwort (*Lunaria*)
  Queen of the Night (*Selenicereus*)

Plants that have white varieties:
  Aster
  Bleeding Heart
  Butterfly Bush ("White Profusion")
  Camelia ("Cornish Snow")
  Camelia japonica ("Ama-no-kawa")
  Clematis
  Garlic Chives
  Cleome
  Columbine
  Cornflowers
  Cosmos
  Dahlias
  Delphinium
  Foxglove ("Alba")
  Gardenias
  Gladeolus ("White Friendship")
  Hibiscus syriacus ("Diana")
  Hydrangeas ("Grayswood White")
  Jasmine
  Lavatera ("Mont Blanc")
  Lilacs
  Lilies
  Love in a Mist
  Pearl Bush
  Portulaca ("Swan Lake")
  Rose ("Iceberg")
  Nicotiana (*sylvestris* and *alata*)
  Poppies
  Snapdragons
  Snowdrops
  Tulips
  Viburnum grandiflora ("Snow White")
  Wild White Violets
  Yucca ("Ivory" and "Nobilis")

Some silver and the green:
  Dusty Miller (*Artemisia stelleriana, Centaurea cineraria, C. gymnocarpa, Lychis coronaria, Senecio cinraria,* and *S. leucostachys*)
  Sage (*salvia*)
  Tarragon (*Artemisia dracunculus*)
  Lamb's Ears (*Stachys*)
  Lavender Cotton (*Santolina*)
  Pincushion flower (*Scabiosa*)
  Sage (*Artemisia*)

Moon Sign Dates 1991 Central Standard Time

Many people like to go by the signs of the moon in carrying out their various activities, so here are the dates for 1991.

Roughly speaking, those things which bear their crops above the surface of the ground should be planted in a favorable sign when the moon is increasing—known as the Light of the Moon. Those things which bear their crops below the surface of the ground should be planted in a favorable sign when the moon is decreasing—known as the dark of the Moon.

In most cases, a number of different dates are given in each category. Just pick the date that is best for your local weather conditions.

● **Things that bear their crops below the surface of the ground should be planted:**
January 6, 7, 8, 9, 10, 13, 14
February 2, 3, 4, 5, 6, 9, 10, 11
March 2, 3, 4, 5, 9, 10, 14, 15, 31
April 1, 2, 5, 6, 7, 10, 11, 29
May 2, 3, 4, 7, 8, 9, 12, 30, 31
June 4, 5, 8, 9, 27
July 1, 2, 6, 7, 10, 28, 29, 30
August 2, 3, 6, 7, 26, 29, 30
September 3, 4, 25, 26, 27, 30
October 6, 7, 24, 27, 28
November 2, 3, 4, 5, 23, 24, 30
December 1, 2, 3, 22, 27, 28, 29, 30, 31.

● **Things that bear their crops above the surface of the ground should be planted:**
January 18, 19, 23, 24, 27, 28
February 15, 16, 19, 20, 23, 24
March 18, 19, 22, 23, 29, 30
April 15, 16, 19, 20, 25, 26, 27
May 16, 17, 22, 23, 24, 25, 26
June 13, 19, 20, 21, 22
July 16, 17, 18, 19, 20, 23, 24, 25
August 12, 13, 14, 15, 16, 19, 20, 21, 24
September 9, 10, 11, 12, 16, 17, 21, 22
October 8, 9, 10, 13, 14, 18, 19, 20
November 9, 10, 11, 15, 16, 19, 20
December 7, 8, 12, 13, 17, 18.

● **The best dates for cultivation:**
January 1, 2, 3, 4, 5, 11, 12, 13, 30, 31
February 1, 2, 7, 8, 9, 12, 13, 14
March 1, 6, 7, 8, 11, 12, 13
April 3, 4, 5, 8, 9, 10, 12, 13, 14, 30
May 1, 2, 5, 6, 7, 10, 11, 12, 28, 29
June 1, 2, 3, 6, 7, 8, 10, 11, 29, 30
July 1, 3, 4, 5, 8, 9, 26, 27, 28, 31
August 1, 2, 4, 5, 6, 8, 9, 27, 28, 29, 31
September 1, 2, 5, 6, 7, 23, 24, 25, 28, 29
October 2, 3, 4, 5, 6, 25, 26, 27, 29, 30, 31
November 1, 2, 21, 22, 23, 25, 26, 27, 28, 29
December 4, 5, 23, 24, 25, 26, 27.

● **The best dates to kill noxious growths:**
January 11, 12
February 7, 8, 12, 13
March 8, 11, 12, 13
April 8, 9
May 6, 10, 11
June 6, 7, 10, 11
July 5, 8, 9
August 4, 5, 8
September 1, 2, 5, 6, 7, 30, 31
October 2, 3, 4, 5, 31
November 1, 28, 29
December 4.

● **The best dates for destroying weeds and pests:**
January 1, 2, 3, 4, 5, 11, 12, 13, 30, 31
February 1, 2, 7, 8, 9, 12, 13, 14, 18
March 1, 6, 7, 8, 9, 11, 12
April 3, 4, 5, 8, 9, 10, 12, 13, 14, 30
May 1, 2, 5, 6, 7, 10, 11, 12, 28, 29
June 1, 2, 3, 6, 7, 8, 10, 11, 28, 29, 30
July 1, 3, 4, 5, 8, 9, 27, 27, 28, 31
August 1, 2, 4, 5, 6, 8, 9, 27, 28, 29, 31
September 1, 2, 5, 6, 7, 23, 24, 25, 28, 29
October 2, 3, 4, 5, 6, 25, 26, 27, 29, 30, 31
November 1, 2, 21, 22, 23, 25, 26, 27, 28, 29
December 4, 5, 23, 24, 25, 26, 27.

● **The best dates for pruning:**
January 1, 8, 9, 10, 13, 14, 15
February 4, 5, 6, 7, 10, 11, 12
March 4, 5, 6, 9, 10, 11, 14, 15, 31
April 1, 2, 5, 6, 7, 8, 9, 10, 11, 12, 28, 29
May 2, 3, 4, 5, 8, 9, 12, 13, 30, 31
June 1, 4, 5, 6, 8, 9, 10, 26, 27, 28
July 1, 2, 3, 6, 7, 10, 11, 28, 29, 30
August 2, 3, 4, 6, 7, 8, 25, 26, 29, 30, 31
September 25, 26, 27, 30
October 1, 23, 24, 25, 27, 28, 29
November 5, 21, 23, 24, 25
December 2, 3, 4, 21, 22, 29, 30, 31.

● **The best dates for picking fruit and harvesting:**
January 1, 2, 3, 11, 12, 13, 30, 31
February 7, 8, 9, 12, 13, 14
March 6, 7, 8, 11, 12, 13
April 3, 4, 5, 8, 9, 10, 12, 13, 14, 30
May 1, 2, 5, 6, 7, 10, 11, 12, 28, 29
June 1, 2, 3, 6, 7, 8, 10, 11, 28, 29, 30
July 1, 3, 4, 5, 8, 9, 10, 26, 27, 28, 31
August 1, 2, 4, 5, 6, 8, 9, 27, 28, 29, 31

● **The best dates for hunting and fishing:**
January 8, 9, 10, 18, 19, 20, 27, 28, 29
February 5, 6, 7, 14, 15, 16, 23, 24, 25
March 4, 5, 6, 14, 15, 16, 22, 23, 24, 31
April 1, 2, 10, 11, 12, 19, 20, 21, 27, 28, 29
May 7, 8, 9, 16, 17, 18, 25, 26, 27
June 4, 5, 6, 12, 13, 14, 21, 22, 23, 26
July 1, 2, 3, 10, 11, 12, 18, 19, 20, 28, 29, 30
August 6, 7, 8, 15, 16, 17, 24, 25, 26
September 3, 4, 11, 12, 13, 21, 22, 23, 30
October 1, 2, 8, 9, 10, 18, 19, 20, 27, 28, 29
November 5, 6, 7, 15, 16, 17, 21, 23, 24, 25
December 2, 3, 4, 12, 13, 14, 21, 22, 23, 29, 30, 31.

● **The best dates for pulling teeth:**
January 15, 19, 20, 25, 26
February 16, 22, 23
March 21, 22, 27, 28
April 17, 18, 23, 24, 25
May 14, 15, 21, 22
June 12, 17, 18
July 14, 15, 24, 25
August 11, 12, 20, 21, 22
September 8, 16, 18, 22
October 14, 15, 20
November 10, 11, 12, 16
December 7, 8, 9, 12, 14, 19.

● **The best dates for getting a permanent:**
January 16, 18
February 14
March None
April None
May None
June None
July None
August None
September None
October None
November 13
December 11.

● **To stimulate the growth of hair, cut on these days:**
January 15, 18, 19, 20, 23, 24, 27, 28, 29
February 15, 16, 19, 20, 21, 23, 24, 25
March 16, 18, 19, 20, 22, 23, 24, 29
April 15, 16, 19, 20, 25, 26, 27, 28, 30
May 13, 14, 16, 17, 18, 22, 23, 24, 25, 26, 27
June 12, 13, 14, 19, 20, 21, 22, 23, 26
July 11, 16, 17, 18, 19, 20, 23, 24, 25

"Moon Sign Dates 1991" brochure. (Reprinted courtesy of Earl May Seed and Nursery L. P.)

64

August 12, 13, 14, 15, 16, 17, 19, 20, 21, 22, 25
September 9, 10, 11, 12, 13, 16, 17, 18, 21, 22, 23
October 7, 8, 9, 10, 13, 18, 19, 20
November 6, 7, 9, 10, 11, 12, 15, 16, 17, 19, 20, 21
December 7, 8, 9, 12, 13, 14, 17, 18.

- **To retard the growth of hair cut it on these days:**

January 1, 2, 3, 4, 5, 11, 12, 13, 30, 31
February 1, 2, 7, 8, 9, 12, 13, 14, 28
March 1, 6, 7, 8, 9, 11, 12, 13
April 3, 4, 5, 8, 9, 10, 12, 13, 14
May 1, 2, 5, 6, 7, 10, 11, 12, 28, 29
June 1, 2, 3, 6, 7, 8, 10, 11, 29, 30
July 1, 3, 4, 5, 8, 9, 27, 28, 31
August 1, 2, 4, 5, 6, 8, 9, 27, 28, 29, 31
September 1, 2, 5, 6, 7, 24, 25, 28, 29
October 2, 3, 4, 5, 6, 23, 25, 26, 27, 29, 30, 31
November 1, 2, 22, 23, 25, 26, 27, 28, 29
December 4, 5, 21, 23, 24, 25, 26, 27.

- **The best dates for shingling and painting:**

January 2, 3, 9, 10, 20
February 5, 6, 12, 13
March 4, 5, 6, 12, 13
April 1, 2, 8, 9, 10, 28, 29
May 5, 6, 7, 12
June 2, 3, 9, 10, 15, 16, 29, 30
July 7, 8, 12, 13, 26, 27, 28
August 2, 3, 4, 30, 31
September 5, 6, 26, 27
October 2, 3, 23, 24, 30, 31
November 5, 21, 26, 27
December 2, 3, 4, 23, 24, 30, 31.

- **The best dates to start plants in the house:**

January 24, 27, 28
February 23, 24
March 24, 25, 26, 29
April 21, 22, 25, 26, 27
May 22, 23, 24, 25, 26
June 19, 20, 21, 22
July 18, 19, 20, 23, 24, 25
August 16, 19, 20, 21, 24
September 16, 17, 21, 22
October 15, 18, 19, 20
November 15, 16, 19, 20
December 17, 18.

- **The best dates to slip houseplants:**

January 18, 19, 27, 28
February 15, 16, 23, 24
March 22, 23
April 19, 20, 27
May 16, 17, 25, 26
June 13, 21, 22
July 18, 19, 20

August 15, 16, 24
September 11, 12, 21, 22
October 8, 9, 10, 18, 19, 20
November 15, 16
December 12, 13.

- **The best dates to plant flowers:**

January 27, 28
February 4, 5, 23, 24
March 4, 5, 23, 31
April 1, 2, 27, 28, 29
May 25, 26
June 4, 21, 22
July 1, 2, 18, 19, 20, 28, 29, 30
August 24, 25, 26
September 21, 22
October 18, 19, 20, 27, 28
November 15, 16, 23, 24
December 21, 22.

- **The best dates for cutting timber:**

January 7, 8, 11, 12, 13, 14
February 7, 8, 9, 10, 11, 12, 13
March 8, 9, 10, 11, 12, 13
April 7, 8, 9, 10, 13
May 6, 7, 10, 11, 12
June 7, 8, 9, 10, 11
July 4, 5, 6, 7, 8, 9
August 3, 4, 5, 6
September 1, 2, 5, 6, 7
October 2, 3, 4, 5, 6, 30, 31
November 1, 2, 3, 4, 28, 29, 30
December 1, 27, 28, 29.

- **The best dates for losing weight:**

January 2, 3, 4, 5, 11, 12, 13, 30, 31
February 1, 2, 7, 8, 9, 12, 13, 28
March 1, 7, 8, 12, 13
April 3, 4, 5, 8, 9, 10, 13, 30
May 1, 2, 5, 6, 7, 10, 11, 28, 29
June 2, 3, 7, 8, 29, 30
July 4, 5, 26, 27, 28, 31
August 1, 27, 28, 29
September 5, 6, 7, 24, 25
October 2, 3, 4, 5, 6, 30, 31
November 1, 2, 26, 27, 28, 29
December 23, 24, 25, 26.

- **The best dates for weaning:**

January 11, 12, 13, 14, 15, 16, 17, 18, 19
February 7, 8, 9, 10, 11, 12, 13, 14, 15, 16
March 6, 7, 8, 9, 10, 11, 12, 13, 14, 15
April 3, 4, 5, 6, 7, 8, 9, 10, 11, 30
May 1, 2, 3, 4, 5, 6, 7, 8, 9, 27, 28, 29, 30, 31
June 1, 2, 3, 4, 5, 23, 24, 25, 26, 27, 28, 29, 30
July 1, 2, 21, 22, 23, 24, 25, 26, 27, 28, 29, 30
August 17, 18, 19, 20, 21, 22, 23, 24, 25, 26
September 13, 14, 15, 16, 17, 18, 19, 20, 21, 22

October 11, 12, 13, 14, 15, 16, 17, 18, 19, 20
November 7, 8, 9, 10, 11, 12, 13, 14, 15, 16
December 4, 5, 6, 7, 8, 9, 10, 11, 12, 13.

- **The best dates for castration:**

January 14, 16, 17, 18
February 11, 12, 13, 15, 16, 17
March 13, 14, 15, 17, 18, 19
April 11, 12, 13, 15, 16, 17
May 10, 11, 12, 14, 15, 16
June 9, 10, 11, 13, 14, 15
July 8, 9, 10, 12, 13
August 6, 7, 8, 10
September 5, 6
October None
November None
December 7, 8.

- **The best dates to slaughter food:**

January 31
February 1, 2
March 1, 2, 31
April 1, 2, 29, 30
May 1, 29, 30, 31
June 27, 28, 29
July 27, 28, 29
August 26, 27, 28
September 24, 25, 26
October 24, 25, 26
November 22, 23, 24
December 22.

- **The best dates for making kraut:**

January 1
February 5
March 4, 5, 6
April 1, 2, 28, 29
May None
June 4
July 1, 2, 3, 29, 30
August 25, 26
September 23
October 27, 28, 29
November 24, 25
December 21, 22.

- **The best dates for making soap:**

January 1, 2, 8, 9, 10
February 4, 5, 12, 13
March 4, 5, 11, 12, 13, 31
April 1, 2, 8, 9, 29
May 5, 6, 12
June 1, 2, 3, 8, 9, 28, 29, 30
July 6, 7, 27
August 2, 3, 29, 30
September 5, 6, 25, 26, 27
October 2, 3, 24, 29, 30
November 5, 25, 26
December 2, 3, 23, 24, 29, 30, 31.

planting by the moon. As a general rule, plant crops that bear fruit above ground when the moon is waxing. Plant root crops in the dark of the moon. Older Welsh tradition says never to plant flowers, trees, or herbs during the waning moon, though most traditions consider this phase a good time to pick herbs that will be used for both magic and healing. A current Mexican-American tradition practiced by at least one person calls for pruning trees at the first full moon in February. The Earl May Garden Center headquartered in Shenandoah, Iowa, distributes brochures to customers each year that provide planting and other lunar advice, the worth of which is, as a company representative cautions, "in proportion to its cost" (free). Still, the number of gardeners and farmers who still honor the moon's rhythms in planting and sowing is sizeable. The large number of popular lunar traditions and beliefs still being practiced the world over is just beginning to emerge. They are included in this work to emphasize how they have persisted, though the work itself is an attempt to establish a foundation for the understanding of belief about the moon in human history. The contemporary beliefs merit another book in themselves.

◑ *Weather and the Moon*

In many times and places it has been and is still believed that the moon influences and predicts weather. Such a belief in England held that if Christmas occurred during a waxing moon, the year would be good; if during a waning moon, bad. Scottish farmers believed that if the moon rose bright and full as a shield, weather fine enough to reap would follow. Irish farmers still believe that a bright clear moon in winter predicts a frosty day to follow—and they are right— a clear winter sky means the air is clear and cold. A moon in a misty sky usually means bad weather, though some have held that to be true only with a new moon, not an old one. Among some English and Welsh people, to see the new moon "with the old moon in her arms" (with the shadow of the rest of the moon visible) meant fair weather. To Scottish farmers and others, the same sight meant bad weather. For others still, the "old moon with the new moon in her arms," meant a storm was coming. The moon has been held responsible for rain, thunder, lightning, and the raging of the seas. One of the most obvious reflections of this belief can be found in an anonymous work known as "The Ballad of Sir Patrick Spens":

> *I saw the Moon late yestereen*
> *wi' the auld Moon in her arms;*
> *And if we gang to sea, master*
> *I fear we'll come to harm.*

Scientific investigation by a number of different individuals and organizations with established reputations, in many cases worldwide, have shown that folklore may not be all wet when it comes to being accurate about the effect of the moon on earth's weather. Though folklore and science use different means to draw conclusions, in more instances than one might think the conclusions are the same. As Paul Katzeff reports, the moon comes into play when we talk about weather because it has an effect on weather. Where patterns of heavy rainfall, tropical storms, hurricanes, typhoons, and coastal floods have been studied, the full moon seems to have some part in the weather.

Color:

Pale moon doth rain,
Red moon doth blow,
White moon doth neither rain nor snow.
                                    —Latin proverb

If on her cheeks you see the maiden's blush,
The ruddy moon foreshows that winds will rush.
                                    —Virgil

The moon, her face if red be,
Of water speaks she.
                                    —Zuni proverb

Frost: New England folk wisdom holds that no frost by the full moon in October means no frost until the full moon in November.

Hurricanes: By studying the dates of sixty years' worth of hurricanes in North America, NCAR (National Center for Atmospheric Research) found that the storms occur more often around new and full moons.

Prophecy: In some parts of ancient China, people believed that if clouds crossed the moon before midnight on the fifteenth day of the eighth month (the time of the midautumn festival), the price of oil and salt would increase; if clouds arrived after midnight, the price of rice would go up.

Rain: In many areas of the world, even today, people believe that when the horns of the new moon are up, fine weather will follow. When the horns are pointed down, expect rain. An NCAR (National Center for Atmospheric Research) study of North American rain storms revealed that the most severe ones do occur a few days after the new and full moons. Meteorological records kept by France and Germany during the first part of the twentieth century indicate more rain falls when the moon is waxing.

Moon changed, keeps closet three days as a queen
Ere she in her prime will of any be seen:
If great she appeareth, it showereth out;
If small she appeareth, it signifies drought.
                                    —1812 proverb

In Wales, the phase of the moon on Michaelmas (St. Michael's Day) determined how much rain would follow.

A pale moon means rain.

Moon Rings: One folk formula for predicting moon rings and rain went like this:

A ring around the moon meant rain. How many stars were in the ring meant how many days it would rain. Six stars or more meant cold weather. Four stars or less meant warm weather.

In China, a ring around the moon was a sign of wind.

Circles round the Moon always foretell wind from the side where they break, and a remarkable brilliancy in any part of the circle denotes wind from that quarter.
                                    —Francis Bacon

A circle or halo round the Moon signifies rain rather than wind, unless the Moon stand erect within the ring, when both are portended.   —Francis Bacon

Haloes predict a storm (rain and wind, or snow and wind) at no great distance, and the open side of the halo tells the quarter from which it may be expected.
                                    —Scottish folklore

Welsh weather wisdom about moon rings was as simple as one, two, three.

One ring meant a storm was coming.
Two meant the weather would be rough (a bad storm).
Three that the weather would be odd (stormy and clear).

A simple way to remember what effect the ring around the moon had on the rain forecast comes from this beautiful little Italian proverb:

Ring near, water far;
Ring far, water near.

A Scottish version of this same idea is stated in two different ways:

A far brugh, a near storm.
When round the Moon there is a brugh
The weather will be cold and rough.

Still yet another way of saying this is: "The moon with a circle brings water in her beak."

Sailors believed that when a star "dogged" or appeared next to the moon, stormy weather was ahead.

A seventy-eight-year scientific study in the United States showed that storms form around new and full moons.

ploughing my father's soil
yellow moon at your back—
even the cricket sleeps

through a hole in my fan   the winter moon

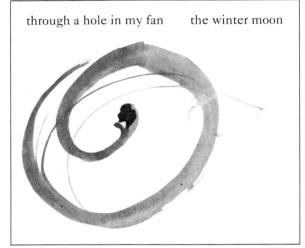

spooning up a moon puddle
        lotus fragrance comes

—*Ann Newell*

WALKING OFF A NIGHT OF DRINKING IN EARLY SPRING (FOR JOE NIGG)

*T*hrough the budding elm branches,
        eyes
of traffic lights blink red to green;
the idled traffic surges forward in the
        dark—
and we stagger on down the alley, joyful,
voices loud and cloudy in the cold.
Where do these hours come from? Hours

when old wounds flare, and the night
opens, and pain boils up into conversation,
as if talk can heal. The sweating bottle

drifts hand to hand, mouth to mouth—
and stars blink through branching clouds,
the blood groping darkly in our heads;

but the Moon's here, too. A bright clarity
over cars and streetlamps, over houses
and leaving trees; going with us.

—*Joseph Hutchison*

AUTUMN

In the night world
of owls and foxes

the cool stars come out

and the moon
is a white rose
floating

—*Jeanne Shannon*

WIND

A fog and a small moon
Bring an easterly wind soon

—*Cornwall*

CHAPTER NOTES
Page numbers are in parentheses at the end of each citation.

Barbara G. Walker summarizes the views of several scholars on Persephone's more ancient identity in *The Woman's Encyclopedia of Myths and Secrets* (Harper & Row: San Francisco, 1983). (47)

English historian Michael Woods, in the TV series "Travels," retraced the fourteen-mile "Sacred Way" from the Acropolis to Eleusis, mentioning the works of Clarke, Pausanias, and Plato. (47)

Briffault mentions in *The Mothers* several triads of goddesses who represent different aspects of the moon. (47)

*The Encyclopedia American*a gives these eight positions of the moon. (47)

This description of the moon was provided by Cordelia Para-Fortier. (47)

Lockyer, Norman. *The Dawn of Astronomy.* M.I.T. Press. Cambridge. 1964 (repr. 1894). (48)

Jacobsen, Thorkild. *The Treasures of Darkness: A History of Mesopotamian Religion.* Yale University Press. New Haven. 1976. (48)

Harding, Esther. *Woman's Mysteries Ancient and Modern.* (Harper & Row: New York, 1976). (48)

Information about the Coligny Calendar can be found in *The Celtic World*, by Barry Cunliffe (McGraw-Hill: New York, 1979). (48)

Brecher, Kenneth, and Michael Feirtag. *Astronomy of the Ancients.* MIT Press. Cambridge, Massachusetts, and London. 1979. (50)

Man, Myth & Magic: An Illustrated Encyclopedia of the Supernatural (Marshall Cavendish Corporation: New York, 1970), edited by Richard Cavendish, provides a basic history of astrology. (50)

Wylie, Francis E. *Tides and the Pull of the Moon.* Stephen Green Press. Brattleboro, Vermont. 1979. (50)

For a comprehensive study of the origin and practice of astrology, see *The Round Art: The Astrology of Time and Space*, by A.T. Mann (Galley Press: New York, 1979). (50–51)

Hesiod's descriptions can be found in *Works and Days*, T.A. Sinclair, editor (London, 1932). (51)

The names given to the Greek days are mentioned by Martin P. Nilsson in *Greek Folk Religion* (Harper and Brothers: New York, 1940). (51–52)

Webster, Hutton. *Rest Days: The Christian Sunday, the Jewish Sabbath and Their Historical and Anthropological Prototypes.* Macmillan Company. New York. 1916. (Republ. by Gale Research Co., Detroit. 1968.) (54)

Morris Jastrow explains the Mesopotamian views of astrology in *The Civilization of Babylonia and Assyria* (J.B. Lippincott Company: Philadelphia, 1915). (51)

Harley, Rev. Timothy. *Moon Lore.* Swan Sonnenschein, Le Bas and Lowrey. London. 1885. Reissued by Singing Tree Press. Detroit. 1969. (52–53)

Trevelyan, Marie. *Folk-lore and Folk-stories of Wales.* Norwood Editions. Darby, Pennsylvania. 1973. (55)

Anne Kent Rush quotes from many cultures in *Moon, Moon* (Random House: New York. 1976). (57)

Alexander Carmichael, compiler of the *Silva Gadelica* and the *Carmina Gadelica*, gathered many customs, poems, charms, and prayers of the Scottish Highlanders, among them much moonlore. (58)

Jablow, Alta and Carl Withers. *The Man in the Moon: Sky Tales from Many Lands.* Holt, Rinehart and Winston. New York. 1969. (58)

Winter, Jeanette. *The Girl and the Moon Man.* Pantheon Books. New York. 1984. (58)

The Mythology of All Races by Louis Herbert Gray recorded a great deal of information about the Yakuts and other peoples of Siberia as well as of tribal peoples in many other regions of the world. (60)

Willetts, R. F. *Cretan Cults and Festivals.* Greenwood Press. Connecticut. 1962. (60)

Paul Katzeff provides a survey of scientific attempts to research the effect of the moon on different forms of life in *Full Moons* (Citadel Press: Secaucus, New Jersey, 1981). (61)

Frazer, Sir James G. *The Golden Bough.* Macmillan: New York, 1922. (60)

The Encyclopedia of Religion. Mircea Eliade, editor. Macmillan: New York. 1987. (60)

These are just three of the many studies and experiments collected by Paul Katzeff. (61)

Julius Caesar and the manuscripts of Irish monks provide information about the Druidic use of herbs. (62)

In 1987 I visited the "bleeding yew tree" at Nevern, reputed by C. Evans-Wentz in *The Fairy Faith in Celtic Countries* (Colin Smyth: Gerrards Cross, 1977) as a center of black magic in the Middle Ages. (62)

The Mexican-American tradition was given to me by a friend who practices it faithfully each year and claims to have the healthiest trees in his neighborhood. (66)

Robin Lane Fox has provided a garden-lover's guide to Sackville-West's enduring Eden in *V. Sackville-West: The Illustrated Garden Book: A New Anthology* (Atheneum: New York, 1986). (63)

C H A P T E R 4

FULL MOON!

"What is there in thee, Moon!
that thou shouldst move my heart so potently?"
–John Keats

Opposite page: Full moon. (Photograph courtesy of Gates Planetarium.)

AS THE FULL moon rises on a cloudless night, whoever we are, wherever we are, we watch her mantle of light spread over the earth, crossing hill and sea, following road and mountain path, lighting the way to and from the city, the town, the village, the hut. Though we know full well that Luna is in the sky above us, the earth is so filled with moonlight at this time that it is not difficult to imagine the moon actually coming down to earth. In the far northern latitudes, in Scotland or Siberia, the presence of the full moon is even more noticeable. While the story told in the previous chapter about the man who visits the young girl tending her reindeer tells the story of the phases of the moon, it also reflects this presence. During certain times of the year, the moon does not even travel across the sky, but simply appears to skim the horizon. In Japan, where use of the lunar calendar continued until 1872, the full moon in September is still celebrated with special moon-viewing parties and the preparation of special food. In the clear skies of Greece even to this day, among people living in the Peloponnesus, the full moon in October is considered special. Its brightness is thought to be more pronounced than at any other time of year. In this part of the world, stories of the full moon still linger in the folk memory.

The moon has had and still has a great influence on the thinking and beliefs of peoples of the Arab world. In a time when the solar calendar had already been adopted, the prophet Mohammed, in a monumental gesture, returned to the use of a lunar calendar which still serves as the basis for the Islamic year. As well as being an important part of Islamic belief, mentioned specifically in the Koran, the moon also figures in Arab storytelling. In her introduction to *Arab Folktales*, Inea Bushnaq describes the decline of the oral tradition in Arab countries. The living word of the Arab storyteller—spoken among women gathered for an evening's sewing session (it was unlucky to tell tales in the light of day), or by men in the coffeehouse, or ordinary laborers at their tasks, or even by professional storytellers who traveled from town to town earning their way through their words—is slowly receding into the background around the world. This activity is now being replaced by radio, television, and the other means of electronic communication. In her collection, drawn from her own research and numerous printed sources which began to emerge in the 1800s as collecting folklore became important, Bushnaq records one story called "Full Moon of the Night."

A young man sees a beautiful girl walk past him, carrying a water jar on her head. Stunned by her beauty, he draws his sword and without harming her or damaging the jar, passes it between her head and the jar. She laughs at him and wishes the love of "Badr-al-Dujja, the Full-Moon-of-the-Night," upon him. He is at once intrigued, and sets off to find this strange and enchanting maiden. When he asks the way to the place where she lives, many do not know. He can only find out that the camels she owns have hair as black as a moonless night. As he makes his way, he finds an old woman spinning black wool. When he asks where she got it, she tells him it is brought by a bird that comes from the far south over the mountains. He follows the bird until he finds a herdsman staking out camels black as a moonless night. In a gesture that might be read as that of a time keeper, since it takes him from one end of the year to the next to accomplish it, the herdsman moves each camel forward one at a time. By the time he has finished, the first one has cleared the pasture and needs to be moved again. For his wages, the old herdsman is allowed to gaze upon Full-Moon-of-the-Night. The young man seeks to do the same, and even to marry her. But the maiden's father insists, as he does with all suitors, that the young man successfully complete a task: he must fight the father's enemies, and win. The young man does, and gains in the end, in spite of the water carrier's jesting curse, the love of Full-Moon-of-the-Night.

Drawing from Greek mythology once again, let us consider another story of the full moon in the person of a woman who, instead of being sought out, visits the earth willingly. Though the *Encyclopedia of Man, Myth & Magic* says that the Greek moon goddess known as Selene was not particularly important when compared to such other lunar deities as Hera, Artemis, or Hekate, other sources give Selene more credit.

In Greek mythology she is one of the earliest symbols of the full moon, a role that Artemis and others would later assume. The story of Selene, who was also called "The Bright One," is a romantic if somewhat bittersweet tale. She was indeed the full moon, the daughter of the sun according to some versions, his sister in others. As she traveled over the earth, lighting up the fields and hills, the oceans, the towns, and all that she touched, she saw a man named Endymion asleep in a field. Some say he was a king, some a prince. Most give his occupation as that of a simple shepherd. Taken in by the beauty of his features, and of his youth, Selene fell in love with him at first glance. Instead of waking him, however, she embraced him while he slept, showering him with her kisses and with her love.

Eventually she gave birth to fifty children by him. Some say these children were the stars. Others claim they represent the fifty months that separate the celebration of the Olympic games. *The Encyclopedia of Religion* makes a case for these fifty months representing one half of the eight-year lunar cycle recognized by the Greeks, called an octaetris. Whatever they symbolize, the story is unusual for a number of reasons. Where so often in mythology and folklore the impregnating, fertilizing power of the full moon is seen to be male, here it is Selene the goddess-woman who finds her way across the fields to her sleeping lover. The tale is bittersweet because the young and beautiful Endymion never awakens. He is asleep, unconscious, unable to fully share in the love Selene bestows on him. But then again, perhaps he is protected in that way from the power of the full moon, for as Shakespeare's Othello later confirmed in words what the rest of the world has long believed in custom and tradition: "It is the very error of the moon, she comes more nearer earth than she was wont, and makes men mad."

Just a few of those notions were recorded by the nineteenth-century antiquarian Timothy Harley. He found the belief that full moon was a time to consider the conclusion of work or business: to cut wood or harvest crops, mow the grass and the hay, and wash the linen (and thus with the decreasing light decrease the stains). Though these observations were made mostly among Europeans, beliefs about the full moon date to the earliest times in human history. For early nomadic peoples all over the earth, the full moon served as both a guide and a way to measure time. The cool silver crescent growing to a full gold and yellow disc served the wayfarer and the wanderer as the lamp of the night, guiding them across valley and plain, to the next stopping place, and the next. Imagine having to wait for moonlight to undertake your journeys (and remember that there are people who, following the guidelines of astrology, still do, though for reasons not associated exclusively with the moon).

Like the early human travelers, there are still plenty of people who wait to travel at night for the coolness, but the idea of traveling by moonlight in our time would be more for enjoyment than necessity. One example of this would be the moonlight ski trips offered by most ski resorts, or other kinds of recreational or leisure activities that can be enjoyed by the light of the moon. After all, the light of the moon is bright enough to do a number of things. Its mirrored light is 2,000 times greater than that of Venus and 24,000 times greater than Sirius, the Dog Star. You could read a book by the light of the moon; the surface reflects 7 percent of the sunlight that strikes it. To return to older times for a moment, for people living in the hot southern countries below the Equator, it has been the moon, not the sun, that has been thought of as the nourishing, cooling, life-giving force. Though we may have some remnants of the archaic stories of these ancient peoples, as Laurens van der Post has conjectured about the stories of the Bushmen, we cannot say for sure what myths they told.

Though the Babylonians placed more emphasis on the time of the new moon, greeting it with shouts of joy and noisy celebrations, they did perform magical rites at full moon or new. Other tribal peoples greeted the full moon the same way the Babylonians did. To the Egyptians, the full moon was the most important phase. According to Webster, one exception to the tradition of celebrating the full moon were the Banyoro of Uganda, who kept as quiet as possible so as not to offend the full moon rising. Katzeff notes that some Native American tribes

considered the full moon to be evil. In the folklore of sailors, the full moon at sea was an evil omen. Plutarch described how Greek carpenters rejected wood cut at the full moon because it was moist, soft, and prone to being wormy.

In addition to having an influence over daily life, the full moon from time to time has also affected the course of history. Herodotus and Pausanias reported that the Spartans did not send aid to the Athenians at the Battle of Marathon because they refused to march out to battle before the time of the full moon.

Others refused the battle of daily life during full moon. Unlike those who believed no work should be done during the dark of the moon, according to Webster residents of some of the Greek islands believed that no work should be done during the few days before full moon, though planting, grafting, cutting trees, and bleaching clothes were good tasks for the few days after the full moon. At a much later date, in the nineteenth century, Marie Trevelyan would find similar beliefs among the Welsh: full moon was a good time to undertake any work that involved cutting or ending: to mow the hay, pluck feathers for a feather bed, even to dig ditches.

These beliefs about cutting wood are clearly at odds with earlier Greek attitudes kept track of by Pausanias, and the contradictions serve to prove how different peoples observed their own unique customs and beliefs within their own regions and times. After the fashion of Stith Thompson, who organized an index to help identify similar themes or motifs in folklore, collectors have always found opposite beliefs the world over. If folk customs are cultural and identifiable and consistent, they are also regional, local, and individual. Each group's experience is tempered by its own environment and values, as well as contact (friendly or hostile) with other groups. The mix has produced a unique recipe with some ingredients the same, some different.

◉ *Moonlight*

Moonlight itself has had its own mystique through the ages. Scientifically we know that moonlight is sunlight reflected from the lunar surface. Not all ancient peoples understood that scientific fact. Some thought the moon shone by its own light, although later epithets such as "She Who Has No Light of Her Own" reveal an understanding of the reflection phenomenon. In his comprehensive study of ancient marriage customs, Robert Briffault intended to rebuff an argument by another scholar that monogamy had been inherent among earlier civilizations. In proving his point, Briffault's work led him into other areas that included the study of lunar beliefs in more traditional societies. He found an early and widespread belief among tribal groups around the world that the essence or spirit of the moon was seen as a primary fertilizing and life-engendering force in nature. In Chapter Three we explored some of the beliefs about the moon as the cause of fertility on earth. By extension, that same belief about the moon applied to humans and has left us with a rich store of mythology, legend, folklore, and story, not to mention the role of the moon as the subject of poems, even in contemporary times.

One of Briffault's many revelations in this regard was the Babylonian belief that the moon controlled both pregnancy and the sex of the child, which was determined by the conditions of the halo around the moon at the time of conception. There is another kind of logic to this, considering that one of the nicknames the Babylonians gave to the moon god was "Father of All." And though the beliefs about the halo around the moon have more to do with weather prediction than gender prediction these days (especially in the age of obstetric ultrasound, amniocentesis, and artificial insemination), the beliefs have endured. The Egyptians believed that the moon not only made women fertile, but that, as Web-

ster recounts, the waxing moon helped the fetus grow inside the mother's womb. In Greece and Rome pregnancy was marked off by counting ten lunations.

Moonlight, and especially moonbeams, have been considered in many places in a whimsical, even magical way. During the Middle Ages a tale was told about how a wise man outsmarted a thief by the clever use of moonbeams. The man knew a thief was hiding on his rooftop, waiting to rob him. He convinced his wife to ask him how he gained his fortune. She agreed, and knowing the thief was listening, the man told her in a voice loud enough to be overheard that he had been a thief himself once, and that before robbing a house he repeated a magic word he knew seven times, before sliding down a moonbeam. The overanxious eavesdropping thief believed what he heard, and tried it. His slide down the moonbeam landed him in the courtyard below, injured, without his booty, and no wiser about moonbeams.

In other places, though, moonlight was taken more seriously. In both Australia and India it was believed that the moon was a male spirit that came down to earth and that the light of the full moon was a force that could impregnate women. The Maori described the moon as "the husband of all women." Katzeff reports that the Buriats of Mongolia believed it took as little light as that generated by a moonbeam to begin life, although pregnancy was considered to be a joint effort between man, woman, and moonbeam. While the man was seen to begin the process, it was through the moonbeam that the woman was able to conceive.

This was one reason women in many cultures kept a caution not to sleep in the light of the full moon. In Brittany, women were careful not to expose their lower torsos to the moon for fear of being "mooned," or made pregnant. This is a custom whose change is interesting to pursue. Currently, "mooning" refers to the act of deliberately exposing one's buttocks for display, either as an insult or a jest, a complete reversal of the idea of concealing the lower part of the body. While the modern custom does not have anything to do with full moonlight, it has retained the name, now attached to those two round orbs that follow us wherever we go.

In Greenland, where the belief was once widespread that women became pregnant by the light of the moon, some people believed the only way they could protect themselves was to rub saliva on their bellies. The Khasians of the Himalayas also believed that the moon god impregnated women who fell asleep in the moonlight. Trigg found that Gypsies once believed in the power of the moon over the fertility of women. Like many other cultures, they believed that the moon's influence determined pregnancy. Slavic Gypsies referred to a mysterious and powerful plant that could be found at full moon on certain mountainsides, whose odor alone was enough to make a woman pregnant. Whether this is an understated way of saying that the right conditions (moonlight and the smell of flowers on a hillside, for example, could probably be traced as the source of many human conceptions!) or this mention refers to a magical plant, we do not know. In Rumania, infertile women offered animal sacrifices to the moon in the hopes of getting pregnant. Perhaps this reflected an older tradition of making offerings to a moon goddess who would have been in charge of the fertility of both animals and humans. According to Leland, among the Romany Gypsies, a pregnant woman would not venture out into the full moonlight, although a child born at full moon was considered to be a blessing, as this old poem reveals:

Full moon, high sea,
Great man thou shalt be;
Red dawning, cloudy sky,
Bloody death shalt thou die.

Pray to the moon when she is round,
Luck with you will then abound,
What you seek for shall be found
On the sea or solid ground.

Some of these ancient beliefs may have to do with the reason the full moon has long been regarded as the only third party lovers never seem to mind having along. Even in our post-Apollo scientific age, the belief in romance and the moon persists. Leftover folklore? Maybe not entirely. According to Ashley Montagu and Edward Darling, that old saw about moon, June, and spooning lovers may have an element of scientific truth to back up what people have

been saying for millennia. It seems that the right chemistry between two people may be further enhanced by the presence of negative ions in the atmosphere—just the sort of condition likely to be present on a beautiful, warm, moonlit June evening. A popular love charm in the Middle Ages was to take a bath in dew. Dew, like rain and the rest of the moisture on earth, was thought to emanate from the moon. According to principles of Tantric yoga, a woman's sexual sensitivity varies with the movements of the moon. Ancient diagrams illustrated different points on the body that would be affected. More recently, a 1978 article in *The New England Journal of Medicine* reported a study that showed increased sexual activity among women at the time of the full moon.

◑ *Love and Marriage and the Moon*

Love and marriage are no longer synonyms, particularly during the present time when surveys report that fewer and fewer American households are organized along the lines of a father, a mother, and children all living together under one roof. But when it comes to looking at moonlore, love and marriage are still found together like the "horse and carriage" of the song lyric.

In older cultures, according to Harley, the preferred time for marriage was at full moon—the Greeks, Romans, East Indians, and Jewish people believed this was true. The Polynesians still do, as Paul Katzeff's survey of scientific studies reports. In the highlands of Scotland, full moon was also once chosen as the best time for marriage; the full moon represented the fullness of passion, fertility, and longevity. When the crescent's horns were showing, it was too easy for passion to grow cold and turn in on itself. Briffault recalls a tradition in the Orkney Islands for brides to visit megalithic circles, also known as temples of the moon. Here is an example in which the customs preserved in folklore may serve to support the suggestions of astronomers that these megalithic Scottish sites may have been ritual rather than lunar observatories, as Alexander Thom has argued. As late as the nineteenth century, young married couples in France scampered around naked in the moonlight among the stones of Carnac in the hope of curing infertility. Research conducted by an American doctor has resulted in an approach to solving the problem of irregularity in the menstrual cycles of women by using light therapy, which we will learn more about in Chapter 6.

The Chinese scholar Wolfram Eberhard mentioned marriage customs among different tribes of southwestern China that had been recorded by folklore collectors. The moon figured significantly in courtship rituals and practices. Young men and women of the Chi'ia-ch'ung Chung-chia tribe began courting by dancing beneath the spring full moon. When they found a partner they were attracted to, they drew brightly colored sashes out of their sleeves, and tossed them toward the one who had caught their eye. This action signalled the beginning of courtship and lovemaking, carried out independently of parents or matchmakers, activity that did not necessarily have to conclude with marriage. The Hua-Miao tribe set aside a special plot of land known as the "moon place" where the young people of the village could begin courting. Among numerous other tribes, the moon was an important partner in the search for love and a mate.

◐ *Moonlight*

Moonlight in general has been the steadfast companion of humans and the human imagination, and its associations with love and romance have been pleasant ones. Special moon-watching parties held just to attend the full moon have been (and still are) an important part of Japanese and Chinese tradition. Taking in the light of the moon has been associated with much love and romance in general, but in some cultures moonlight is not considered so enchanting, and watching the moon was actually considered a dangerous activity to be carefully avoided. The Bedouins warned strangers against gazing at the moon for too long, as it was not healthy to do so. The belief that the moon could provoke epilepsy, dropsy, and a host of other diseases recalls the early human fear that such misfortune might be brought on by the Babylonian moon god Sin.

Plutarch warned against sleeping in the light of the full moon, for fear of becoming mad. The same warning was issued to the author's mother by an Irish-American grandmother during the 1930s, and is still believed in many parts of the world today by people who are several generations away from their ancestral roots. Among the Welsh, Trevelyan also found the belief that sleeping in the moonlight could cause blindness or madness, especially in children. And curtains or shutters were an absolute necessity, since moonlight shining through the kitchen window was considered powerful enough to break the dishes. Women from a tribe in New South Wales believed that if they or their babies looked at the full moon, the children would come down with thrush. In Mexican culture, although the full moonlight is viewed as a mostly beneficent force, a practice is still reported among people of Mexican heritage of not allowing the moonlight to shine on the belly of a pregnant woman. If it cannot be avoided, a silver talisman is worn for protection.

Webster reminds us that older German customs extended the idea of avoiding moonlight and recommended abstaining from certain kinds of activities. Spinning and sewing were not to be done by moonlight, as the rays would

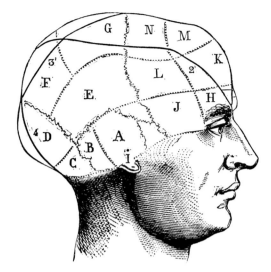

cause linen to weaken. It was also believed that what was sewn at that time would become the shroud. Clothes hung out in the moonlight were believed to cause the one who then wore them to be moonstruck. Tools left in the moonlight would break, and water from a well where the moonlight shone, if drunk, would fill the drinker with the evil effects of the light.

As mentioned earlier, the moon does not look the same from all vantage points on earth. For people living in the Arctic areas, for example, the light of the moon is much brighter than it is in other places, as it not only reflects off the ice, but at certain times merely skims the horizon, appearing to hover just above the earth, and not without a sinister, brooding aspect. Is it any wonder, then, that in Siberia the Chukchi people avoided looking at the moon for too long for fear of losing their wits?

Lunacy has long been associated with the effects of the full moon upon human beings. There is scarcely a culture in the world where we cannot find some mention of this connection. The Greeks looked to Hekate as the bringer of madness. As Esther Harding recounts, so fearful were they of her powers that they left a ritual meal called "Hekate's Supper" near crossroads, places thought to be specially favored by her. It was customary to leave the meal and walk away quickly without turning back.

The remnant of another legend of lunar madness whose age is impossible to date comes from the west of Ireland, and lies in the name given to a valley there, called *Gleann na nGealt* in the Irish Gaelic. The name is often translated as the "Valley of the Mad" and the "Valley of the Lunatics," though it has also been described as referring to the color of the moonlight on the night when the moon is full. The word *gealt* refers to a lunatic or crazy person, and is related to *gealach*, the word for moon. As Steve MacDonagh, an Irish publisher and writer tells it, tradition held for many years that the valley was once a place where mentally disturbed people went, hoping for a cure. It has even been rumored that Mad Sweeney of Irish literary fame spent his wildest years here, perched in the trees, feasting on cresses and spring water, which were later held to have curative power.

During the Middle Ages in Europe it was commonly believed that the moon was the cause of insanity, although according to Katzeff, one fellow who disagreed with that idea was St. Jerome, who told his followers that while the moon was widely believed to be the cause, demons were actually at fault. In Wales, Trevelyan found that lunatics were thought to have been exposed to moonlight as children. People who could never stop talking were described as "moon led." We have already mentioned the belief in Greenland that women avoided moonlight for fear of becoming pregnant. In Icelandic folk belief, if a pregnant woman exposed her face to moonlight her child would be born insane. Reflecting the hold this notion had in Europe, in 1845 in England the Lunacy Act was passed. This law was the first to recognize mental disturbance as a disease—although the phases of the moon and the kind of disturbance produced by each were named in the course of the legislation. Katzeff notes that on the contrary side of this argument, the English poet Thomas Chatterton told his friends that he was more alert and intelligent at the full moon.

In the United States, the effect of the moon upon mental disturbance has been dismissed by many as superstition, but after reading Paul Katzeff's chapter on "Madness" in *Full Moons*, the last laugh may be on ourselves for not paying better attention to what hundreds of generations have been saying in folk belief for thousands of years. Katzeff discusses studies conducted in places where people are not laughing about lunar effects, in psychiatric hospitals and mental health centers that record a statistically significant amount of increased activity in the disturbed behavior of patients. Likewise, crisis centers and hotlines, emergency rooms, as well as police departments and psychiatrists have come to recognize and accept, even when their scientific training argues against it logically, that something odd happens to the human frame of mind in correspondence with new and full moon. Is this wacko journalism reported in untrustworthy publications? No. A number of scientific studies, considering all sides of the issue, have been reported in such publications as *The New England Journal of Medicine, Lancet*, the *American Journal of Psychiatry*, the *Journal of Psychiatric Nursing and Mental Health Services, The Skeptical Inquirer*, and *Sky and Telescope*.

Two studies published in 1978, based on data collected between 1956 and 1970, proved to be quite controversial, and remain so. Miami psychiatrist Dr. Arnold Lieber and clinical psychologist Dr. Carolyn Sherin decided to see if there was any scientific basis to anecdotal information about a lunar effect on human beings, namely that at the time of full moon human behavior changed. Analyzing homicide statistics from Dade County, Florida, and Cuyahoga County, Ohio, according to the lunar synodic cycle, Lieber and Sherin reported that a causal effect existed, and that homicide increased at full moon and new moon. Many remain skeptical about Lieber and Sherin's work. A study that countered their findings appeared only two years later. Lieber questioned its validity as it did not compare the same kind of data. The Lieber-Sherin study analyzed time of attack; the second study (conducted by Drs. A.D. Pokorny and J. Jachimczyk) analyzed time of death. Nicholas Sanduleak, writing in a 1985 issue of *The Skeptical Inquirer*, refuted the Lieber-Sherin study by reanalyzing the Pokorny-Jachimczyk study. Sanduleak ultimately made a case for a combined lunar-solar effect, ironic in light of Lieber's words: ". . . we can conclude that many aspects of behavior reflect the net effect of both solar and lunar timing." Though it has quieted in recent years, the controversy still exists. With renewed interest in further moon

NUMSKULL STORIES

There are a number of stories about fools and the moon, called "Numskull Stories" by folklorists. They are told about humans as well as animals. An older version of a typical numskull story comes from China: a man walking near a lake or a river or a pond at the time of the full moon sees the huge beautiful orb reflected there. With his fishing pole or his net or his hands, he tries to capture the moon, and is mocked by others for his efforts. Though the poets have managed to turn this image of fishing for the moon into a beautiful metaphor, in the numskull stories the fisher is viewed a fool. The same sort of story shows up later in England. Here we can find an origin for the word "moonraker," applied to those who raked the water in order to capture the moon.

Sometimes the fool is a stranger who arrives in town, and is heard greeting the new moon as if it were the old moon. When asked why he does this, since obviously the moon is new, he says he has never been here before, and that certainly each town must have its own moon.

A Zulu tale from South Africa pokes fun at the hyena who, while carrying home a bone in his mouth, was stopped by the appearance of the full moon in a lake. Thinking it a big piece of meat, he put his bone down and tried without luck to retrieve it from the water. While he was busy at this, another hyena came along and stole his bone, leaving him with only a mouthful of water for his meal and his efforts.

exploration, perhaps it will surface yet again.

It is hard not to wonder what might happen if more attention were paid to some of this information. The Japanese people, for example, have a long and familiar history with the moon. Commenting on one aspect of this influence, Laurens van der Post, during his years as a prisoner of war in a Japanese prison camp, came to understand and document a change in the behavior of the camp guards toward prisoners near the time of new moon. It was a time when cruelty toward the prisoners increased. His careful observations allowed him to prepare the men under his command for a counter response. For thousands of years humans have been noticing something astir at the new and full moons. Remember, these are also the times when the moon has the most effect on the ocean tides. The question has been raised: if the moon can influence tides, can it also influence the actions of humans, whose bodily fluids resemble the composition of ocean salt water?

As for other medical events, Katzeff reports that plastic surgeons in India would not operate at full moon because they believed the danger of abnormal bleeding at that time to be quite real. A Florida physician who studied the records of more than one thousand tonsillectomy patients found an astounding connection between those who experienced abnormal bleeding and the full moon—an effect later confirmed by two additional and separate studies. A dentist in Colorado once confided to patients who were close friends that he had noticed more bleeding among patients at the time of the full moon, and that whenever possible he discreetly tried to schedule certain procedures when the moon was on the wane.

If human violence appears to be more rampant at particular phases of the moon, studies of suicide conducted across the country show that a relationship might exist between suicide and the moon. In Buffalo, San Francisco, Reno, and Cuyahoga County, Ohio, studies point to a connection between full moon and suicide. In studies from other parts of the world—Australia and Winnipeg, for example—first quarter suicide attempts seem more likely. It is important to point out that in these studies what researchers are looking for is not a relationship between the light of the moon itself and human behavior, but what effect the gravitational forces between the earth and the moon might have on humans (and the other living creatures on earth as well) during certain phases of the moon. The gravitational effect of the moon is known to be stronger at both new and full moon.

Some less deadly human activities have also been compared to the lunar rhythm. Paul Katzeff reports a phenomenon that scientific researchers have found—that of people adapting to a lunar rhythm. In one case, *Science* magazine reported the case of a healthy young man who was often plagued with insomnia. It was discovered that his circadian rhythm matched that of the lunar day. Experiments conducted with people remaining in caves or in underground living situations for long periods of time have also revealed a tendency for humans to adapt to a lunar rhythm. Cases have also been studied of the appearance of migraine headaches and asthma in accordance with lunar rhythms. Whereas older folklore held that the moon caused certain diseases, medical journals from Britain and the United States once argued a case for tropical diseases, as well as ulcers and urological problems, following a lunar rhythm. Alcoholism has been included in this pattern. Epilepsy has long been associated in the folk tradition with the moon. The word epilepsy itself comes from a Greek word that means "to seize upon from the moon." While many have given this no more than passing notice as folklore or superstition, a serious medical study described the records of patients whose attacks arrived punctually with the full moon. Another name for sleepwalking, pre-Michael Jackson, was moonwalking. Modern medical cases refer to a possible link between sleepwalking and the full moon.

Another kind of power attributed to the full moon is one mentioned by Briffault and others: the Greek belief that witches needed the moon in order to complete their work. Pliny recorded that the witches of Thessaly could draw the moon down from the sky; to counteract the possibility, people often created a great deal of noise to keep the moon from hearing the women's incantations. Pindar also commented on the origin of "drawing down the moon," saying that Aphrodite taught her son Jason how to perform this ritual, which in essence meant drawing the power of Hekate to oneself, the power that was significant in relation to the moon. The full moon was thought the best time to work witchcraft in India and among the Mongolian Tartars (where it was practiced exclusively by the women). A belief existed in the Shetland Islands that witches needed to soak up the moonlight in order to go about their work. The Roman occult practitioner Cornelius Agrippa believed that all magic was worked on earth through the intercession of the moon.

Margot Adler, the contemporary chronicler of the practice of Wicca, mentions the continuing tradition of "drawing down the moon" in relation to the power of the full moon. In a modern tale set in

Greece, the English writer Mary Stewart had one of her characters describe "the moonspinners," three women who were seen in the woods, spinning. The cloth they spun was drawn down from the moon onto spindles. When the spindles were full and the moon was dark, the women went to the ocean to wash the spun stuff. There it unravelled, trailing out across the water until it found its way back up into the sky and formed once more into the moon. A writer's imagination at work, or another version of drawing down the moon?

◐ *Animals and the Moon*

Since we have devoted a good deal of attention to the effects of the full moon and moonlight upon human beings, let us turn to the other creatures that share the planet with us, and see what their associations to the moon have been. Chapter 2 discussed how different cultures saw certain animals as legendary inhabitants of the moon and talked briefly about how some of those legends came to be. There are really two ways to reflect on the relationships of animals and the moon. The first is to consider them in light of the mythologies, legends, folklore, and customs that have developed around the world. The second is to consider how the mythological observation relates to any scientific understanding of the effects that different phases of the moon (especially the full moon) might have on animals. The natural associations between animals and the moon developed by different cultures are many and wonderful to consider. Two of the most fantastic full-moon creatures are the

Opposite page: Apollo 17 (last lunar mission) view of the full moon. (Photograph courtesy of NASA).

werewolf and the vampire. Mention of the werewolf occurs in Greek mythology with the story of Lycaeon, who was changed into a wolf because an angry Zeus refused his blood sacrifice of a child. Several classical writers mentioned werewolves: Plato, Herodotus, and Pliny among them. Petronius made fun of the belief in werewolves in the *Satyricon*, but as Paul Katzeff points out, the Romans believed heartily that the goddess Diana, who was mistress of the woods and the wild creatures in it, had the power to turn anyone who offended her into a werewolf. Since she was also the goddess of the full moon, it makes good mythological sense that under the influence of her light, she could wield tremendous power.

This idea of a human who transforms into a wolf (or other creature; there have also been werebears, werelions, werejackals, and even werecrocodiles in other cultures) and then kills and eats the flesh of other humans and animals predominated throughout Europe in the Middle Ages. We should keep in mind that throughout much of history, the wolf has been so feared that it has been virtually exterminated in both Europe and North America. An old tradition in Europe held that if a person were conceived at the new moon or fell asleep on open ground in the moonlight on a Friday night, he or she (most werewolves have been male, it seems) was in danger of becoming a werewolf. An earlier version of the change from human to beast indicates that these creatures tried to escape from the light.

The requirement of the transformation having to take place in full moonlight occurs in many tales, and in most Hollywood folklore. For example, a combination of the herb wolfbane and a full moon caused the metamorphosis for Wolfman Lon Chaney. Some scholars believe that traditions about werewolves can be traced to ancient initiation rites into animal cults like those sacred to Diana, while others find in them a deep-seated and ancient human fear of both predator animals like the wolf and the internal fear of the "beast" in us all.

The vampire, a unique creature of eastern European origin popularized by the novel *Dracula* by Bram Stoker, was a corpse returned to life who stalked new victims at night. Though vampires are associated with darkness, the traditions surrounding the vampire do not mention moonlight specifically, although Hollywood versions of this theme often use dramatic moonlight.

Animal Behavior

Because of the early recognition of the moon's influence on ocean tides, life within the fathoms has also had a special link to the moon. Greeks and Celts both noticed the moon-tide connection. So did the Maoris, the Eskimos, the Hawaiians, and the ancient Babylonians. Chinese, Arabic, and Icelandic, too, peoples all knew about tides. Tides are not equal across the earth because of the many factors that affect them—such as the tilt of the earth's axis, the earth's orbit around the sun, and the resistance encountered when water meets land. There are numerous good technical and scientific sources to consult on the moon's effects on the tides.

In a mythological connection with tides and water, however, the moon is often depicted as a deity that rules over water, moisture, rain, and the oceans. This was true in China, Japan, Australia, central Asia, and Brazil, among many other areas. Esther Harding and other contemporary women's studies scholars have pointed out that moon goddesses the world over can be found as the guardians of springs, wells, rivers, lakes, and streams—those places usually sacred to fertility goddesses. An example of how this sort of feeling and devotion has been carried forward in modern times can be seen in the numerous water sources still sacred to the Blessed Virgin Mary in Ireland and throughout many other Catholic countries of the world where the old moon goddesses assumed new identities with a change in religious traditions.

In Chinese culture the moon has always represented *yin*, the receptive feminine element, and thus associated with the dark, moist, cool, watery elements of nature. This is true of other Asian countries as well. Harley found that in Mexico and Peru, the water deities were honored at full moon. The Persians, like the ancient Indians, believed the moon was responsible for the earth having enough water; places in Persia that were lush and fertile had the name for the moon, *mah*, attached to them. In a different sort of idea, Pliny thought moonlight caused water to evaporate slowly and gently, and in fact increased its amount. These notions of associating the moon with water and tides parallel the ideas about the moon being responsible for the fertility of the earth as well.

In addition to ocean tides, scientific research has led to the discovery of atmospheric tides and terrestrial tides, which at least four scientific studies have indicated correspond to the pull of the moon on the earth. Atmospheric tides are more subtle and harder to measure. Terrestrial tides were discovered when distances between several places on earth were compared with previous calculations. The gravitational pull of the moon, though too subtle to be noticed on a daily basis, has caused the earth to rise nearly two feet or more in some places.

In the fourth century B.C.E., Aristotle noticed a connection between marine animals and the full moon. A century later, a Chinese scholar named Lu Pu-Wei made similar observations, that the muscles and gonads of certain sea creatures enlarged or shrank as the moon waxed and waned. Greek and Roman literature is filled with references to the effects of the full moon on fish, and according to Katzeff, the belief still holds today among fishermen the world around. For example, crabs are thought to be "full" at full moon and "empty" when the moon wanes, and North Atlantic fishermen have recorded bigger catches of herring at full moon. Reports of fishermen along the East Coast of the United States indicate that blue crabs shed their shells and thus grow soft at full moon. Crabs rise to the surface and lay their eggs at full moon. Another scientific study reported by Katzeff revealed that scallops spawn at full and new moons, as do the oyster, grunion, and several other sea creatures.

Scientific experiments such as those conducted by Frank A. Brown, Jr., have found that many sea creatures (oysters, for example) follow a lunar pattern for other behaviors such as feeding. The chambered nautilus creates a new twist to its shell on a lunar monthly pattern, giving it a unique association to the moon that was recognized in earlier cultures. Similarly, the snail emerges in and out of its shell like the moon emerging and disappearing in the sky. And in another comparison, the snail extends and retracts its horns. One particular snail is even called a moon snail. The quahog clam is another ocean dweller that follows both a daily and a monthly lunar pattern in opening and closing its shell.

Other water creatures with a special affiliation with the full moon include turtles, which dwell in both the sea and in fresh water. An early and persistent natural observation was that they also hide in the dark mud and re-emerge like the moon does. The shells of some of them contain a special message for certain people, as we shall see in Chapter 6. Sea turtles are specially drawn to the light of the full moon at a certain time of the year. They migrate to the southern coast of Florida in the late summer and lay their eggs at full moon. The

eggs hatch at the time of the full moon about two months later. In order to protect the turtles, bright artificial lights have been banned from the beaches during the nesting season so as not to confuse or distract the animals, who react to the moonlight. They have mistaken bright artificial light for that of the moon, and instead of moving back into the water, have gotten onto roadways, with disastrous results. Though the turtles have often been threatened by human predators as well as those they face in their own ocean environment, they are now protected at breeding time and have become a source of wonder, not plunder, to their human watchers. The frog is another water creature that, like the toad and the turtle, hides in the mud and reemerges like the moon. The frog was a creature used in many older moon rituals.

Although snakes are still considered to be truly slimy creatures, in fact they are not. The truly slimy creatures are worms, and they have their own special, if surprising, link to the moon. Scientific studies have revealed the relationship between the moon and the spawning and mating habits of several types of worms. One of the most well known (of those that are known outside the scientific community) is the palolo worm of Fiji. Recorded by an Englishman named William Burrows, the twice-annual spawning of this creature during the last quarter moon in October and November made for quite a predictable spectacle as the worms wriggled their way to the surface and mated. Astronomer

Anthony Aveni discusses how the Trobriand Islanders of New Guinea use the appearance of the palolo worm to keep and measure their own time. Directly and indirectly, the moon and its relationship to natural events, still sets the clock. Katzeff reports several studies that have to do with the lunar rhythms of worms and their relatives. One, from Wood's Hole, Massachusetts, describes a worm that swarms during the summer and early fall months at full moon. Another, though it has been known for some time, describes how eels begin their migration from European rivers to the Sargasso Sea after full moon. A third, in the *Journal of the Fisheries Research Board of Canada*, reported that a particular sea worm in Java swarms for three nights after the full moon throughout the year. Likewise, in Indonesia a worm known as "Wawo" swarms on the second and third nights after full moon during March and April. Not to be outdone by their showier relatives, even the humble earthworms follow a lunar pattern in their breathing.

Not only water creatures have been linked to the different aspects of the moon. Those who walk or crawl upon the land have their own connections. The snake, because of its self-regenerating nature, and because it also sheds its skin, like the moon appearing and disappearing, has long been thought a creature of the moon. Mircea Eliade added that the snake was also thought to be eternal, and to represent fertility, two more qualities in common with Luna. Reflecting this belief, a creation myth from southeastern Africa described a love affair between the wife of the moon and a snake. A legend mentioned in Chapter One from the Native American Blackfeet described a love affair between the moon and the Snakeman. Although used in ceremonies at the new moon phase as well as the full moon, the snake's association with the moon probably dates to prehistoric times.

As for other land animals and the moon, the Egyptian Horapollo wrote that baboons stood up and saluted the moon, and that when the moon was dark the baboons would not eat or look up at the sky. Mircea Eliade is just one of many who comments on the way that the hibernation and reappearance of the bear were compared to the phases of the moon. The ancient Egyptians, and the Greeks after them, believed that a cat's eyes changed as the moon changed. The black cat, as the familiar of witches, has been associated with both the new and the full moon. Associations between the cat and the moon most likely date to prehistoric times. Dogs, wolves, and coyotes are all known to howl at the moon. Briffault tells us that Hekate's companion was a dog whose bark was the mark of worship, and whose howling announced her arrival. The close association between horned animals and the moon has been discussed in Chapter Three, but the deer were sacred to the moon as they were the special animal of the goddess of the hunt and the full moon, Diana. It is possible that the nocturnal feeding habits

WITCHY PLANTS FOR A FULL MOON

Bat-plant (*Tacca chantrieri*)
Belladonna (*Atropa*)
Blood lily (*Haemanthus*)
Blood twig dogwood (*Cornus sanguinea*)
Bloodberry (*Rivina*)
Bloodflower (*Haemanthus coccineus*)
Bloodleaf (*Iresine*)
Bloodroot (*Sanguinaria*)
Bloody butchers (*Trillim sessile*)
Bloody cranesbill (*Geranium sanguineum*)
Cat's claw (*Macfadyena unguis-cati*)
Cat's ears (*Calochortus tolmiei*)
Cat's foot (*Antennaria*)
Chokeberry (*Aronia*)
Dead nettle (*Lamium*)
Deadly nightshade (*Solanum*)
Death camas (*Camassia*)
Devil flower (*Tacca*)
Devil in a bush (*Nigella*)
Devil's apple (*Mandragora officinarum*)
Devil's backbone (*Pedilanthus*)
Devil's bit (*Liatris spicata*)
Devil's claw (*Proboscidea louisianica*)
Devil's ivy (*Scindapsus aureaus*)
Devil's pincushion (*Coryphantha robustipina*)
Devil's tongue (*Sansevieria*)
Devil's walking stick (*Aralia spinosa*)
Devilwood (*Osmanthus americanus*)
Ghost plant (*Graptopetalum paraguayense*)
Ghost weed (*Bupherbia*)
Graveyard tree (*Plumeria*)
Luna witch hazel (*Hamamelis*)
Moonlight witch hazel (*Hamamelis*)
Poison lily (*Crimum*)
Poison spurge (*Euphorbia*)
Toad flax (*Lineria*)
Toad lily (*Tricyrtis*)
Witch hazel (*Hamamelis*)
Witch's broom
Woody nightshade (*Solanum Dulcamara*)
Wolfbane (*Aconitum*)
Wolfberry (*Symphoricarpos occidentalis*)

of deer also contributed to their special attachment to Diana.

Ancient hunters took advantage of the moonlight in pursuing their prey. So do modern ones. An article written in 1987 for a hunter's magazine tells of the author's modern-day determination to study the moonlight habits of deer—do they feed more often at new and full moons? It is a question many modern-day hunters would like answered. To think that hunting according to the phases of the moon is a habit left behind with our hunter-gatherer ancestors is not true. Many contemporary hunters and fishers are avid followers of Luna, as the demand for lunar and tide tables from these sports enthusiasts indicates. An article published in 1990 provided fishing charts developed by Neil Rothery for the United States. Combining the best of old and new world

wisdom, Rothery used lunar tables developed by the Maoris of New Zealand as sources for his computerized annual angling predictions.

Curious about folkloric hearsay that deer hunting was either best (or worst) when there was no moon, a new crescent moon, or at full moon, author Tim Lewis decided to find out for himself by studying the lunar habits of deer for nine months. Following a standard statistical method of charting, and armed with copies of John Alden Knight's *Solunar Tables*, and Doug Hannon's *Moon Times*, Lewis recorded the times that deer appeared in a certain vicinity, making all the possible adjustments for other possible factors besides the phase of the moon. The results? As he says himself, "nothing conclusive," indicating that he intended to continue his study. He did identify some trends that led him to recom-

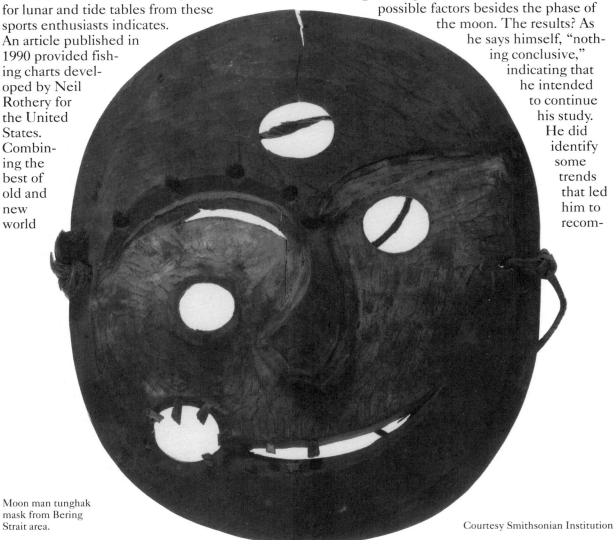

Moon man tunghak mask from Bering Strait area.

Courtesy Smithsonian Institution

mend, among other things, that hunters plan their outings in conjunction with the dark of the moon or full moon. Lewis would seem to be in good company, as Katzeff informs us that even St. Augustine and Francis Bacon believed in the effects of the full moon on animals.

Other creatures whose activities have been linked especially to the full moon in a less dramatic way include hamsters, lemurs, and rats. A study by Frank A. Brown, Jr., and Young H. Park showed that hamsters have a higher metabolic rate at full moon, and that the activity of rats follows a lunar cycle. Another study reported by Katzeff indicates that lemurs follow a lunar pattern of sexual activity that peaks just before full moon. A third study by biologist J.L. Harrison revealed that certain types of forest rats in Malaya mate at the full moon.

The creatures of the air should not be left out when considering lunar effect or influence. Birds have both their mythological and scientific place as well. It was said that Akla, a bird that belonged to Buddha, had feathers made of moonbeams. Doves, peacocks, and swans all have associations to the moon. Doves were the special bird of the Greek goddess of love, Aphrodite, who had clear ties to the moon. Katzeff mentions the existence of an African, belief similar to the European one of a stork delivering newborn children: western Africans once referred to the "Moon Bird," which was sent by the "Great Moon Mother." On a more scientific note, the scholar J.L. Cloudsley-Thompson found that Scandinavian grouse followed a lunar pattern in mating habits, and that lemmings and game birds also follow a complex lunar pattern of mating and reproduction. The nightjar is also most active at full moon.

Is it strange or weird that so many creatures follow a lunar pattern in their behavior and activity? Not at all. Like the many forms of life on earth, they are responding to certain kinds of stimuli, in this case light and the effects of gravity. What is interesting is that many of these same activities have been noted, albeit not in scientific notation, for thousands of years in mythology, legend, folklore, and story. In a fitting mythological metaphor about the animals of earth and the moon, according to Fitzhugh and Crowell, the Bering Sea Eskimos believed in a deity that had control over the animals and lived in the moon. Known as a *tunghak*, this deity was often represented in masks used by the shamans to "travel to the moon" (a phrase that in another context meant sexual intercourse) to plead with this spirit for success in hunting and other good fortune. Many of the masks of the Bering Sea Eskimos reflect a lunar theme and have the look of the old "man in the moon" as well. As far as the animals were concerned, it was believed that a hole had to be cut in the side of the moon so that the animals could get out. In an interesting parallel on earth, the house where the women of the tribe lived had a hole cut in it during the spring to allow exit. In these beliefs and practices lies a metaphorical expression and understanding of the moon's participation in the activities of the natural world of humans and animals.

If the presence of the full moon does not guide our lives in the same way it once did, it will probably never cease to allure and enchant us. No matter how much may be known about the astronomical realities of our sister in the sky, because of the beauty she brings to our world month after timeless month, shining like an eye, a marble, a mirror, a disc that combines the best of silver and gold well enough to have a color of her own, we will continue to honor her in our own ways. Maybe that means packing the family or friends off to the planetarium for a knowledgeable explanation. Maybe it means finding a clear hilltop away from the city to set the telescope up on. Maybe it means pausing at the end of a tiring day and just glancing up to see what we have always seen—Luna rising, still mysteriously, still unbound, in the sky.

HYMN TO SELENE

O Muses, sing of the far-flying moon,
you honey-voiced daughters of Zeus, son of
   Kronos,
who know our songs well.

From heaven streams the light from her head.
It floods the earth, and in its brilliance
all beauty comes forth. The black sky
brightens with her glow. Her rays fill the night
as she bathes in the radiant ocean and dons
garments that shine through a million miles,
as she yokes her burning team and races,
flecked with lightbeams, quarter by quarter
to fullness. Her course run
she shines her brightest from the height of the
   heavens
and shows herself as a sign to us mortals.

Zeus once lay with her, and she bore
the maiden Pandea, incomparably beautiful.
Hail, white-armed goddess, shining Selene,
you of the glistening flows of gold hair.
I begin my songs with you

and turn them now to the demigods
whom our singers exalt with crystalline voices

— translated by Gregory McNamee

BOMBER'S MOON: NEW YORK, 1944

*M*anhattan, honeycomb of light,
was dark "for the duration."
A full moon
whitened the sky over the city.
The air held a September softness,
resting before the excitement of October.

Suddenly air alerts warbled.
The hive stopped buzzing
and an eerie quiet spread.
Skyscrapers changed to silver spires:
a vast cathedral,
silent as a snow field.

Louvered traffic lights,
invisible from above,
signaled to empty streets.
No vibration from the subway:
the sidewalk, hollow five minutes ago,
felt solid under my feet.

I was herded into the lobby
of a small East-side hotel.
No panic, no pushing,
we stood silent,
watching through glass doors
crisscrossed with adhesive tape.

Soon I slipped outside
to stand entranced by the quiet,
the moonlight,
beautiful but deadly.

—Betty Chancellor

CHAPTER NOTES
Page numbers are in parentheses at the end of each citation.

The Illustrated Festivals of Japan (Japan Travel Bureau, Inc., 1985). (72)

Bushnaq, Inea. *Arab Folk Tales*. Pantheon Books. New York. 1986. (72–73)

The Encyclopedia of Religion. Mircea Eliade, editor. Macmillan. New York. 1987. (73)

Man, Myth & Magic: An Illustrated Encyclopedia of the Supernatural. Richard Cavendish, editor. Marshall Cavendish Corporation. New York. 1970. (73)

Harley, Rev. Timothy. *Moon Lore*. Swan Sonnenschein, Le Bas and Lowrey. London. 1885. Reissued by Singing Tree Press. Detroit. 1969. (73)

Laurens van der Post discusses this idea in *A Mantis Carol* (Island Press: Washington, D.C., 1975). (74)

Spence, Lewis. *Myths & Legends of Babylonia & Assyria*. George G. Harrap & Company. London. 1916. (74)

Webster, Hutton. *Rest Days: The Christian Sunday, the Jewish Sabbath and Their Historical and Anthropological Prototypes*. Macmillan Company. New York. 1916. (Republ. Gale Research Co., Detroit. 1968.) (74, 75, 77)

Trevelyan, Marie. *Folk-lore and Folk-stories of Wales*. Norwood Editions. Darby, Pennsylvania. 1973. (74, 78)

Thompson, Stith. *Motif-Index of Folk Literature*. Indiana University Press. Bloomington. 1955-58. (74)

Briffault, Robert. *The Mothers*. Abrdg. Gordon Rattray Taylor. George Allen & Unwin Ltd. London. 1927. (75, 76, 81, 85)

Katzeff, Paul. *Full Moons*. Citadel Press. Secaucus, New Jersey. 1981. (74, 75, 76, 78, 80)

Alta Jablow and Carl Withers have retold this tale in *The Man in the Moon: Sky Tales from Many Lands* (Holt, Rinehart and Winston: New York, 1969). (76)

Trigg, Elwood B. *Gypsy Demons and Divinitie*s. Citadel Press. New Jersey. 1973. (76)

Leland, Charles Godfrey. *Gypsy Sorcery and Fortune Telling*. University Books. New Hyde Park, New York. 1962. (76)

Montagu, Ashley, and Edward Darling. *The Ignorance of Certainty*. Harper & Row. New York. 1970. (76)

Evan Hadingham mentions this fairly well known folk custom in *Early Man and the Cosmos* (Walker and Company: New York, 1984). Alexander Thom published his notions of similar megalithic sites in Scotland in *Megalithic Lunar Observatories* (Clarendon Press. Oxford. 1971). (76)

Eberhard, Wolfram. *Studies in Chinese Folklore and Related Essays*. Indiana University. Bloomington. 1970. (77)

Trevelyan gathered this tale from the David Jones Family Manuscripts. (77)

This tradition was described to me by Jose Espinoza as being in current practice. (77)

Esther Harding describes the context of the power the Greeks felt the dark of the moon had over them in *Woman's Mysteries Ancient and Modern* (Harper & Row: New York, 1976). (78)

Gearrfhocloir Gaeilge-Bearla (Rialtas na hEireann: Baile ath Cliath, 1981). This Irish-English dictionary and inquiries among residents of the Dingle Peninsula revealed these translations for Gleann na nGealt. (78)

MacDonagh, Steve. *A Visitor's Guide to the Dingle Peninsula* (Brandon Press: Ireland, 1985). (78)

Lieber, Arnold L. *The Lunar Effect: Biological Tides and Human Emotions*. Anchor Press/ Doubleday. Garden City, New York. 1978. (79)

Sanduleak's study was reported in the Spring 1985 issue of *The Skeptical Inquirer*, and was summarized in the "News Note" column of *Sky & Telescope* for July 1985. (79)

Van der Post, Laurens. *The Night of the New Moon*. Hogarth Press. London. 1970. (80)

Stewart, Mary. *The Moon-spinners*. M. S. Mill and William Morrow. New York. 1963. (81)

For a definitive study of contemporary witchcraft, see Margot Adler's *Drawing Down the Moon* (Beacon Press: Boston, 1986). (81)

Both Eliade and Webster list peoples who noticed a connection between the moon and the tides. (82)

Katzeff reports on atmospheric and terrestrial tide studies. (82, 83, 84, 87)

Eliade, Mircea. "The Moon and Its Mystique" in *Patterns in Comparative Religion*. Sheed & Ward. London and New York. 1958. (85)

Interview with Florida residents Fred and Judy Parsons. (83–84)

Aveni, Anthony. *Empires of Time*. Basic Books, Inc. New York. 1989. (83–84)

Rothery, Neil. "Fishing by the Stars." *Outdoor Life* (14): 66-70. July 1990. (86)

Lewis, Tim. "Moonshine Bucks." *Nebraska Game & Fish* (11):50-53. December 1987. (86)

Fitzhugh, William and Aron Crowell. *Crossroads of Continents: Cultures of Siberia and Alaska*. Smithsonian Institution. Washington, D.C. 1988. (87)

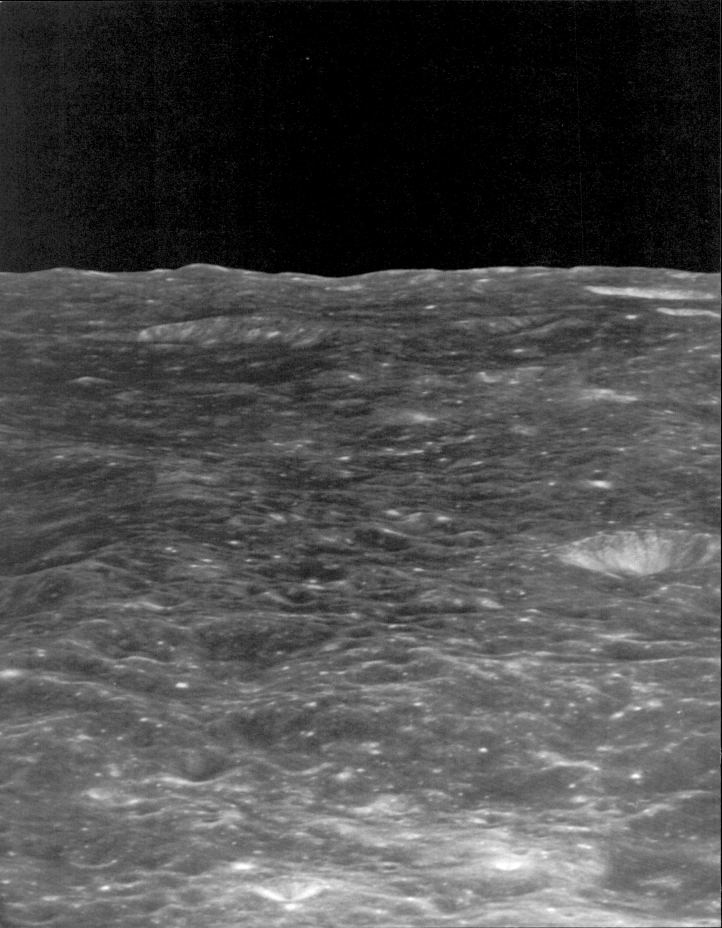

C H A P T E R 5

THE DARK ONE

✴

Far Side, Dark Side

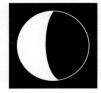

*"Everyone is a moon
and has a dark side which he never shows anybody."*
–Mark Twain

Opposite page: Apollo 8 view of the lunar surface. (Photograph courtesy of NASA).

MANY PEOPLES believed that the moon descended to the underworld during its dark phase, an idea that has served as the model for multiple myths throughout the world. One of the best known of these is the figure of Christ descending into Hell after his crucifixion and death, and then rising again on the third day. There were many deities who took the road to the Underworld long before he did, however. Isis endured a kind of harrowing of hell in her search for the scattered pieces of the corpse of her husband Osiris, which had been scattered by Set, the god of darkness and death. The Babylonian moon god Sin and the Greek moon goddess Selene, like the young Persephone, also descended to the shadowy Underworld. The tales of the Greek heroes Odysseus, Orpheus, and Aeneas recount similar descents. The goddess or god who traverses both the light and the dark worlds is nothing new to spiritual belief.

But there was one who went before all of these. Her name was Inanna, the Sumerian goddess known as the "Queen of Heaven and Earth," also known as Ishtar. She had many manifestations, and we must remember that before monotheism older cultures had a different psychological and emotional approach to their gods and goddesses, perceiving in them many different qualities and abilities. In what may be one of the most careful and beautiful retellings of an ancient myth brought forward across the centuries (indeed across the millennia) for our times, folklorist Diane Wolkstein and renowned Assyro-Babylonian scholar Samuel Noah Kramer collaborated for ten years to render Inanna's story in a way that accommodates the differences in language, culture, and time. This is not a story most of us heard while growing up, either in school or in church. After learning the story of Inanna as told by Wolkstein and Kramer, having Genesis as the starting point for spiritual and human beginnings seems comparable to starting the history of the airplane by beginning with the jet engine.

Wolkstein and Kramer's work is 227 pages long. In it, Inanna's stories and hymns are retold in a poetic narrative, accompanied by historical and mythical background. Inanna's myth is complicated. Like a literary archaeological dig, it reveals many layers. It tells the story of a cultural change, of a time when a society shifted from a pastoral to a more settled agricultural state, when the status of the female deity was beginning to change as well. The figures who represent that change are Inanna and her shepherd-lover Dummuzi, known also as Tammuz. In their many fascinating guises (which sometimes seem only confusing to us), Inanna and Dummuzi are also deities. Inanna is "Queen of Heaven and Earth," an epithet frequently given to the mother goddess as well as to the moon. We know from other study of Assyro-Babylonian culture the significance that was attached to the moon. Inanna was known as the daughter of the moon god Sin, and was also recognized as the personification of another heavenly body closely associated with the moon, the planet Venus. As Venus, she was also called Ishtar, the goddess of love and war. With so many associations to the moon, it would not be out of place to read at least part of Inanna's story as a moon myth.

The story that Wolkstein and Kramer reveal comes from a translation of cuneiform inscription; it may be the oldest poem uncovered in the world so far. Upon the death of her sister Ereshkigal's husband, Gugalanna (also called the Bull of Heaven), Inanna travels to the Underworld to comfort her sister, who rules there. As goddess of the Underworld, Ereshkigal is of course associated with death and darkness. We can see in her the qualities we also recognize in Greek Hekate, and so many other gods and goddesses who represent the dark side of the moon, as well as death and black magic.

Inanna is not naive about traveling into the dark realm her sister rules. She senses the danger of her journey and prepares for it by giving her servant, Ninshubur, special instructions to follow if she does not return in three days. The directions sound much like the ceremonial lament sent up during the dark of the moon by the people of this ancient culture. Inanna tells her servant to:

Set up a lament for me by the ruins
Beat the drum for me in the assembly places.
Circle the houses of the gods.
Tear at your eyes, at your mouth, at your thighs.

Inanna further instructs her servant to travel to the temples of Enlil, god of the air; Nanna, the father of Inanna; and Enki, the god of the ocean. These are three of the most powerful deities and include the moon god himself, known both as Sin and as Nanna.

As Inanna begins her descent, she must pass through seven gates. She is not accorded special status because she is Ereshkigal's sister, but must enter the world of darkness and death in the same manner as anyone else. At each gate she must remove some piece of clothing or some symbol of her office: her crown, a small necklace of lapis lazuli, then a larger double strand of lapis, her breastplate, her gold ring, the lapis measuring rod and line, and finally her robe. Much like the waning moon decreasing in its final stages, Inanna at last stands naked in the dark before the judges of the Underworld.

Unlike other tales about the disappearance of the moon into the darkness, this one tells what happened to Inanna while she was in the Underworld. Her sister, whose look alone was powerful enough to bring about death, turns her eye upon Inanna. Even though Inanna has come to grieve with her, Ereshkigal's grief is so fierce that she turns the full force of it upon her sibling and kills her. Inanna's corpse is hung up like a piece of meat on a hook, where it begins to rot after three days. Meanwhile, above ground the faithful Ninshubur awaits her mistress' return. When the third day comes and goes, Ninshubur does as Inanna has instructed. She goes in turn to the temples of Enlil, Nanna, and Enki and implores them to help Inanna return to earth. Enlil and Nanna answer that Inanna got what she deserved by traveling to the Underworld. Enki, in sympathy with Inanna, offers help. He creates two small creatures from the dirt beneath his fingernails. To one of them he gives the "breath of life," to the other the "water of life." He also gives them special instructions on how to behave once they enter Ereshkigal's presence.

The two little creatures, small enough to enter the Underworld unnoticed, find Ereshkigal wailing in her throne room. As Enki has instructed, they do nothing but mourn with her. They do not give her advice. They do not tell her everything will be all right. They do not tell her to look on the bright side or not to think about her loss. They honor her grief and grieve with her. When she cries, they cry. When she moans, they moan. Finally, she notices them and asks who is there. They present themselves. Because they are the first to truly mourn with her, she rewards them, as Enki knew they would, with the gift of anything they want. They ask for and receive Inanna's corpse, restoring it with the breath of life and the water of life.

Restored, Inanna returns with them to the world above, but not before she must pay another price. The Underworld is one of true balance: if one soul leaves, another must enter. Inanna ascends from the Underworld accompanied by demons who search for the soul they will claim. Along the road they see first Inanna's daughter and then her son, and seek to take them. Inanna begs them not to, as she loves her children dearly. They love her, too, as evidenced by their state of grief at their mother's absence. Farther along the road they spot Dummuzi, Inanna's consort. Instead of grieving, however, Dummuzi has dressed himself up in his finest robes. He shines like the sun in his pride. Inanna's anger is swift and furious. She commands the demons to take Dummuzi in her place. They chase him, but Dummuzi, like Inanna before him, also prays to another god for help, this time to Utu. Utu responds to Dummuzi's call by transforming him into a serpent which the demons could not catch.

This story in its totality is far more than a moon myth, but it is not hard to recognize the dying and rebirth of the moon in Inanna's journey, given what we know about the importance of the moon's return from the darkness in the cultures of Assyria, Babylonia, and Sumeria. These were people who faithfully observed the moon's journey across the sky, who mourned and were fearful at its absence, and who celebrated its return with special ceremonies. Older cultures did not always just "look on the bright side." They not only recognized the dark side, but acknowledged and honored it as a part of their daily lives. In our own culture, we are often quick to quote the old cliche about the only sure things being "death and taxes." We do not have any problem talking about taxes. Yet the remarkable impact of the work done by Elisa-

The University Museum, University of Pennsylvania (Neg. #S8-6829).

Hymn to Sin.

beth Kubler-Ross and others on death and dying reveals how hard it has been for us to talk about death, much less fully acknowledge its certainty in our lives. Perhaps lunar myths and legends about the dark side can help us understand one of the events that links us all.

◑ *Bad Luck and the Dark of the Moon*

The dark of the moon was generally considered to be an unlucky time. Arabians and Athenians alike looked to the last three days of the month that way, as an inauspicious time, and nearly every kind of activity ceased. Some tribes like the Akamba of India even extended this idea of standstill to birth, believing that no animal or human gave birth when the moon was not visible. One place in particular where we can examine how an ancient culture viewed the dark of the moon, known as "the day of sorrow," is in Babylonia. Priests were entrusted with the task of watching, recording, and reporting the moon's movements through the sky at all times. Prayer rituals and sacrifices were carried out during this time. One of the entreaties to the moon god Sin has survived.

Since astrology as well as astronomy seems to have had its beginnings in the cultures of Akkadia, Sumeria, and Babylon, and among the Chaldeans, where the fate of the state was un-questionably connected to the state of the heavens, there was great rejoicing when the moon returned. For hundreds of years the scientific and Judeo-Christian traditions of the West have tended to view the connections that ancient people made between the life of the heavens and daily life as nothing but the super-stitions of ignorant people. Drawn to the brink of disaster because of our careless disregard of the delicate balances required by Nature, we are starting to take a closer look at the early re-lationship humans established with both their

earthly and their heavenly surroundings. This is not a paean to astrology, but perhaps if we could learn some of the purposeful attention that related the natural world to human lives that older and different cultures enjoyed, we could benefit from it.

When viewed for itself in a more natural state, it seems only logical that an air of evil would surround the dark of the moon. Webster collected information that the Kikuyu of Africa, who saw the sun and moon as husband and wife, believed that the two quarreled and that the sun killed the moon each time she dis-appeared. During the time she was gone, most activity ceased. Equitorial African tribes be-lieved the new moon just emerging was hungry and vengeful, and tried to stay out of sight. They believed that the moon, if it saw them, would kill them.

It is hard to find a place in world culture where the dark of the moon has not been asso-ciated with death. Mircea Eliade mentions Ed-uard Seler as the scholar who noted that the moon would have been among the first objects in nature that humans would have watched "die." It disappeared for three days (or more, depending on weather and atmospheric condi-tions), completely dead or dark or out of sight, and then emerged and began to grow whole once again. The moon may have been the first model for belief in a deity, either a god or a goddess, who dies or descends into the under-world for three days only to be born again. The story that has become so familiar to us that we have almost come to believe that it originated with the Christian narrative is just the most re-cent telling of an ancient human myth. Briffault found that among the indigenous people of Australia the moon was thought to control life, death, and resurrection. In a statement that complements Seler's idea, the modern archaeo-astronomer James Cornell also points out that "For ancient man [sic], the discovery of the stars may have been the first step toward scien-tific, or at least cognitive awareness. . . ."

Consequently, the dark of the moon has long been associated with death and death rituals. In addition to those other inhabitants of the moon discussed in Chapter Two, many notions existed about the moon as a land of the dead.

From the earliest times, the soul was associated with the moon. In some cultures, dead souls were thought to dwell on the moon. In other cultures, it was the lost or damned souls that could be found there. The Upanishads, Hindu writings composed between the eighth and sixth centuries B.C.E., speak of two roads the soul could follow after death: the road of flame and the road of smoke. The road of smoke leads to the moon, to ancestors, and to reincarnation. The Upanishads further taught that the moon was a way station for souls; there they awaited another reincarnation or continued on their path to perfection. Eliade mentions a belief in ancient Iran that good souls passed through the moon on their way to the sun and then on toward the light of the supreme deity, Ahura Mazda. This parallels a belief recorded among the Inuit, that at death the soul is lost and travels first up to the moon and eventually on to the sun. The same theme can be found in Plato's *Republic*. Pythagoras popularized the notion that the Elysian Fields were on the moon. Plutarch believed that the moon was a place where the souls of the just received a purification. In the ancient world of Babylonia, the moon god Nanna-Sin, at whose return people rejoiced by shouting and celebrating, was, in his dark aspect, associated with death. Belief held that on the last day of the month the moon traveled to the underworld; there the moon god sat in judgment of the dead souls.

Evan Hadingham points out that while the Scottish archaeologist Alexander Thom argued that megalithic sites at Kintraw, Clava, and at

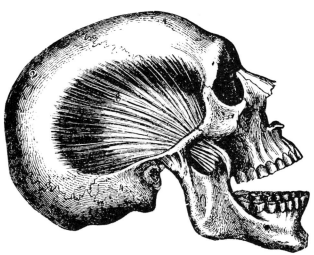

Callanish in northern Scotland could have served as lunar observatories, other evidence points to the possibility that the sites were used as shrines and ceremonial locations related to the moon. In a cairn at Kintraw, for example, a false doorway or gateway seems to be aligned to the moonrise, and may be part of a belief that the dead would watch the path of the moon through the sky. In *The Mabinogion*, the mythological cycle of nearby Wales (which is culturally linked to ancient Scotland), Prince Pwyll leads a group of his followers to the Celtic Otherworld by passing through just such a doorway. Though Pwyll's story is not conclusive evidence, it certainly points to a similarity in belief.

Extensive work by Mircea Eliade, Samuel Noah Kramer, and others has revealed that the symbol of the moon was used in Sumerian, Assyrian, and Babylonian funeral carvings and reflected the belief that the moon was a place where the souls of the dead reposed. The symbol of the crescent moon was also used in Egyptian, Greek, and Roman funeral carvings. E. Wallis Budge, who collected the inscriptions inside the Egyptian pyramids, found recorded instructions in the *Book of the Dead* that certain prayers be recited at new moon and at special full moon dates. To the Bushmen of South Africa, the horns of the new moon pointed upward was a sign of death. Charles Hardwick, writing about African tribal beliefs, quotes the work of M. Du Chaillu, who traveled among the Ashango and later described the lunar beliefs of people he met. Even though they believed the sun and moon to be the same age, they told a story about an argument between the two. Each one claimed it was the oldest, and they insulted each other back and forth in the attempt to prove it. Finally, the moon claimed that it had more companions than the sun, pointing to all the stars. The sun answered back by saying that if the moon had not killed so many people on earth, the sun would have more company. The Ashango believed that along with darkness the moon brought witchcraft, evil, sickness, and death. They believed that death came at the new and full moons.

Aristotle was among the first to note a belief later popular throughout Europe that people died with the ebb tide, a notion that persisted well into the twentieth century among sea-faring and coastal peoples, and was recorded in the British Isles.

The time of the dark of the moon was deathly still in other ways, as nearly all normal activity ceased—field work, cooking, planting, journeys, sometimes eating and even playing. Children were often cautioned to make no noise during this time, so as not to offend or upset the moon. This was not an auspicious time for marriage or birth, and in emulation of the moon's disappearance, many communities literally came to a standstill. In parts of India, even the steers were given a rest from their hard work in the fields.

While such a notion of standstill may seem quaint, archaic, or even foolish to present-day cultures or societies that propel themselves nonstop at any time of day or night, season, or lunar phase, the Sabbath or a day of rest (which existed in many cultures, not just Judeo-Christian) most likely has its origins during the pause in human industry during the dark of the moon. Samuel Noah Kramer tells us that the Sumerians believed the moon descended to the underworld each month on the day it was not visible. The *Encyclopedia of Religion* records that they called this time "the days of laying down." The word *sabbatu* apparently comes from the Assyrians and meant "a day of rest for the heart." The Akkadians, who developed the week and devoted its days to the sun, moon, and planets, denoted the Sabbath with words that meant work was forbidden.

Both Jain and Buddhist traditions honor a sabbath period. Called *posaha* among the Jains, this was noted as a time of abstinence from not only work but all pleasures of the senses as well, including sex and even incense. According to Hutton Webster, the Buddhist sabbath seems to be related to an older Vedic lunar celebration of change in the phases of the moon. The Buddhist restrictions extended from avoiding certain activities to abstaining from particular kinds of foods. Similar practices were found in Tibet, and among Chinese Buddhists four sabbath-like days were observed at the changes in the moon's phases. In India, study of the Vedas was partially governed by the time according to the moon. Although many other

HOW THE WORLD TURNS

*T*he original lunar deities were described as spirits that oversaw wisdom, writing, knowledge, the creative powers (including both earthly and human fertility as well as artistic endeavor), and the laws of both nature and humanity. Though these presences recognized as well the virtue of intuitive ability, prophecy, oracle, and inner wisdom, akin to the notion of Sophia, the numinous being that haunts the "Wisdom" literature of the Bible. Times have changed. The solar gods and spirits and consciousness have come to dominate our thinking, our outlook, and our lives. Once the lunar deities were thought to "illuminate" human life. In the list of words below, consider how that sense has changed, even reversed itself, as you consider which words apply to the moon or to the sun.

Night	*Forsaken*	*Pity*
Illusion	*Golden*	*Logic*
Day	*Silver*	*Torment*
Delusion	*Rays*	*Reason*
Dark	*Sweat*	*Rejection*
Evil	*Sweet*	*Rational*
Illumination	*Profusion*	*Heaven*
Hallucination	*Peace*	*Emotional*
Wisdom	*Ascend*	*Heavenly*
Blissful	*Descend*	*Ethereal*
Peaceful	*Affinity*	*Surreal*
Serene	*Divinity*	*Intuition*
Divinity	*Grief*	*Cerebral*
Despair	*Anguish*	

prohibitions were also in force, study was forbidden on the day of the new moon, the eighth and fourteenth days, and on the full moon. In Japan, three days were observed: the first day of the month, full moon, and the final day of the old moon. In ancient Iran four days were observed in connection with the moon. Even though the Egyptians were probably using a solar calendar by the fourth millennium B.C.E., celebrations from a previous lunar calendar were still held on the first and the fifteenth of the month. These older traditions, transmitted through cultural contact, clearly seem to have been updated or at least brought along into the Judeo-Christian systems, and can ultimately be traced to observances that paused to consider seriously the phases of the moon.

If the dark of the moon was a time to be quiet, either in honor or fear of the lunar absence, the Canaanites, Hindus, Jews, Teutons, and Moroccans all believed that the dark of the moon was the best time to commit foul deeds. In England and other countries the dark of the moon was the best time to pick herbs used for working charms. It was also the best time to acquire a lucky rabbit's foot (the left hind foot), provided that the rabbit was killed near a cemetery by a cross-eyed person. Webster informs us that the Dravidian people of India had firm beliefs about the dark of the moon being an evil time. No one went to the fields on the last day of the month. A birth at that time signalled a death. Calves or foals born then were sold. People abstained from eating cooked food on the last day of the darkness, a prohibition similar to those discussed previously. In medieval religious thought, on several occasions theologians mentioned that even the devil blamed his own evil misdeeds on the moon.

While the full moon was considered the most powerful time to work most modern witchcraft, the dark of the moon was considered best in other times and places, such as Greece. Hekate, who represented the dark of the moon and its true power as far as the ancient Greeks were concerned, was the guardian of witches. The dark of the moon was considered the best time to pick herbs specifically used in both black magic and healing. Curses and charms were most effective if uttered in the darkness, but it

was also the best time to work white magic. Briffault remarked that Germans were especially on the lookout for evidence of witchcraft on Monday (Montag), the "moon's day," and that along the Gold Coast the word for the moon was the same as the word for witchcraft. Pope Innocent VIII officially banned witchcraft in 1459, nearly two hundred years before the hideous witchcraft trials and burnings of the Inquisition took place throughout Europe.

In the new scholarship on women's studies and women's spirituality, the issue of witchcraft and its relationship to the old religion and the passing of the old ways has been discussed quite thoroughly. Readers are encouraged to study some of the courageous and groundbreaking work by writers and scholars such as Elaine Pagels, Charlene Spretnak, Starhawk, Hallie Iglehart, Monica Sjoo, and Barbra Mor, to name a few. Likewise, the best study of the status of contemporary paganism and witchcraft and its relationship to the moon can be found in Margot Adler's *Drawing Down the Moon*. The notion of contemporary paganism and witchcraft is a volatile one, and one which evokes immediate and mostly fearful response, given the emphasis that has been placed on devil worship and cults. The study of paganism and witchcraft, however, is an important part of the study of human thought and history.

◉ *Eclipse*

Another feature of the dark side of the moon is the solar eclipse, which occurs when the new moon passes directly between the earth and the sun. Throughout history, more often than not people viewed eclipses with uncertainty and fear. It was almost always an evil omen that presaged ill luck for the individual, the family, the state, the nation—even the world—and was often thought to predict war, famine, plague, blight, destruction, and other horrors. For example, the story of the destruction of the Athenian fleet before the battle of Syracuse was blamed on an eclipse. The Athenians delayed their expedition against Syracuse because an eclipse, considered to be a bad omen, occurred at the time of their scheduled departure. Many cultures abstained from work, food, drink, and

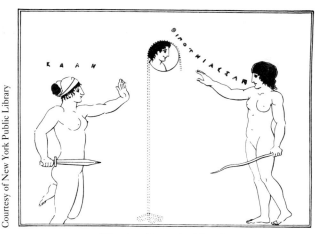

"Drawing Down the Moon"

even sexual intercourse during an eclipse. Webster notes that in ancient Jewish culture, where eclipses were viewed not just as dangerous but evil, people fasted, a natural kind of sacrifice in order to try and propitiate the forces that controlled nature, and thus existence itself.

In Tahiti, a world and several lifetimes away, Harley mentions that an eclipse was seen as a time when the earth was filled with evil. Prayer in the temple was in order, to appease a god who had perhaps been offended, even accidentally. In southern India it was usual for people to go inside and close up their houses during an eclipse. Chinese merchants closed their businesses. Trevelyan found that in Wales eclipses were feared and were thought to foretell, as the Babylonians and Sumerians believed, some national danger or disaster, as the sun hid its face from view. Fearful that the shadow of the eclipse would cause the water to become impure, Welsh people once covered their wells during eclipses.

Many cultures recorded lunar eclipses—the Babylonians and the Chinese were just two among many. Chinese astronomers were the first, as far as we know, to make a written record of a lunar eclipse in 1136 B.C.E. Stories of eclipses had existed from one thousand years before that date, and a common popular belief even at the later time was that an eclipse was caused by a dragon or other monster eating the moon. Officials of the ruling class, fully aware of the approaching eclipse, were always suc-

cessful at "saving the moon." One sad story from the reign of Chung K'ang has survived, however; the emperor's astronomers slipped up on their predictions on one occasion because it seems they were too busy drinking (Chinese poets had a known fondness for wine, flowers, and moon-watching, but apparently the astronomers preferred one over another). Their lapse caused a panic. They were executed for their waywardness, so critical was the public prediction of eclipses to the state.

The famous Dresden Codex, one of the few written records preserved from pre-Conquest Mexico, is actually a table of lunar eclipses recorded by the Maya, and contains a calendar and almanac for predicting eclipses. The Maya paid attention to the movement of the moon, sun, stars, and planets, and incorporated their movements into their ritual and social calendrical systems. As described by archaeoastronomer James Cornell, the lunar tables in the Dresden Codex follow a pattern of 177 days (six lunar months, from full moon to full moon) and 148 days (five lunar months)—reconciled with a period of eclipse. Another noted astronomer, Anthony Aveni, comments that the Dresden Codex records an eclipse table which uses the same cycle used by the Chaldeans in the Old World. Called the Saros Cycle, it represents a cycle of thirty-five similar kinds of eclipses. Most of us do not know what phase the moon is in on a given day without consulting an almanac or a lunar calendar, much less the cycle for lunar eclipses. It is no longer necessary for us to keep such careful track of the lunar phases, so we believe. Consequently, any group of people or culture who historically kept such information may seem to us mysterious, obsessed with time and the heavenly bodies, or even mystical. Developing a lunar eclipse table from scratch takes some work, certainly. It demands careful concentration and attention to detail over a long period of time. But that is precisely what people of many cultures did as part of their daily lives —they observed the natural world carefully and consistently over generations, eras, eons, millennia. When the only power illuminating the dark was oil, candles, and the stars and moon, the powers of observation and concentration had a different focus than they do now.

Since often the easiest way to explain a complicated subject, or even an unknown one, is to tell a story about it, cultures did just that to explain the lunar eclipse as they did with other lunar events. In Babylonian mythology, the moon darkened because seven horrible spirits attacked it and tried to destroy it. At the bidding of the chief god Anu, the god of the ocean and the sun god were sent to help. The seven wicked ones were overcome by the flames of the sun god, which, in one way of looking at it, is exactly what happens.

The Buriat also found an interesting way to explain both lunar and solar eclipses, according to *The Mythology of All Races*. In their version, a monster named Alkha once darkened the world and made the gods so angry that they cut him in two, leaving him a head but no body. He ate the sun and the moon, causing them to disappear as they do temporarily during an eclipse; but, they both fell out through his head and appeared once again. An Egyptian tale of the lunar eclipse involved the god Set, who chased the moon, known as the Left Eye of Horus, and struck it blind. In India the belief flourished that the lunar eclipse was caused by a serpent or monster devouring the moon. In Hindu belief, a story whose elements are frequently echoed in surrounding cultures tells how a demon spirit named Rahu, who had stolen the drink of immortality, chased the sun and moon through the sky because they told the warrior Vishnu what he had done. Harley further recounts that in Asian countries in general, people shouted and made noise by banging together pots and pans or whatever instruments they had in order to frighten the dragon so it would let go of the moon. Katzeff mentioned an exception to this in southeast Asia where a frog was believed to have swallowed the moon at eclipses; the same belief held true at one time in Persia, India, Finland, Lithuania, Africa, Borneo, and Italy. The element of the chase existed also in Scandinavia, where the lunar eclipse was caused by two wolves, Skoll and Hati, who chased the moon. Other peoples of Mexico also had their stories. To the Tlaxoaltecs, as Harley tells it, since the sun and moon were husband and wife, an eclipse was a domestic quarrel. According to Gyles and Sayer, the Totonac people also believed that eclipses were the result of quarrels between the sun and the moon, and that the sun and the moon shining with equal brightness will signal the end of the world.

Several ancient writers and astronomers commented and puzzled over the eclipse phenomenon. The Chaldean Berosus was incorrect when he declared that the moon dimmed because she turned her dark side to the earth. In another step toward scientific theory in place of story, both Aristotle and Pythagoras, watching lunar eclipses and noting the curved shape of the earth's shadow on the moon, concluded early on that the earth was round. In turn, they agreed with Plato that the eclipse was caused when the moon fell into conjunction with the sun. Anaxogoras (b. 499 B.C.E.) was the first to understand the real cause for the eclipse, but was considered an atheist for his belief and thrown into prison for his attempts to explain it. Harley recounts a little-known story about the way Christopher Columbus used his knowledge of a forthcoming eclipse to free and feed himself and his men, who were being kept prisoner during one of their journeys to the New World, by saying he would take away the light of the moon if they were not cared for. The eclipse occurred on March 1, 1504.

Though the thought of monsters or wolves or torso-less creatures is an exciting way to tell the story of lunar and solar eclipses, in fact the phenomena are caused by light and shadow. A lunar eclipse occurs when the Moon, Earth, and the Sun line up on the same plane in their orbits, with Earth between the Moon and the Sun. Earth's shadow falls across the Moon. Not every eclipse is total. Some are partial. Others are penumbral, which means that the sun's reflected light on the moon is dimmed but not obscured. Eclipses occur in the sequence they do because of the tilt in the plane of the moon's orbit. Even though we know the scientific explanation for a lunar eclipse, no one wants to miss the opportunity for viewing one when it occurs.

This sort of darkness, as well as the dark phase of the moon and then the dark side of the moon itself, has found an unusual mode of expression in religious iconography in the person of the Black Virgin. Her worship emerged in places such as Africa, South America, Spain, Portugal, and Mexico, but she is also found throughout Europe, including Scandinavia, Switzerland, France, and Poland. Though some scholars have claimed that Europeans came into contact with the Black Virgin during the Crusades and brought her worship back into Europe, the famous Black Virgin of Chartres pre-dated Christianity. The "Shulamite" spoken of in the Song of Solomon may represent an earlier form of the Black Virgin, obviously pre-Christian. Now most often recognized in the form of the Virgin Mary, she has a much older heritage as the dark of the moon. One interesting example of her history and worship can be found in Ireland.

In the medieval maze of Dublin streets, within walking distance of Grafton Street and Saint Stephen's Green, is a Carmelite Church that holds a special dark treasure. Stepping along through the unfamiliar paths can be dizzying—the street and lane names change every block or so, weaving one into the other like lost pieces of history. Though strange at first, the challenge of keeping track of the names, or of finding the right street, becomes a quest in its own right. The treasure will certainly be worth it, though it would be no surprise to ask another traveler for directions and run the risk of being told perhaps that, oh no, the street has not been here for 250 years. But the turns, straight on twice, then left, then right, bring the traveler to the destination—a small stone church tucked into a street that seems more like a lane, as if one or the other had always been there.

For the middle of the day, the Carmelite church seems full, almost bustling. People come and go. Old women whisper to each other, bowing their heads reverently as they pass the friar who seems to be standing guard near the entrance. The young women and boys talk openly amongst themselves—no whispering, though no disrespect either. The friar is only giving directions. The guidebook says the treasure is above the main altar, but the main altar lies straight ahead and the treasure is nowhere in sight. To come all this way, across a continent and then an ocean and a country, to find the treasure missing? No, the friar chides gently, and points. Simply turn around, and there she is, over the right shoulder (is it good luck or bad to spot the dark moon over the right shoulder?). The treasure. The Black Virgin. Our Lady of Dublin. The Dark Moon.

She is well dressed and kept there above the altar toward the back of the church. She wears silk and gold, accenting her lovely wooden skin, dark as a moonless night. Her child, holding a pomegranate in his hand, reaches out in a more human way than some of the other representations of the Christ Child—her lovely boy, almost wiggling out of her arms, like any infant. She is proud and dark and silent. They come to her, the faithful and the needy. Believers cluster at her feet like stars. Her story is similar to the one told over and over about others like her, nearly four hundred of them altogether throughout the world—in Africa and Mexico and Spain and India, yes, but also in Chartres and Czestochowa and Einseideln. Somehow, they now say, the statues were burned or painted or broken or destroyed or stolen, then burned and painted again. Where the wood is ebony or teak, the stories do not hold. Even where they do, there is an older story behind them. In the case of Our Lady of Dublin, it is said of her that during Cromwell's time the statue was desecrated, burned, and then used as an animal trough, only to be later recovered by a priest and restored to a place of honor above first one church altar and then another. A clue to her older history lies in the reasons people still come to her. This chapel is a favored place for weddings. More than that, if the marriage proves childless, young couples seek the power of her grace and blessing, as young couples have always sought out the moon for such blessings.

She is today the representation of the Roman Catholic Blessed Virgin. She is a sister to the Black Virgin of Chartres Cathedral, built, as tradition would have it, like so many churches, on a pre-Christian worship site. Though there are two Black Virgins recognized at Chartres, the altar of one is near a well, known to be the oldest site there. The old Gypsy festival of Sainte-Marie-de-la-Mer described by Anne Rush has similar overtones of an older lunar celebration in its reverence for the Black Virgin. Celebrated on May 24–25, the ritual involved walking to church and maintaining a vigil in the crypt where a statue of Sara Kali, a form of the Black Virgin, was kept. The devotion involved hanging all sorts of garments around, touching the statue, and then touching the garments to it and other objects for healing and blessing. The four hundred or so statues of the Black Virgin throughout the world (some original, some replacements, some replicas) can be traced to a tradition of honoring the dark side of the moon goddess. Many scholars have pursued this trail and their arguments are convincing.

We live in times that have been described as having a "solar consciousness" about them. We are admonished to look on the bright side, not worry, be happy, have a nice day. We have little patience with sadness or death or grief, and depression. Even unpleasant thoughts frighten us into silence. We do not like to talk about them. We avoid the dark, whether the shadowy side of the street or the shadowy side of life. This has not always been the case. In many traditional cultures and throughout history, both the dark side and the light side have been recognized, each for what they are and what they mean to human existence. Nothing better symbolizes both the light and the dark than the moon does. It has both, constantly moving into or out of one into the other, without rest; it is ever-changing and yet ever the same.

There are dark female deities in many cultures. Diana of Ephesus was depicted as both black and white. Kali of India is the dark devouring female image. Coatlicue of Mexico is the mother-creator and the destroyer. She

brings life, and she takes it away. She is light and dark, like life and death itself. The Egyptian goddess Isis and her son Horus were often presented as the Black Madonna and her child. Their story was associated with life, death, and resurrection. The Ainu of Japan dressed their personification of the moon in a black and white garment.

The Black Virgins, most scholars believe, represent a remnant of this awareness of both dark and light brought forward into Christian iconography. The Virgins are also connected with the notion of Wisdom. Not the wisdom we can gather during a lifetime of experience, but the Wisdom of the universe, the hidden feminine presence once known as Sophia, described in what has come to be called the Wisdom literature of the Bible and in the Gnostic texts known as the Nag Hammadi manuscripts, discovered in 1945. In older cultures, wisdom was also connected with the moon. Lunar deities, both female and male, are quite often the caretakers of wisdom and knowledge, bringing it to humans, showing them the way through the laws of language, writing, and natural and social order. These representations persist in the figures of the Black Virgins, whose names and qualities also provide clues: protector of children, of women in childbirth, bringer of fertility, overseer of birth. Her image has been discovered nailed to an oak tree; another site was miraculously uncovered by a special light; and yet another discovered by ani-

Diana of Ephesus

mals that led the way—all qualities that through the centuries were attributed to the moon. In personifying this aspect and bringing it closer to human life, previous generations visualized the spirit of the moon on earth through these little dark goddesses who have successfully made the transition from one religious system to another. Throughout the countries where the Black Virgins reside, devotion to them is still widespread and fervent. The painting of the Black Virgin of Czestochowa in Poland counts among her most ardent admirers none other than His Holiness Pope John Paul II.

◑ *The Far Side of the Moon*

Black Diana of Ephesus

There is one other aspect of the moon that we know more about scientifically than mythologically, and that is the far side of the moon, known to us as the dark side because it is always turned away from earth. Here, by the way, would be a good subject for the creation of a modern myth: to explain why the far side always faces away from the earth in story form. It is one of those scientific realities that is so simple and elegant as to appear unbelievable or unexplainable. As every text on the topic will say, the reason the moon always shows the same face to the earth is because the moon takes the same amount of time to complete its orbit around the earth as it does to complete one of its own revolutions. Some people advise trying to simulate this with an apple and an orange, both turning. Others suggest one person moving in a circle around one person seated. Still others say the best thing to do is find the right person who can explain it to you. Another method is to get two bottles. Move one of them around the other, letting one complete a full but slow circle. Another way to consider it is that if the moon were not itself moving, then it would eventually be completely exposed as it turned. A modern story might help us all understand this better.

Many myths speak to the dark of the moon and the hidden nature of the moon, but the far side itself has remained a great mystery to humanity even into the current century.

The Russian satellite named Lunik III returned the first photographs of the far side of the moon to the earth during its voyage in 1959. Subsequent American space shots, notably during the Apollo mission, also photographed the far side of the moon. Probes have landed there, but so far no one from earth has set foot on the far side. A book of predictions, based on scientific fact, that even now reads like a possible mythology for the far side of the moon, described the potential for setting up a cosmic observatory on the far side, one that could listen and watch deep space. During the piloted Apollo flights, orbit to the far side of the moon was a time of wonder and worry, since communications with earth were cut off, unable to penetrate the moon itself. The far side is physically quite different than the near side, with a pockmarked countenance that shows its history of being struck by thousands of meteors from space. We have much to learn about the far side yet, both scientifically and mythologically. But let us continue on our search of the mythology and mystery of Luna, to find out how humans first used the mythological beliefs about the moon to construct for themselves a scientific way of measuring time by creating calendars.

Photograph courtesy of NASA

Apollo 8 moon view of the farside.

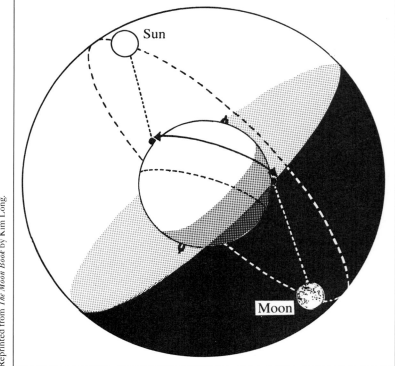

Reprinted from *The Moon Book* by Kim Long.

Sun

Moon

The moon's rotation around the earth.

CHAPTER NOTES
Page numbers are in parentheses at the end of each citation.

The summary of Inanna's tale is from *Inanna Queen of Heaven and Earth* by Diane Wolkstein and Samuel Noah Kramer (Harper & Row. New York. 1983); likewise, the quoted passage. (92–94)

Webster, Hutton. *Rest Days: The Christian Sunday, the Jewish Sabbath and Their Historical and Anthropological Prototypes.* The Macmillan Company. New York. 1916. (Republished by Gale Research Company. Detroit. 1968). (95)

The chapter entitled "The Moon and Its Mystique" in *Patterns in Comparative Religion* by Mircea Eliade (Sheed & Ward: London and New York, 1958) is one of the most informative and evocative discussions of the importance of the moon to human life. This observation alone, about the moon presenting to humans by its own changes the notion of death and dying (and rebirth), is worth pondering for weeks. (95, 96)

Briffault, Robert. *The Mothers.* Abrdg. Gordon Rattray Taylor. George Allen & Unwin Ltd. London. 1927. (95, 98)

The Upanishads. Translators Swami Prabhavananda and Frederick Manchester. New American Library. New York. 1948. (96)

Hadingham, Evan. *Early Man and the Cosmos.* Walker and Company. New York. 1984. (96)

Walton, Evangeline. *The Prince of Annwn: The First Branch of the Mabinogion.* Ballantine Books. New York. 1974. (96)

Budge, E. A. Wallis. *The Book of the Dead: The Hieroglyphic Transcript of the Papyrus of Ani.* University Books. Secaucus, New Jersey. 1960. (96)

Hardwick, Charles. *Traditions, Superstitions, and Folk-Lore.* Arno Press. New York. 1980. (96)

Webster, Hutton. *Rest Days: The Christian Sunday, the Jewish Sabbath and Their Historical and Anthropological Prototypes.* The Macmillan Company. New York. 1916. (Republished by Gale Research Company. Detroit. 1968.) (97)

Kramer, Samuel Noah. *The Sumerians: Their History, Culture, and Character.* University of Chicago Press. Chicago. 1963. (96, 97)

Trevelyan, Marie. *Folk-lore and folk-stories of Wales.* Norwood Editions. Darby, Pennsylvania. 1973. (99)

Aveni, Anthony F. *Skywatchers of Ancient Mexico.* University of Texas Press. Austin and London. 1980. (99)

The Mythology of All Races. Gray, Louis Herbert. Marshall Jones. Boston. 1916. (100)

Katzeff, Paul. *Full Moons.* Citadel Press. Secaucus, New Jersey. 1981. (100)

Gyles, Anna Benson and Chloe Sayer. *Of Gods and Men: The Heritage of Ancient Mexico.* Harper & Row. New York. 1980. (100)

This description of the Black Virgin of Ireland, Our Lady of Dublin, comes from my own visit to the Carmelite Church in June 1986. (101–102)

Ean Begg's *The Cult of the Black Virgin* (Arkana: London and New York, 1985 o.p.) is particularly enlightening on this dark subject. In addition to a gazetteer of sites where Black Virgins exist or have been found, he provides a thorough history of the research to date. (101)

Esther Harding mentions the Black Virgin in her unparalleled discussion of ancient women's rites and their relationship to the moon in *Woman's Mysteries Ancient and Modern* (Harper & Row: New York, 1976). (101–103)

Elaine Pagels discusses the notion of Wisdom-Sophia in *The Gnostic Gospels* (Vantage Books: New York, 1979). (102)

Ean Begg provides the names of the Black Virgins in the Gazetteer section of *The Cult of the Black Virgin* (Arkana: London and New York, 1985 o.p.). (102)

Rush, Anne Kent. *Moon, Moon.* Random House. New York. 1976. (102)

THE GREAT MEASURER

✴

The Original Moon Calendars

*"God created the moon and appointed its houses
in order that men might know
the number of years and the measure of time."*
–The Koran

Opposite page: Sunday Chart by Jobst Crossmann.

Mayan altar tablet of holy days—Altar of the Cross.

ONCE UPON A TIME in a place called the Here and Now lived a woman who was obsessed with time. She lived in a period of history called the Twentieth Century, although the name given to that time was only according to one certain way of counting. There were also other ways. To keep track according to Chinese reckoning, the current year, 1991, could have been counted as 4689. One way of describing the year she lived in was 1991 A.D., or Anno Domini (the Latin version), or the "Year of Our Lord" (the English version). A.D. was an especially appropriate way to distinguish the year for anyone who happened to be Christian, because it marked and divided time from the beginning of the birth of Jesus Christ, a date established in 532 A.D. when the Abbott Dionysus Exiguus declared December 25 to be Christ's birth date, and March 25 to be the date of his conception. A.D. is not appropriate, however, for someone who happens to be Jewish or Buddhist, for instance. For that reason another distinction in time has been recently made, and thus the year can also be described as 1991 C.E., or in the Common Era, a rather more inclusive way to characterize the counting of the last nearly two thousand years.

Now, this woman in the Here and Now is constantly faced with different ways to organize and divide her time. She follows many calendars: civil, ritual, social, and natural. Consider the civil divisions of time she must keep track of. First of all, there is the solar year according to the Gregorian calendar that begins on January 1 and ends on December 31, a 365-day period that nearly everyone she comes in contact with recognizes and follows. Unless, of course, she has to deal with the United States government, which operates, for the purpose of commerce, on a calendar called a fiscal year. Although it also encompasses a 365-day period, it begins on October 1 of the solar year and ends 365 days later on September 30. This woman also lives in one of the fifty states of the United States of America. That particular state also follows a fiscal year, but, determined to be as unique as the city-states of ancient Greece, divides that solar year to fit the needs of its own marketplace between July 1 and June 30. This woman's birthday falls on June 30, so she has no trouble remembering the end of the state's fiscal year.

There is another way of dividing time that has persisted into her own "Age of Aquarius," also known as the space age, the information age, the new age, and the electronic age. That is the division of astrological time, developed by ancient skywatchers in Mesopotamia, and remembered even now. She knows, for example, that she was born under the astrological sign of Cancer, which is ruled by the moon. The astrological calendar has its own sort of progression in time, based on the apparent motion of the sun, moon, and planets through twelve star groups known as the zodiac, discussed in a previous chapter.

In addition to the more arcane methods of considering time, there are also other civic calendar protocols to be observed. April 15 is a special economic festival within the calendar of the United States government, since by that date all income tax owed must either be paid or the date due extended by special application. This particular occasion has its own set of calendrical rules and deadlines. Other economic calendars are established by banks and businesses. Financial cycles come in a variety of choices: thirty days, sixty days, and ninety days are frequent time periods for payment of loans and bills, although longer cycles can be established to purchase increasingly larger items. For example, a three-year cycle to make car payments is not unusual, nor a thirty-year cycle to complete home mortgage installments, or even longer to pay off corporate debts, to buy a building, a company, or a country. It is often a wonder how we keep track of all these cycles; true havoc prevails when we don't!

Another set of civic rituals that must be accounted for within each year are the official holidays of the United States government, and of the fifty states and territories. Though most of these have their own particular origin in history, they are subject to change by a vote in either the Congress or the state legislature, so that the birthday of a famous president may or may not be celebrated on the actual date of its occurrence. Since there is no model that interlocks all these separate calendars, it is interesting to observe this woman and her companions keeping track of so many different divisions of time all at once. Because of the complexity and number of calendars she and those living in her time are forced to obey, they have become obsessed with recording their every movement in ritual books known by such names as FiloFax and Daily Reminder.

There are also several ritual calendars that must be observed by this woman and people like her everywhere. If she is Chinese, her year begins on the first new moon of the first lunar month, which finds the moon in the constellation of Aquarius. If she is Jewish, her ritual year, as adopted in the fourth century C.E., begins at the new moon in the month of Tishri (in the fall) and continues on a nineteen-year cycle that can be adapted to coincide with certain holy days. This flexibility, always necessary when working with a lunar calendar, and called intercalation, allows for a ritual year that can range from 353 to 385 days. If she is Roman Catholic, for instance, her ritual year follows the life of Christ and begins as many former lunar calendars did, in the dark of the year, at Advent, on the fourth Sunday before Christmas. If she is Islamic, her year follows the lunar way of marking time, as the prophet Mohammed determined. She will observe certain holy days of the year, such as Passover, Easter, or Ramadan, that are still regulated by the appearance and disappearance of the moon.

If this woman has children, they must also observe a nine-month school calendar which once began early in September, and now fluctuates between August and September, and in some places has been extended to include all twelve months of the solar year. There are also social calendars that must be obeyed. There are seasons to consider, such as the opera, theater, and tourist, the latter of which can vary from place to place, given the climate and the attraction. Membership in clubs and organizations means following yet another calendar, perhaps weekly, monthly, quarterly, and so on, likely to culminate in an annual or semiannual event that marks a turning point of some sort for the group. Sports also follow their own particular seasons: baseball, basketball, cricket, soccer, and hockey, to name only a few. And then there is the football season, which ranges from Little League for youngsters to professional for adults. At the professional level, it has become somewhat of a moveable feast during the past twenty years in the United States. What once began in the fall of the year, usually in September, now opens unofficially with the first broadcast of preseason games.

Other social activities are usually regulated on some sort of a calendrical system, such as weekly piano lessons and aerobics classes, television programs, or special functions. And if there is any need to communicate this information to friends, relatives, or colleagues outside the immediate area, this woman must also be aware of the twenty-four time zones in the world, should she want to FAX or phone her colleagues in Tokyo, Dublin, or Washington, D.C. Anyone trying to coordinate one or more of these particular calendars knows what a full-time task being a day or night or seasonal planner can be, and probably has a better understanding than most why this might have been a full-time job in many cultures.

Then there are the natural cycles of time. In temperate areas of the world these fall into roughly the four seasons of winter, spring, summer, and autumn. There are many places in the world that do not have four seasons, however; countries that lie along the equator, for example, or those near the arctic areas. Some have two, winter and summer. Some have one, winter or summer. In some areas, the seasonal division is made according to the rainy season and the dry season. Weather patterns follow a calendar of their own, such as the hurricane, monsoon, tornado. Farmers and gardeners everywhere in the world, whether working on a large scale or a subsistence level, must follow different planting tables that outline the maximum period of growth for a given area. Fortunately or unfortunately, a way has been found to artificially extend the hours of daylight during the summer months, and thus put off the darkness. Called Daylight Savings Time, it is a complicated system that affects both agricultural output and the schedules of children riding school buses, but can be easily reduced to understanding by a simple nursery-rhyme mnemonic: "Spring forward, Fall back."

Always related to agriculture, the normal periods of gestation for animals or rooting for crops must ordinarily be followed, although with the advances of artificial insemination and the mechanical approach to much husbandry (including human), body clocks can be set to different rhythms than they once were. Even at that, nine months is nine months. This woman will also have her own body rhythms to adhere to, although contraception has allowed her the choice to change that, too, and perhaps her awareness of it as well. She will mark off the calendar of her life, the passing of time measured in years, decades, and then parts of centuries. She may count her time in generations as well, and if she is able to do this, she will know well perhaps the meaning of time, of dividing time, of creating time.

If we think other cultures have been "obsessed" with time—the Maya, for example, are often accused of this—we should stop and think about this woman, measuring her days in almost too many ways to keep track of. How did she get into this situation of having to balance so many cycles of time all at once? Is she a magician? A mystic? Does she rely on some higher power to help her find her way through this complicated maze of calculation and prophecy? Sometimes at the end of a long hard day in a long hard week in a long hard month at the end of a long hard year, this woman probably sits at her upstairs window and watches the moon and sighs and wonders how she came to have so much time on her hands that she must balance.

◉ *Lunar and Solar Calendars*

While the changes of night into day and day into night would have given our early ancestors the most immediate sense of the passage of time, watching the moon traverse the night sky would have provided a better sense of the continuous passage of time and is probably the oldest method of actually measuring time. Notations of lunar cycles and lunar phases on pottery, sculpture, and burial sites in Old Europe dates to approximately thirty-two thousand years ago, according to the work archaeologist Marija

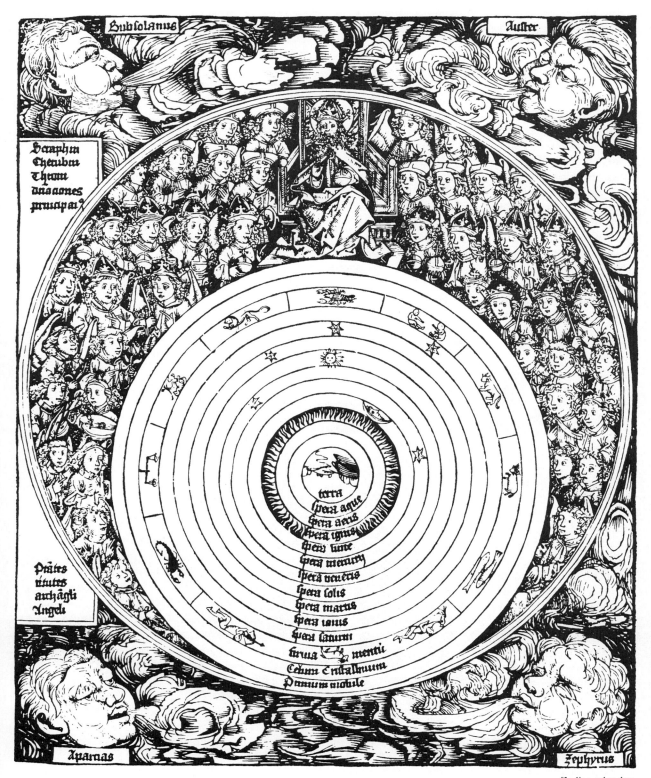

Zodiac calendar.

Gimbutas has done during the last thirty years. The moon's obvious changes could be easily related to events on earth in what would come to be the daily, weekly, monthly, and annual cycles that some humans would eventually describe as decades, centuries, eons, eras, and millennia; of course, these segments of time follow a decimal system that many other cultures did not use.

Generally speaking, the older a culture is, the more likely it is to contain elements of lunar measurement. The traditional cultures of the Americas, Africa, Australia, and Oceania all provide such examples. Even Egypt, so well known to us as the civilization of the sun god, shows traces of a prior method of lunar reckoning. There are hints within mythology that give the older calendar away. The myth of the Egyptian moon god Osiris, which has become as well known as the myth of his determined companion Isis, is a moon myth. When Osiris disappears, having been murdered, Isis searches everywhere for the dismembered pieces of his body, cut up like the moon appears to be as it wanes. Inscriptions on papyrus manuscripts reveal that a hieroglyphic crescent moon was used to symbolize "month," and that a lunar year was still in use as late as the Twelfth Dynasty in Egypt.

The astronomer Sir Norman Lockyer hypothesized that as early as 6400 B.C.E. southern Egyptians who worshipped the moon gods Osiris, Thoth, Khonsu, and Chnemu moved into northern areas where sun worship prevailed. The southerners brought with them the use of a lunar month of thirty days, which equalled a lunar year of 360 days, and one that was subject to necessary intercalation. By 3200 B.C.E. the priests at Thebes had established the worship of Amen-Ra, the sun god. Contemporary archaeoastronomer James Cornell remarks that the Egyptians had to develop a solar calendar to be able to predict the annual flooding of the Nile, once thought to be

caused by the moon, another clue to earlier lunar leanings. It was the Egyptians who divided the day into twenty-four hours, twelve of daylight and twelve of night. In 631 C.E., by requesting his followers to adopt a lunar calendar instead of the lunar-solar calendar used by the Arabians, Mohammed was actually returning to an older method of measuring time, one that persists among his followers today. The Islamic year dates from 622 C.E., the year of the Hegira, or Mohammed's flight to Medina. In Peru, among the Inca, a civilization which held a special place of honor for the sun, the measurement of time was kept according to lunations, and this practice still survives in many places.

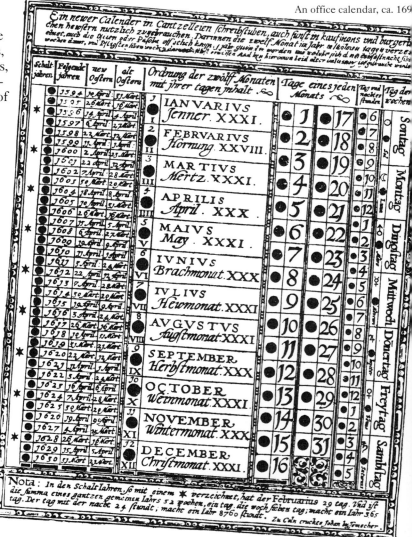

An office calendar, ca. 169

◑ *Women and the Moon*

Though we will discuss spiritual connections between the moon and women in Chapter Seven, for now let us consider the menstrual cycle and its link to the moon. In many cultures, old and new, the moon is held to be the cause of menstruation. Even the words for it show the connection, whether, as Briffault records, it is referred to as "moon-change" or "le moment de la lune" (French, "the moment of the moon"), or simply "moon sickness" or "the moon." In still other cultures, for instance in Indian Zaire, among the Mandingo of western Africa, in Australia and parts of New Guinea, the word for moon and menstruation are synonymous. In Latin, the word *menses* doubled as a meaning for "month" and "menstruation." In Greek, the word *katamenia* served the same purpose.

It made sense to the Babylonians that the moon caused menstruation in women, since they believed that the moon goddess Ishtar, the goddess of love, also menstruated. Since they believed that this event took place around the full moon, they ceased normal activities and celebrated a "Shabathu" or "sabattu," from which we get our word Sabbath and the notion of a day of rest. A Jewish tradition holds that the rabbis gave as the cause of menstruation Eve's relation with the serpent in the Garden of Eden. Likewise, many other cultures have maintained the belief that the snake, by its lunar association to the moon because of its apparent self-generation and fertility, shedding its skin to begin a "new life," is the cause of menstruation. A similar notion about the moon as a woman menstruating was held by East Indians and by some Native American tribes. More modern epithets such as "the curse" and "my aunt" or "the friend, my girlfriend," or "the visitor" have replaced references to the moon. Anthropologist Helen Neuenswander conducted a more recent study of time concepts among the Cubulco Achi people of the central highlands of Guatemala. She found that the moon's path through the sky, considered as a single journey from the time of its rising to its disappearance each month, is called "our grandmother's road." In describing the moon's location in the sky at a given time, the Achi use precise gestures to describe where "grandmother" is on her path. Her placement is used to keep track of agricultural cycles as well as menstrual and birth cycles.

With the advent of the birth control pill, women's cycles are less in tune with lunar movements and are set instead to an artificial rhythm. However, with increasing concern and awareness of natural cycles in every phase of life, from eating the right food to taking care of the environment, women seem to be paying more attention to the natural rhythms of their own bodies, and how those rhythms match that of the ever-changing orb in the sky. Paul Katzeff describes a German study of ten thousand women conducted earlier in the twentieth century that revealed that menstruation began more often at full or new moon than at any other time during the month.

A couple of theories exist about why cycles of the moon and menstrual cycles are in accord. One links the menstrual tides with the ocean tides, observing that similar effects follow. Another theory put forth by Charles Darwin holds that cycles may be a result of humankind's long affiliation with life by the sea. Still another theory offers that it is the effect of moonlight, whose artificial creation has been successful in regulating menstrual cycles that are out of kilter, that stimulates the monthly cycle. While not everyone may agree with the Maori conclusion that the moon is the true husband of every woman, or that the first menstruation is proof of intercourse with the moon, the metaphors are worth exploring for their rich attempt to understand both the natural world and human life within that world. Proof of the desire to become more attuned to natural rhythms once again has surfaced in a number of books on the new scholarship on women. One such example comes from writer Hallie Iglehart, who describes menstruation and moon rituals that might be re-established for women seeking such a connection.

Though the menstrual cycle belongs exclusively to women, Katzeff discusses several studies that make a case for the existence of male periods, also linked to the moon. From the

1920s to the late 1970s, studies have revealed the existence of such a phenomenon. It would appear that human hormonal changes occur most often at full moons, and sometimes at new moon—again, the two times that the lunar effect on tides is also the greatest. Katzeff mentions a more well-known case study of a bus company in Japan; when the accident rate among drivers increased to disturbing proportions, a study of the circadian rhythms of the all-male work force revealed lunar patterns of activity. When the schedules were aligned with these patterns, the accident rate decreased enough to be statistically significant.

◐ *The Meaning of Measuring*

The meaning and etymology of many words provide clues to the long history of establishing the measurement of time according to the moon. Briffault found that early humans believed that the moon created time: the English word that means "to measure" is derived from the root word *mas*, a name for the moon, not the other way around. The moon was there first. Measuring came later. The origin of the word fortnight, still in common use in the British Isles, refers to a period of fourteen nights and days, and can be traced to a measurement of the time between new moon and full moon. An archaic word, sennight, refers to a measure of seven nights and days, roughly the time it takes for one lunar phase to change, the basis on which the familiar week developed.

When it came to naming periods of time, the way older cultures went about it provides some interesting information, as calendar scholar Hutton Webster further discovered. Some peoples used the different phases of the moon to indicate the time for certain events. Tribes in Australia used the particular phase of the moon to describe certain festivals and feasts. In parts of New Guinea, any period of time longer than a day was described by referring to the phase of the moon. In some places people gave each day of the moon a different name, in accordance with the change in the moon. This was true in traditional Hawaiian culture. Such a practice is simply a different and larger, and perhaps more

precise, pattern of repeating the names of the week four or five times within the common month. Some cultures counted from new moon to new moon; others from full moon to full moon; still others kept separate counts from new moon to full and then from full to new again. Each approach reflects a unique way of viewing the moon and its role in the tribal life as a handy and obvious timepiece. In studying how ancient people used the heavens to learn to measure time, we can also see how other aspects of civilization developed. From naked-eye observation of the skies followed the development of magical, religious, and spiritual beliefs, along with the progression of different elements of society: political, cultural, and social.

The way to divide time into its largest segments according to the moon would be by the light phase and the dark phase, the two fortnight periods from new moon to full and then from full moon back to new. Yet the cultures of the world have devised a number of ways to keep a lunar count. The seven-day week is most familiar to us, and it is perhaps surprising that such a division of time has been adopted in so many cultures as a way to measure the month, considering the many choices offered throughout history. As we might expect, the number twenty-eight figures largely in many cultures around the world, as does the number seven, which is often considered a sacred number. The seven-day week eventually came into use in India, but was borrowed from other cultures; it was sacred to the Akkadians, who created the week. Seven is closely tied to the phases of the moon, which can be divided into four separate units by seven (although seven is the number that always carries a remainder with it, given the uneven nature of the moon's cycle).

There have also been weeks of five, six, eight, nine, and ten days, each developed according to a need and a view. The Yoruba of West Africa once followed a lunar month consisting of six weeks of five days each. Other evidence of six-day weeks has been found in Africa. The five-day week, developed to follow the economic activities of the marketplace, has been found in Malaysia, Africa, and southeastern Asia. Some tribes along the African Gold

THE GREEK YEAR BEGAN WITH

Autumnal equinox	Crete, Miletos, Rhodes, and Sparta
Vernal equinox	Chios
First new moon after summer solstice	Athens and Delphi
First new moon after winter solstice	Boiotia and Delos

HAWAIIAN NAMES FOR THE DAYS OF THE LUNAR MONTH

Hilo (new moon)	Hoku
Hoaka	Mahealani (full moon)
Kukahi	Kulu
Kulua	Laaukukahi
Kukolu	Laaukulua
Kupau	Laaupau
Olekukahi	Kaloakukahi
Olekulua	Kaloakulua
Olekukolu	Kaloapau
Olepau	Kane
Huna	Lono
Mohalu	Mauli
Hua	Muku (dark of the moon)
Akua	

NORTHEASTERN NATIVE AMERICAN NAMES OF MOONS
(From various tribal nations, compiled by Joseph Bruchac)

October	Moon of Falling Leaves
	Moon of Freezing
November	Harvest Moon
	Corn Moon
	Moon When Deer Shed Their Horns
December	Cold Moon
	Long Night Moon
	Little Manitou Moon
January	Big Manitou Moon
	Snow Moon
February	Starving Moon
	Hunger Moon
	Moon of Wind Scattering Leaves Over the Snow Crust
March	Maple Sugar Moon
	Strong Wind Moon
	Crow Moon
	Moon of Wakening
April	Frog Moon
	Wild Goose Moon
	Moon of New Grass
May	Planting Moon
	Corn Planting Moon
	Moon When Ponies Shed
June	Moon of Strawberries

	Hatching Moon
	Rose Moon
July	Raspberry Moon
	Thunder Moon
	Sun House Moon
August	Mating Moon
	Chokecherry Moon
	Moon of Spawning Salmon
September	Hunting Moon
	Moon of Leaves Turning Color
	Moon of Spiderwebs on the Ground
	Moon of Wild Plums

OSAGE
The following names were collected by John Joseph Mathews, a member of the Osage Nation:

January	Single Moon by Himself
	Frost-on-Inside-of-Lodge Moon
	Hunger Moon (old name)
February	Light-of-Day Returns Moon
March*	Just-Doing-That-Moon (*spring begins)
April	Planting Moon
May	Little-Flower-Killer Moon
June	Buffalo-Pawing-Earth Moon
July	Buffalo-Breeding Moon
August	Yellow-Flower Moon
September	Deer-Hiding Moon
October	Deer-Breeding Moon
November	Coon-Breeding Moon
December	Baby-Bear Moon

OTHER COMMON NAMES FOR THE MOONS
Names currently in common use in the eastern United States for the full moons of each month are:

January	Wolf Moon
February	Snow Moon
March	Sap Moon
April	Pink Moon
May	Flower Moon
June	Strawberry Moon
July	Buck Moon
August	Sturgeon Moon
September	Harvest Moon
October	Hunter's Moon
November	Beaver Moon
December	Cold Moon

In his long poem, "Hiawatha," (1855) Henry Wadsworth Longfellow adopted Native American names for the following months:

April	Moon of Bright Nights
May	Moon of Leaves
June	Moon of Strawberries
September	Moon of Falling Leaves
November	Moon of Snow-Shoes

Coast chose a seven-day lunar week, but found it necessary to start the days at different times to keep in tune with the moon's phases. A popular and mathematically practical ten-day division called a decade existed among the Maori and the Hawaiians, as well as in China, Japan, and throughout southeastern Asia. Inscriptions reflecting the use of a decade in Egypt have been found in the pyramids. Hesiod's writings provide evidence that the Greeks used a decade as early as the eighth century B.C.E. Few cultures seem to have used a nine-day unit of time, although mention of it exists among the ancient Germans and in Irish and Welsh texts. Multiples of nine predominate throughout Celtic literature and thought. And the Classic Maya used a nine-day "Lord of the Night" cycle, although its connection to the lunar count is uncertain.

Many cultures did not find a need to count time in months, days, or years. For some, descriptive use of the twenty-eight day lunar month was enough to record festivals, historical events, or other occurrences important enough to be remembered and passed on. Though the Chinese did not limit themselves to the confines of a lunar month or year, and were keeping careful historical and cultural records thousands of years before other cultures, they had a fascinating way of naming the days of each month. Poetically described as the "mansions of the moon," twenty-eight names were used for the days of the lunar month to record the moon's transit through the heavens. The Babylonians similarly cataloged "moon stations," which described the constellations that the moon appeared to pass through in its journey across the sky. The same practice existed in India and was recorded in Hindu texts. The Babylonians kept track of lunar cycles, as we know. Jastrow, the Babylonian scholar, believed that the Babylonian year began in the spring. He cited inscriptions which tell how the god Marduk, after defeating Tiamat, the goddess of chaos, restored order and directed the moon god Sin to mark the days by illuminating the night. The laws that Sin recorded were said to come from the sky. If we consider that Sin's "laws" were natural ones used to regulate time, a different understanding of the myth emerges.

How did we leap from watching the moon and carefully recording its movements to using wall calendars as a way to measure and predict our lives? Obviously the step was gradual and determined. Most of us learned in school the origins of the current calendar in use, the effort of Julius Caesar and his Egyptian astronomer to reconcile the lunar and solar ways of counting time. But the road to a common calendar was a long one, filled with many mysterious turns and detours.

When thinking about how cultures developed their calendars, it is important to consider the purpose and definition of the calendar. What would it be used for? How was it determined? What was the physical and magical or spiritual view of the people who developed it? The calendar of a Bronze Age Briton would not resemble at all the calendars and date books we hang on our walls or carry in our briefcases, intended for us to divide months, days, and hours of the solar year. Calendars of earlier times may have had entirely different purposes. For instance, a calendar meant to guide agricultural activities was very different from one meant to regulate religious or civil functions. Many cultures still measure time by the lunar method in one way or another. The Islamic observance of Ramadan, held during the ninth month of the Islamic calendar, begins with the sighting of the crescent moon and continues through one lunar cycle, ending when the next new crescent appears. And if the plethora of lunar calendars available around the world is any indication, many people are returning to this ancient way of reckoning, or at least attempting to reconcile it with more modern sensibilities.

According to most authorities on the subject, as cultures developed agriculture they came to rely increasingly on a solar rather than a lunar calendar. The ever-changing Luna is not usually reliable as a guide for seasonal changes. In some cultures this switch from one method of time keeping to another also reflects a different direction in the political structure of the state. Many cultures adjusted their calendars to keep track of the variety of times and events important to the people. This included the events of the agricultural seasons (when to plant and when to harvest, for example), as well as the

(Intercolary month)	RIVROS MAT	GIAMON- ANM	EDRIN- MAT	RIVROS MAT	GIAMON- ANM	EDRIN- MAT	RIVROS MAT
MAT	ANAGAN- TIOS ANM	SIMIVIS- ONN- MAT	CANTLOS ANM	ANAGAN- TIOS ANM	SIMIVIS- ONN- MAT	CANTLOS ANM	ANAGAN- TIOS ANM
SAMON- MAT	OGRON- MAT	EQVOS ANM	SAMON- MAT	OGRON MAT	EQVOS ANM	SAMON- MAT	OGRON- MAT
DVMANN- ANM	CVTIOS MAT	ELEMBIV- ANM	DVMANN- ANM	CVTIOS- MAT	ELEMBIV- ANM	DVMANN- ANM	CVTIOS MAT

(Intercolary month)	EQVOS ANM	SAMON- MAT	OGRON- MAT	EQVOS ANM	SAMON- MAT	OGRON- MAT	EQVOS ANM
MAT	ELEMBIV- ANM	DVMANN- ANM	CVTIOS MAT	ELEMBIV- ANM	DVMANN ANM	CVTIOS MAT	ELEMBIV- ANM
GIAMON- ANM	EDRIN- MAT	RIVROS MAT	GIAMON- ANM	EDRIN- MAT	RIVROS MAT	GIAMON- ANM	EDRIN- MAT
SIMIVIS- ONN- MAT	CANTLOS ANM	ANAGAN- TIOS ANM	SIMIVIS- ONN- MAT	CANTLOS ANM	ANAGAN- TIOS ANM	SIMIVIS- ONN- MAT	CANTLOS ANM

A representation of the Coligny calendar, based on Celtic lunar measurement.

events that had been marked for so long by use of the lunar calendar (festivals, and special ritual days and times within the year). They did this through the process called intercalation, exercising great individuality and resourcefulness in coordinating different cycles of time.

The Jewish calendar followed solar years but lunar months. *The Encyclopedia of Religion* mentions that the Hebrew word *yera* refers to both the month and the moon. As in the earliest times, and still today in other Middle Eastern cultures, the month began when an official eyewitness sighted the new moon, which was celebrated with a feast. The months were named according to the agricultural activity taking place at the time. The Jewish people still follow a lunar calendar to determine the dates of religious observances, but like many people around the world, use the Gregorian calendar for daily life. Webster reports that the Masai of Africa, nomadic cattle herders, used a lunar calendar of thirty days counted not from the new moon but from the fourth day after the new moon.

Willetts comments that the Egyptians added an extra month every nine years out of twenty-five, creating a twenty-five year cycle that is important to understand when trying to learn about the lunar aspects of the culture. Creation of such a cycle indicates intercalation, or making the celestial events agree with human ones. Intercalation occurs in both lunar and solar calendars, but greater efforts are needed to bring the lunar calendar into line with seasonal events. In Mesopotamia, an extra month was added every seven years out of nineteen, creating a nineteen-year cycle. A nineteen-year cycle, called the Metonic cycle after the Greek

astronomer Meton, figures importantly in Celtic lore as well. It describes the amount of time it took for the new moon to occur on the same day of the solar year as it had at the beginning of the previous cycle. According to Caesar and other classical writers, evidence of lunar reckoning among the Celts existed in the fact that they measured time by "a night and a day," rather than a day and a night. In a story from the Ulster Cycle of mythology (also known as the tales of the Red Branch Knights), Nessa, the mother of Conchobar mac Nessa, tricked the king then in power by requesting that her son be allowed to reign for "a night and a day." Once her wish was granted, Conchobar did not have to leave the throne, since "a night and a day" was metaphorically the perpetual measure of all time. Like many contemporary remnants of a lunar calendar still to be found embedded in the solar calendar, the special days of Celtic celebration began at night. Celtic new year, called Samhain, began near the darkest time of the year, at the beginning of what is now November. Still celebrated as the Christian holy day known as All Souls' Day and All Hallows' Eve, it is of course the popular secular holiday called Halloween, celebrated on October 31. The fortnight, a lunar measure still in use, is frequently mentioned in Celtic literature.

One of the most important artifacts from the Celtic world is an actual calendar known as the Coligny Calendar, now in a museum in Lyon, France. Though the inscriptions are in Latin, the calendar shows the Celtic measure of time. The Coligny Calendar divided the lunation of twenty-nine or thirty days into two parts, a dark half and a light half. These periods were considered good (MAT) and bad (ANM) days for different kinds of activities. The good days occurred during the first part of the cycle, the bad days clustered, as they did in so many other cultures, at the end. Webster mentions that the word *atenoux* was always used for the second half of the month. It is thought to refer to the full moon, since it has been translated as both "great night" and "renewal." The Coligny Calendar shows an awareness of greater cycles of time as well. Its sixteen columns of four months equal a five-year cycle of sixty-two lunar months, plus two months of intercalation. In turn, the Coligny Calendar may be part of an even larger nineteen-year cycle, previously mentioned, to have been an important measure of time for the Celts. Gerald Hawkins believes this same lunar measurement was calculated at Stonehenge.

The Greek city-states were independent when it came to both time-keeping and political rule. They used a combined lunar and solar calendar, though each month began with the new moon. In certain places in Greece, a practice existed that later surfaced in Rome, that of criers announcing the new moon. Each city-state kept its own calendar, though they all followed a similar structure. To get a better sense of this, just imagine that each of the fifty states in the United States were able to regulate its own seasonal and ritual aspects of the calendar. Like other cultures, the Greeks alternated between twenty-nine and thirty days in a twelve-month cycle. In three years out of every eight, a thirteenth month was inserted, thus creating an eight-year cycle that came to be known as the *oktaeteris*. Understanding the nature of such cycles demanded careful observation over a long period of time. Though tedious and requiring great attention to detail, determining the cycles would have been no great task to cultures and civilizations who were constantly watching the moon anyway.

The first Roman calendar was lunar, made up of ten lunations beginning in March and extending through December, which left a gap in the winter. Intercalations were added in February, when the year ended. The priests regulated the Roman calendar according to the festival days and determined days on which no work

could be done. According to *The Encyclopedia of Religion*, in Rome, the person who watched for the new moon was known as a pontifex minor. Upon seeing it, the pontifex called out to the goddess Juno. The new moon was sacred to her, while the full moon (or Ides) was special to Jupiter. The time of the new moon was known as the Kalends, a word that comes from the verb *calare*, "to call." In it we can see the root of the modern word "calendar." The Ides marked the thirteenth or fifteenth day of the month, and the less important (ritually, anyway) Nones, sometimes known as the "half moon," on the fifth or seventh. In either 45 or 46 B.C.E., Julius Caesar, with the help of an Egyptian astronomer, adapted the lunar calendar to a solar orientation, in order to bring civil time and natural time into accord. It became known as the Julian Calendar. The commission appointed by Pope Gregory XIII further altered it in 1582 to the form currently in existence, giving it both its name and its structure. The Gregorian calendar was developed in response to the need to regulate the date of Easter.

We have become so accustomed to the familiar names for the months adopted with the use of the Gregorian calendar that we take for granted how such naming came about, and forget that there was much that preceded it. Some cultures named the months after what they saw happening in them. The naming of the months often reflected activities such as the life cycles of animals, plants, birds, and other natural phenomena. Working from a cryptic Welsh riddle, Robert Graves deduced what he believed to be an alphabet-calendar developed by Celtic peoples, according to the time that trees budded, flowered, or produced fruits and berries during an annual cycle. As the Celts followed a lunar calendar, the tree alphabet-calendar, if Graves is right, provides a more insightful look at the way they considered time.

Shepherds, farmers, and ancient astrologers alike watched, measured, and named their months according to lunations. Webster mentions that examples of this kind of naming can be found in China, Japan, and Babylonia, as well as among the Hebrews, Celts, Germans, and Slavs. Native American culture provides some clear examples of this method of reckoning, and of an individual approach to the naming. The names given to the "moons" by Native American tribes in the northeastern United States, for example, are different from those used by tribes in the western part of the country. Observation and naming is local, unique, and according to the nature of the countryside and its events.

In Polynesia, one tribe gave a separate name to each night of the month, based on the phase of the moon, as did the Hawaiians. We know that Babylonian months officially began at the new moon. Each had its own name, which reflected the major natural and human activities undertaken during each time period.

Sometimes the fascination with older cultures far removed from our own time and place tends to make us forget about older cultures that are quite near to us. Most of us have been introduced to the history of civilization through courses with titles like "History of Western Civilization," which were developed on the premise that civilization began with Egypt, Greece, or Rome. While of course these cultures are significant to our understanding of ourselves and our place in the world, they are also only part of the picture. For instance, as Sir Norman Lockyer and others have pointed out, the Greeks thought the Egyptians, for all their cultural achievements, to be quite backward and unsophisticated, Old World "hicks," as it were. Many cultures preceded those of Egypt, Greece, and Rome, and laid the foundations for them. It is hardly sensible to study the history of Egypt without studying the history of Africa, yet we have done it. Likewise, it is hardly sensible to study the Americas (South, Central, or North) without trying to understand their history prior to 1100 C.E., 1492 C.E., or 1519 C.E. Yet we have done that, too. In this discussion of the development of the calendar from lunar cycles and times, let us turn for a moment to what has always been described as the "New World," or the Americas, although that name, like so many others in history, is not really accurate from the point of view of the people who had

The eighteen Mayan months.

119

been living there some 25,000 years or so before the Europeans arrived. The Olmec culture, for example, peaked around 700 B.C.E. Mayan culture had reached a high level of sophistication by 400 C.E., a time the Roman Empire was coming to an end. In Teotihuacan, a pre-cursor of Aztec culture, trade in obsidian was at its most active around 650 C.E. Zapotec culture was contemporary with that of Teotihuacan, between 500 and 1000 C.E.

The ancient Americans were sky watchers along with everyone else. They had been observing the movements of moon, sun, planets, and stars long before the Spanish conquistadors arrived on their shores. As the Dresden Codex reveals, the Maya recorded an eclipse table. Many valuable books and codexes kept by the peoples of Central America were burned by the conquerors, who, without understanding their contents, assumed the material to be worthless heathen rantings. They were wrong. The books they burned, the products of independent New World literary traditions, may have provided a greater understanding of the way these cultures perceived the universe—knowledge that now must be pieced together the hard way because of the gaps and missing pieces in the historical and archaeological record.

Archaeoastronomers describe the system of observation used by the Aztecs as "positional astronomy." The system was used to align ceremonial centers and buildings. The intricate and complicated Aztec ceremonial calendar has received special attention from scholars and students alike in the last many years, and is perhaps the best known of the time-discerning methods of the pan-Mesoamerican peoples of Central and South America, each of whom developed a unique application of its use. The word "discerning" is used rather than "keeping" because the Aztec calendar contained much more than just a strict calendar measurement of time in the way we think of it currently. It was used and regulated to fit the purpose of ritual among the Aztecs, the Maya, the Toltecs, and the Mixtecs.

To say that Mayan culture peaked around 400–800 C.E. is accurate in one sense and inaccurate in another. The culture flourished in different ways at different times. As Dennis

Tedlock, author of the newest translation of the Popol Vuh, the sacred book of the Maya, has discovered firsthand and shared with others, the Mayan culture is still very much alive in the highlands of Guatemala among the Quiche people. The Maya had (and have) several ways of time reckoning that were used concurrently, and, in the same way as the woman from the twentieth-century tale of Here and Now that introduced this chapter, used and understood them in a way that was immediate for their own lives. Also, every lunation had its own name— the glyphs say: "its holy name was . . ." as part of the lunar count. When we stop and think about the use of the several different cycles used to keep track of time in our lives, perhaps we can gain a little perspective on the Mayan understanding of time. We should not think they are identical, however, as the time periods used by the Maya were cyclical rather than linear.

9-day cycle	Lords of the Night sequence
29.52592-day cycle	lunar month (compare to 7 minutes difference from current lunar measurements)
260-day cycle	ritual calendar, made up of one of 13 numbers combined with one of 20 day names
365-day cycle	"vague year," made up of 18 months of 20 days each and one five-day period
365.242500-day year	astronomical year (compare to the modern year of 365.241198)
584-day cycle	measured from the time Venus appears as the morning star until reappearance as the morning star
819-day cycle	819-Day Count

Using a similar system, the Toltecs kept two calendars: one was a solar calendar of 365 days, the other was a ritual calendar of 260 days. A larger cycle of 52 years was also kept. Another way of indirectly marking and celebrating the calendar was the use of day names of birth used as personal names by the Toltecs and Aztecs.

Not far away from these centers of pre-Columbian culture dwelt other cultures native to North America. Radiocarbon dating indicates that Native Americans were on the North American continent between 40,000 and 70,000 years ago. Archaeoastronomer James Cornell reports that astronomical efforts were concerned primarily with the sun; the lunar calendar measured phases. Yet very few tribes marked time according to the day, as the Commanche did. As Hadingham and others, most notably tribal people themselves, have noted most Native Americans reckoned time by "nights" or "sleeps," and named certain times of the year by "moons," reflecting in the names the progression of natural events. With our rationalistic love for order, organization, and standardization, we may assume that each tribe had a set number of names for a set number of moons for each year. This is not the case. Names were often different even within the same tribe. Early observers reported that some tribes had names for twelve moons, others for only six. The customs of naming were and are unique, reflecting an individual and local relationship to the natural and spiritual environment. Western culture has often made the mistake of assuming that everyone holds the same world view, and that if they do not, that standardization in such matters would certainly be the better way. In studying the many ways of seeing nature, and in this case specifically the moon, we can see how false a view that is. Among the various Native American cultures, naming traditions reflect a local look at the moon.

In another kind of observation, Joseph Bruchac, a contemporary writer and publisher of *The Greenfield Review* in Greenfield, New York, and of Abenaki ancestry, has pointed out a special calendar in general use among Native Americans. The calendar is elegant, simple, and portable. It is the turtle shell. Bruchac describes thirteen plates (one for each lunar cycle in a year) and twenty-eight smaller plates around the edge (one for each day in the moon) of every turtle's shell. Actually, every single turtle shell does not bear this exact number of plates, but the observation is true enough. More than that, given some thought, this knowledge reflects an incredibly careful attention to the surrounding environment. To connect the slow-moving creature on the ground with the luminous creature moving through the sky is as poetic as it is practical, and has about it an air of reverence we seem to be striving in many ways to bring back into our lives.

Although for many thousands of years now we have by and large adapted to a solar consciousness through use of the solar calendar and the awareness of the sun as the determiner of our days and lives, there are still many elements of the lunar calendar embedded in our own. Wherever we have feasts, festivals, holy

FESTIVALS

Special festivals that celebrated different aspects of the moon could once be found in nearly every culture. Here are some examples.

- **Africa:** Pygmies had a new moon celebration just before the rainy season began. Like the Chinese festival of Yue-Ping, it was a celebration for women only (the men had their own sun feast). The women covered themselves with white clay, appearing to look like ghosts, thus honoring the moon's association with dead souls, and prepared a drink from fermented bananas. The feast consisted of singing, dancing, and offering prayers to the moon.

- **Burma:** The full moon in October brings with it the most important celebration of the year, at the end of the Buddhist Lenten season.

- **Celtic Countries:** The Celts celebrated four major divisions of the year, all begun in the evening. Modern practitioners of Wicca have adopted these older lunar festivals for contemporary ritual celebration and practice:

    Samhain, or Celtic New Year, now recognized as the eve of October 31.
    Imbolc, a celebration of light now recognized as February 2 (also known as Candlemas).
    Beltane, another light and fire festival celebrated on May Eve.
    Lughnasa, a harvest festival that begins on the eve of August 1.

- **China:** A festival once called Yue-Ping (Loaves of the Moon), celebrated from ancient times on the fifteenth day of the eighth month. Now a mid-autumn festival called the Moon Festival, the Mid-Autumn Festival, or the Festival of the Moon Lady. This was originally a celebration in which only women and children participated. Special moon cakes were made, though now they are mostly bought at the bakery. Also, special fruits were bought at this time. The image of the hare in the moon and the lady in the moon often appeared in the house, and special preparations were made to await and celebrate the rising of the full moon. This festival is still widely celebrated by Chinese people. In Hong Kong, where it is also called the Mooncake Festival, it has become a special celebration for children, highlighted by the appearance of beautiful lanterns made in the shapes of dragons and rabbits and other animals that are paraded through the streets during the evening. Chinese New Year is also a lunar celebration, marking as it does the beginning of the year according to the lunar calendar.

- **Egypt:** The ancient moon god Horus was called "He of the Lotus." Like the lotus itself, he was associated with the moon. The festival of "He of the Lotus" was celebrated at new moon, the same day the pharaohs were crowned.

- **England:** Harley mentions a celebration in Lancashire similar to an ancient custom of making cakes in honor of the Queen of Heaven, a practice the prophet Jeremiah railed against in the Old Testament. Many scholars have considered this to be a vestige of former moon worship.

- **France:** "La Lunade," an old midsummer festival known in Limousin, was associated with the moon. As with other Celtic celebrations, it began in the evening, at moonrise.

- **Greece:** M.P. Nilsson noticed that most Greek festivals occurred during the first part of the month. The first day the new moon was seen, called Noumenia, began the lunar month. Dichomenia was the full moon. It was mentioned by classical writers including Homer and Hesiod. Described in the Odyssey, it was thought to be a good time for marriage. Business was conducted as usual, but like the sabbath day celebrated in other Mediterranean cultures, certain activities were suspended, apparently in honor of Apollo and Hera, a moon goddess from even older times. The twelfth day of the month was also a particularly favored day. A festival called the Karneia was celebrated at full moon in the month of Karneios. Young single men who carried clusters of grape vines paraded and then chased one who was covered with animal skins. To catch him brought good luck.

- **India:** The eighth day after the new moon was regarded as a festival day.

- **Native American** *(Blackfeet):* A special celebration was held in August, four days before the new moon. The tribe stopped and set up camp and ceased all ordinary activities. They fasted and built sweat lodges. A young woman was selected from the tribe to represent the moon, whose husband was the sun.

- **Rome:** The Ides (full moon) of May were celebrated by the Vestal Virgins to regulate the water supply. A celebration in honor of Diana was held on August 13 (compare with the Greek festival of Hekate) to ask that no storms would appear and to celebrate the harvest.

days, or holidays that begin in the evening, most likely we are participating in an event left over from when time was counted by nights, according to the moon, rather than by days, according to the sun. The references to midnight courts and councils in both literature and history, and to other celebrations that also began at night are clues to the previous existence of lunar time-keeping. Edmund Spenser's famous poem, *The Faerie Queene* and Brian Merriman's poem *The Midnight Court*, both drawn from the same tradition out of older Irish-Celtic mythology, are two such examples that update poetically an old memory of such courts and councils. The name of one of our days of the week, whether in English as Monday or German as Montag, means literally "the moon's day." Perhaps that is why the rhyme that describes the personality of children depending upon what day of the week they were born says of the "moon day's child" that he or she is "fair of face," like the bright-faced moon. There are probably many more elements within our calendars and timetables that we can trace to an earlier lunar heritage among our human ancestors. Knowing about them may not change the course of our lives, but it can certainly provide us with a deeper appreciation of the work and human effort that has gone into being able to look up at the calendar on the wall and ask, "What day is it?" And even beyond that, there seems to be something in us that does want to know and understand the lunar rhythms once again, if the growing lunar calendar and moon watch industry is any evidence. So, shine on, Harvest Moon, Mating Moon, Deer-Hiding Moon, Chokecherry Moon, Moon of Mating Salmon. . .

FOOD

*F*ood that was special to the moon goddess or god, or had a special meaning or affiliation with moon festivals, included dates, olives, bread, cakes, wine, fish, rice, apples, peaches, pomegranates, and plums. In some cases the association is obvious, such as fish with the sea and the moon's influence over the sea. Others are not so obvious, but still quite understandable; the olive, for instance, was the fruit of a tree that once symbolized the moon.

- **Bread:** Even if the connection is no longer remembered or only incidental, an Italian bakery in Denver bakes semolina bread in large "half moon" loaves.

- **Cookie Cutters:** Crescent moon cookie cutters, no longer as easy to find as they once were, are popular items with antique collectors.

- **Croissant:** This bread of French origin is popular even today. It literally means "crescent" and may have as its origin a special bread prepared for a moon festival.

- **England:** The hot-cross buns sold on Good Friday as late as the nineteenth century were a remnant of earlier celebrations dating to a time when cakes in honor of the moon goddess Astarte were made and marked with crescent horns. Though the cross replaced the sign of the crescent, the tradition has been traced historically through Jewish passover bread, the Greek sacramental bread, and the European Christian Easter rites.

- **Egypt:** Another possibility for the origin of the hot-cross buns may extend back to Egyptian moon worship. Bun is an ancient Greek word. At Herculaneum two buns marked with a cross, an Egyptian symbol, were found. A *boun* was a cake shaped like two horns to form a crescent.

- **Greece:** Round cakes called selenai were made to honor Artemis.

- **India:** At the full moon during Kunar (September-October), food is left on the rooftops to soak up the moon's rays. It is then given to relatives to eat, to share with them the energy of the moon.

- **China:** Special moon cakes are made to celebrate the lunar festival on the fifteenth day of the eighth month (according to the Chinese lunar calendar). The making and selling of mooncakes existed also in many cultures throughout the ancient Middle East, and were found at Greek festivals and dated back to Biblical times and before.

The prophet Jeremiah, in a time when the moon goddess was falling out of favor, issued a stern warning: "Do you not see what they do in the cities of Jerusalem? The children gather wood and the fathers kindle a fire, and the women knead the dough to make cakes to the Queen of Heaven and pour out libations to other gods, in order to anger me."

An archaeological dig in Israel uncovered a mold of Astarte, that same "Queen of Heaven," which may have been used to bake cakes in celebration for such a feast.

- **United States:** Moon Pies have now become part of the fast-food junk culture. A homemade Black southern version consisted of marshmallow in the middle and graham cracker crust; as one woman discovered, in the North these same desserts are called Jack Horner Pies.

- **Taboos:** Many cultures had taboos against food at certain times of the moon. Many instances have been recorded of abstaining from food, and some of the provisions are quite specific: cooked food, meat, certain kinds of meat, drink. It is not uncommon to find abstinence from food required during or near the dark of the moon, a time generally held to be full of misfortune and evil. The exceptions are no less interesting, such as those imposed on a tribal leader in Uganda, who had to fast for twenty-four hours at the time of the full moon.

- **Moonshine:** Beat the whites of 6 eggs into a very stiff broth; then add gradually 6 tablespoons of powdered sugar, beating for not less than 15 minutes; then beat in 1 heaping tablespoon of preserved peaches, cut in tiny bits; to serve, pour in each saucer some rich cream sweetened and flavored with vanilla; on the cream place a liberal portion of the moonshine.

— *Scannell's Treasure House of Knowledge, 1891*

MOONCAKES

*T*hough most mooncakes are purchased from the bakery these days, here is a recipe that is slightly easier than the original.

Mock Moon Cake (Hoan Jo Bang)
by Rhoda Yee

Yield: 1 dozen

40 jujube nuts (Chinese red dates), about 1 cup chopped
1 cup sesame seeds
6 tsp sugar
9 sheets filo dough

Preparation: Soak the whole dried jujube nuts in ½ cup water for 2 days. Take out seeds and put through blender with the soaked liquid and sugar. Add sesame seeds, mix well.

Wrapping: Cut filo dough lengthwise into 4½ inch wide strips. Stack strips on top of each other and cover with slightly damp cloth. Fold each strip into halves crosswise 3 times. Cut 2 folded strips into 4½ inch circles and the third strip into a 3 inch circle. Line buttered or greased muffin tins with the 4½ inch circles. Place filling in cup until ½ inch from top. Place the 3 inch circle of dough over the filling and seal edges with beaten egg. Brush top with oil. Bake at 350 degrees for 20 minutes. Cool for 10 minutes. Cake should unmold easily especially if you use Teflon coated muffin tins. (Be sure to oil each strip separately before folding and cutting).

Do-ahead notes: These delicious little cakes will keep for a week or more. Reheat by baking in a 300-degree oven for 10 minutes or until heated through. The crust will be light and flaky.

Photograph courtesy of Denver Art Museum

Serving dish (detail) showing "Man in the Moon" motif, either Haida or Bella Bella, from British Colombia, ca. 1830s.

EVENING CELEBRATIONS

*M*any remnants of the lunar calendar still exist in modern culture. Celebrations like these that begin the evening or night before a holiday or a holy day are just such remnants.

- **Chinese New Year:** Celebrated on the evening and for several days after the beginning of the new year, according to the lunar calendar (determined by the first new moon of the lunar month in which the moon appears in the constellation Aquarius).

- **Christmas Eve:** Christian replacement for eve of the winter solstice.

- **Easter** *(Christian):* A moveable feast established as the first Sunday after the full moon past the spring equinox.

- **The Eve of St. Agnes** *(Christian):* Celebrated on the eve of January 21, this was a night given over to young girls who wished to glimpse into the future and see the prospects of their married lives.

- **Halloween:** An abbreviation for All Hallow's Eve, the Christian replacement for Samhain, the beginning of the Celtic New Year.

- **Hanukkah** *(Jewish):* Celebrated for eight nights beginning on the twenty-fifth of Kislev.

- **Holy Saturday** *(Roman Catholic, Greek Orthodox):* Celebrated the evening before Easter, this ritual is performed in the dark and recalls the time that Christ spent in the darkness before resurrection.

- **Mabsant** *(Wales):* An age-old local celebration that marked the feast of the patron saint; begun in the evening. Discontinued because it degenerated into a drunken orgy that attracted all the wrong elements.

- **Mid-Autumn Festival** *(China, Japan, Viet Nam, most Asian countries):* Celebrated on the fifteenth day of the eighth month according to the lunar calendar. Also called the Moon Festival and the Mooncake Festival. In China, once known as Yue-Ping (The Celebration of the Loaves) and the special day of Chang-O, the Lady in the Moon. In Japan considered to be the most beautiful moon of the year, called the Harvest Moon *(Chushu no meigetsu)* and celebrated by preparing special foods and having moon-watching parties.

- **Passover** *(Jewish):* Commemoration of the Exodus that begins on the evening of the fourteenth day of Nisan and continues for seven or eight days.

- **Pentecost** *(Christian):* Celebrated the seventh Sunday after Easter, this holy day commemorates the evening visitation of the Holy Ghost upon the Apostles.

- **Ramadan** *(Islamic):* The ninth month of the Islamic year, a time of fasting and prayer; ends with the sighting of the new moon at the beginning of the tenth month.

- **Sabbath** *(Jewish):* Begins at sundown on Friday of each week.

- **St. John's Eve** *(Christian):* Replacement for eve of the summer solstice, Midsummer Night's Eve.

- **Yom Kippur** *(Jewish Day of Atonement):* Like other Jewish holy days, this one also begins in the evening.

CHAPTER NOTES
Page numbers are in parentheses at the end of each citation.

Kim Long summarizes different lunar calendars in *The Moon Book* (Johnson Books: Boulder, Colorado, 1988). (112)

Marija Gimbutas discusses evidence for recording lunar cycles in *The Language of the Goddess* (Harper & Row: San Francisco, 1989). (112)

Lockyer, Norman. *The Dawn of Astronomy*. M.I.T. Press. Cambridge. 1964 (repr. 1894). (112, 119)

Cornell, James. *The First Stargazers: An Introduction to the Origins of Astronomy*. Charles Scribner's Sons. New York. 1961. (112, 121)

Briffault, Robert. *The Mothers*. Abrdg. Gordon Rattray Taylor. George Allen & Unwin Ltd. London. 1927. (113, 114)

Paul Katzeff mentions synonyms for the moon and menstruation in *Full Moons* (Citadel Press: Secaucus, New Jersey, 1981). (113, 114)

The use of "our grandmother's road" by the Cubulco Achi to describe one lunation is contained in a paper by Helen Neuenswander, "Vestiges of Early Maya Time Concepts in a Contemporary Maya (Cubulco Achi) Community: Implication for Epigraphy," originally presented at the 77th annual meeting of the American Anthropological Association, Los Angeles, California, November 14–18, 1978. (113)

Iglehart, Hallie. *Woman Spirit: A Guide to Women's Wisdom*. New York. Harper & Row. 1983. (113)

Eliade, Mircea. "The Moon and Its Mystique" in *Patterns in Comparative Religion*. Sheed & Ward. London and New York. 1958. (113)

Katzeff, Paul. *Full Moons*. Citadel Press. Secaucus, New Jersey. 1981. (113, 114)

Webster mentions the use of the word "sennight" in *Rest Days: The Christian Sunday, the Jewish Sabbath and Their Historical and Anthropological Prototypes*. The Macmillan Company. New York. 1916. (Republished by Gale Research Company. Detroit. 1968.) (114, 117, 118)

George Smith discusses the early use of the number seven among the Akkadians in *The Chaldean Account of Genesis* (new edition revised and corrected by A. H. Sayce, Scribner's: New York, 1880). (114)

Northeastern Native American Names of Moons (From Various Tribal Nations) reprinted with permission from Joseph Bruchac. (115)

The list of Osage names for the moons compiled from John Joseph Mathews' *Talking to the Moon* (University of Oklahoma Press: Norman, Oklahoma, 1945). (115)

Complete information about the Chinese moon stations can be found in Harry T. Morgan's *Chinese Symbols and Superstitions* (P.D. and Ione Perkins: California, 1942). (Republished by Gale Research Company: Book Tower, Detroit, 1972.) (116)

Jastrow, Morris. *The Civilization of Babylonia and Assyria*. J.B. Lippincott Company. Philadelphia. 1915. (116)

The Encyclopedia of Religion. Mircea Eliade, editor. Macmillan. New York. 1987. (117)

Willetts, R.F. *Cretan Cults and Festivals*. Greenwood Press. Connecticut. 1962. (117)

Though dense, frequently difficult to follow, and often undocumented, Robert Graves' *The White Goddess* (Farrar, Straus and Giroux: New York, 1948) presents a challenge to any reader interested in the Celtic infrastructure. (118)

The source of this table was provided in an interview with Lorenzo Cruz, who studied and taught classes on the calendars of the Aztec and Maya for nearly twenty years. (121)

The information about Native American use of the turtle's shell as a lunar calendar was provided in correspondence from Joseph Bruchac during August 1990. (121)

THE GREAT MOTHER

✳

Moon Worship

Every Great Mother. . . is a moon goddess.
–Robert Briffault
The Mothers

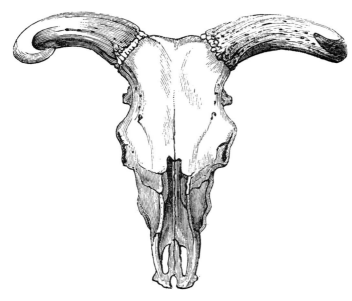

THE MYTHS of the Great Mother goddess, who also often appears as a moon goddess and whose worship is clearly evident many thousands of years ago, are so numerous and interesting that it seems impossible to present just one for consideration. Some of the finest scholarship on the subject today takes up hundreds of pages, making it even more difficult to find one that best shows the link between the Great Mother and the moon goddess.

To begin with, who or what is the Great Mother goddess? To readers familiar with the new scholarship in women's and religious studies, the concept will be more familiar. Others may have never heard of her before, since the major world religions have been devoted for thousands of years to the fixed concept of a male father god as the one and only acceptable deity—at times even on pain of punishment. Yet the cultural, historical, literary, and archaeological records all bear other evidence that the human perception of god was not always male. The idea of a mother goddess at any time in history is terrifying for some people to accept. It questions the core of dogma and belief. Yet the truth is seldom as frightening as the imagined truth. That is what Wisdom does; she upsets the comfortable apple cart of beliefs and turns the known world on end. Consider, for example, the displacement of Newtonian physics by Einstein's many discoveries about the universe. Gaining new knowledge and understanding about the human presence in the universe can be and is an exciting and surprising adventure. Remaining open to it and going forward with the explorer's nature makes it even more so. Still, the fear of knowledge one does not want to be presented with or investigate can be overwhelming. The following true story, which took place only a couple of years ago, illustrates the kind of fear and misunderstanding that surround the notion of the Great Mother goddess.

A woman was walking in a park near her home when she was approached by a man handing out leaflets, inviting her to a free movie. It turned out that a local fundamentalist church had taken over a nearby movie theater, and was using it to conduct worship services and show films that supported its religious position. The young woman politely declined the flyer, saying "No thank you" to the man.

"No thank you! You're going to say 'no thank you' to the Lord Jesus Christ?" was his surprised response.

"Yes," she replied. "No, thank you."

"Well, all I can tell you, ma'am, is that God loves you."

"And the Goddess loves you," came her answer.

He turned on his heel like a precision marcher. "The Goddess! The Goddess!" Within a few seconds, his face contorted in the unmistakable look of rage. "The devil is in that Goddess! That's devil worship!" He began a ramble of words and phrases, continuing to raise his voice until other people in the park gathered around to see what was happening. He shouted and shook his fist at the woman and continued to talk about the devil and the Goddess in one breath, coming closer to the woman as he did. His face by this time was red with anger. The veins in his neck bulged. The woman, though terrified, but without raising her voice, insistently told him that if he did not stop she would call the police. With that, he retreated, still shouting at her as he walked through the park. He had no notion that although he was poised and dedicated to imposing his own religious ideas on others, frozen in the conviction that they alone were correct, others perhaps did not share his beliefs. The mere mention of the word Goddess—not even her name, not even the beliefs surrounding her history in the world—was enough to send him into an instant rage. Some would say fear triggered the rage. Some would blame ignorance. Whatever the reason, his is an attitude that refuses to even consider, much less acknowledge, a part of human history.

In an attempt to learn more about human religious and spiritual origins, a temporary return to the opening of Chapter One is in order—to a time somewhere between the fifth and second millennia. Having left the stone and bone artifacts of the African continent behind, the stones and bones that held Alexander Marshack's attention so completely, the journey shifts northward to Europe this time.

This is not modern Europe, but Old Europe, the unique culture of 6500–3500 B.C.E., the land and people prior to the arrival of Indo-Europeans from the east, best understood perhaps through the work of archaeologist Marija Gimbutas. Gimbutas has made it her life's task to gather and study the artifacts and the culture of the people who honored a Great Mother goddess, the giver and taker of all life.

Among the thousands of artifacts Gimbutas has collected and studied, many present the possibilities for myth. Many of the animal and human images contained in them emerge in later mythologies. There is one whose story has the pull of the moon about it, though as a scientist Gimbutas of course presents the information in a straightforward and scientific way. For the sake of this present work, here is a story about the Great Mother, who is also a moon goddess, developed from Gimbutas' description.

It is an ordinary day in this time so long ago. You are a woman. The day has followed an ordinary night, with the crescent moon in a clear sky, growing strong and round again, like the horns of animals you have seen, deer and cattle. You notice these things around you, the look of the horns in the sky and those of the animals on the ground. Your daily life depends on keen observation. You know how both keep growing, and how the one in the sky disappears and returns. There is a connection. The large one above must help the small one below.

You have seen other things, too, on your way along the track that leads to water and back, in a field nearby. A dead bull has been buried there. Only its horns remain above ground. You have seen this all before. The flesh rots, the corpse decays and turns back into the earth. The horns, too, eventually crumble and return to the earth. Yet the horns in the sky always return, full of new small life. And soon, out of the horns buried in the ground, life will also emerge. You have seen it. You will see it again—bees and butterflies and other creatures emerging from the dead bull, crawling or flying out of the horns. You will see life emerge from death, as you often do, sure that the life in the sky encourages the return of life on earth. From the bull come bees, butterflies. By turn, they all come from the power of the horns in the sky.

The mother who gives life takes it, and taking it, restores it again. She is powerful, the one you honor and remember so well that you have drawn the horns of the earth animal and the horns of the sky animal on the vase you carry. And you will leave the memory behind on other vases and dishes and sculptures you create: bees, butterflies, the crescent horns. Mother Life. Mother Death. Mother Moon.

Though this is a fanciful version of what might have happened, Gimbutas makes the case for this belief and event occurring, based on the motifs used on vases and dishes she has found in the culture of Old Europe during the last thirty years or so of searching. She offers additional evidence of the once-common belief that bees and butterflies came from dead animals, particularly bulls, quoting from Antigonos of Karystos (ca. 250 B.C.E.) and later Ovid, Virgil, and Porphyry. Granted, this conclusion is one drawn by observation without benefit of microscopic examination, yet it provides a wonderful example of the way a mythical symbol develops.

◐ *Mother-moon Goddess*

Esther Harding also discussed the ancient presence of a Mother Goddess at the back gate of civilization. She refers to the goddess called Dea Syria and Magna Mater, the Great Mother. The goddess has many names. From western Asia and Asia Minor her worship progressed and endured, and changed. She came to be known in one of her oldest forms (old in contemporary terms, that is) about 3000 B.C.E. as Ishtar. Yet Ishtar was already old by then, having been a figure of worship already for thousands of years. Later, around 1700 B.C.E. she was represented by Isis. From prehistoric times she had been Anu in western Europe, where her name is still embedded in the hills of western Ireland known as the Paps (or breasts) of Anu, showing her close connection to the earth as well as to the moon. She is Cybele, Anahita, Annis, Anatis, Nana, Rhea, Ge, Demeter, Tellus, Ceres, and Maia, to name only a few. She is day and night, earth and moon. And, in spite of literal argument to the contrary, she is manifested most recently as the Virgin Mary.

She is the persistent subject of the old record and the new.

The American poet Marge Piercy wrote a book entitled *The Moon is Always Female*, taken from a poem of the same name. Though Piercy's poem is a protest of violence against women, she brings up a thought-provoking question: was the moon always female? In poetry, yes. But in *The Mothers*, while Briffault argued that lunar worship preceded solar worship, he also believed the tradition of male lunar deities to be older than that of female lunar deities. Yet he seems to contradict himself. In one instance he claims that the original lunar deities of Greece and Rome were male, but later describes the "Moirai," a triad of Greek goddesses who represented the moon and were "older than the gods." He adds that male moon gods predominated in nearly every corner of the world: Australia and the Oceanic cultures, Northwest America, Mexico (here he said the old moon gods were male and the new female), in the Caribbean, South America, Asia and the Middle and Far East, and in Africa and the Scandinavian countries.

According to Briffault, as cultures changed from pastoral to agricultural, the gender of the gods changed, too. He describes myths and stories of how the moon became female and was thus more frequently associated with women and their activities. The sun became male, growing to be recognized as a fertilizing force in nature. Briffault believed that a further clue to the gender switch lay in some of the early names given to the sun gods. For example, for a sun god to be called a weaver, a spinner, or to go by the name of "the Hidden" or "the Obscure," all qualities and names given to the moon, was an indication of the sun god's once lunar nature. A striking example from Greek mythology is Apollo, whose name even today evokes the image of the sun god. Yet Apollo was connected with the darker hidden arts of prophecy, divination, and the control over disease, all associated with the moon. Delphi, the site of the famous Greek oracle and perhaps the place most notably associated with Apollo, was once sacred to the earth and moon goddesses Gaia, Themis, and Phoebe. Priestesses at Delphi were called Melissai, a name for the moon.

In the Greek, Latin, Italian, Spanish, and French languages, the word for the moon is feminine. Yet Briffault recorded that Greek peasants thought of the moon as masculine. In the Germanic languages, it is masculine. The ancient Sanskrit word for moon is masculine: *mas*. In another observation, Harley notes that the moon is sometimes considered to be the husband of the earth, sometimes the wife.

The Mythology of All Races records that Turks living in Siberia once thought of the sun as Mother Sun and the moon as Father Moon or Old Man Moon. They considered each a living being, and were known to greet them, swear oaths by them, and to undertake activities dependent on the phases of the moon. Anne Kent Rush notes that to the Armenians, the word Amazon meant "moon woman." The moon was the emblem of the Amazons, who were said to have founded several major cities in Africa and Asia Minor.

In old Norse, the moon was masculine. Harley says the moon was mostly a male deity, and cites examples of words and stories from India, Egypt, Arabia, Slavonia, Lithuania, Sweden, and South America. However, female moon deities also existed in India, Egypt, Arabia, many of the Scandinavian countries, and South America. The deities of Mexican cultures have had both female and male aspects. Ancient Syrians believed the moon was androgynous.

Many tribes throughout the Pacific Northwest of the United States considered the moon to be a male deity or spirit. Other tribes of the Central, Southwest, Plains, and North Central regions saw the moon as a woman, however. A few of her enduring names include Changing Woman, The Eternal One, Grandmother, and the Old Woman Who Never Dies. Quite often, as Briffault tells it, this woman has two sons: the dark one and the light one. As in many other mythological systems, one rules over death, one over life. One is called "The Slayer," one the "Controller of Water." Together the three of them represent the cycles observed in the life, death, and rebirth of the moon.

As Briffault also mentions, however, it is important to keep in mind that in the mythology of more traditional cultures, deciding on the gender of a spirit was and is often determined to suit the occasion. This is not an easy concept for those whose deities have had a fixed and certain gender for several thousands of years to understand immediately. Where lunar deities are concerned, in many cultures and historical times, the gender varies. The moon is sometimes male, sometimes female.

Briffault did not have the benefit of the research of Marija Gimbutas and others who succeeded him. There can hardly be a question about both the quantity and quality of Gimbutas' work and its relationship to the idea that the worship of a Great Mother goddess was the focus of spiritual belief during the time period she studies, from 7000 to 3500 B.C.E. Later evidence from cultures surrounding Old Europe and from other cultures throughout the world reveals that the presence of the Mother Goddess once dominated spiritual belief, and that her absence, not yet total, in the human experience, has only been a recent one. For example, only female deities have been found on Crete. And as Gimbutas and Harding and a host of others inform us, the worship of the Mother Goddess is inevitably linked to the moon. Before turning to that more exclusive connection, however, there is a need to explore the extent of lunar worship a little further.

◉ *Lunar Worship*

Robert Briffault was the first person to state that in all cultures moon worship existed before solar worship. It seems clear that once agriculture became an established feature of a culture, the sun became more important on a practical level, regulating the economy and thus the larger creation of a state. Anne Kent Rush claims that the struggle between matriarchal and patriarchal culture, and consequently between lunar and solar deities, took place around 1500 B.C.E. But the moon, in addition to being magical and mysterious, was used first. There was no need to regulate time before agriculture became a settled endeavor, or before the state became institutionalized. Briffault went so far as to say that there is no culture in which a solar pantheon precedes a lunar one. He mentions that in some cultures, Polynesia for instance, the moon was always uppermost in

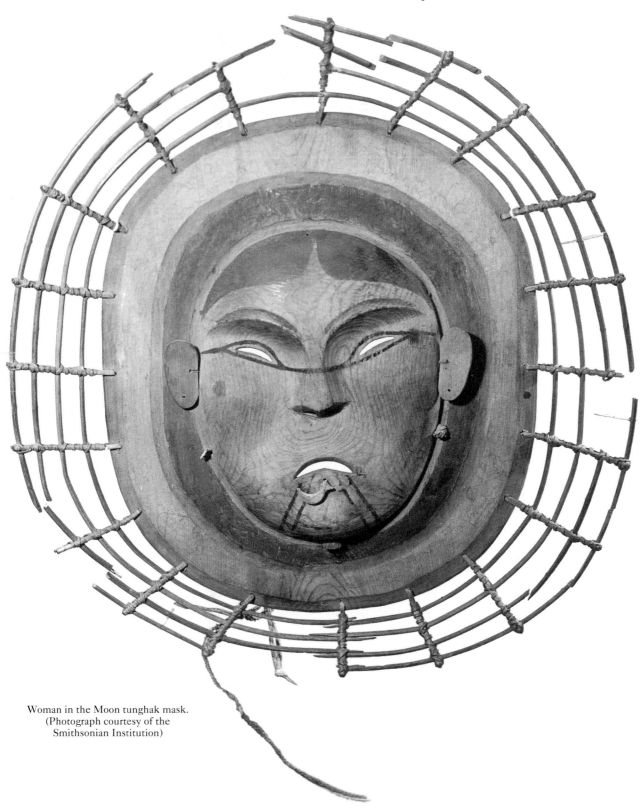

Woman in the Moon tunghak mask.
(Photograph courtesy of the
Smithsonian Institution)

the psychic and spiritual belief. He says also that moon worship was exclusive among Indonesian peoples and in parts of Borneo. The people there called the moon "Mother" and honored her with perpetual fires, harvest songs, and sacrifices. They prayed to her for children, prosperity, good harvests, and for the fertility and protection of their fields and animals.

Another example can be found in the mythical genealogy of the Babylonian moon and sun gods. The moon god was the father of the sun god Shamash, which is another way of saying that the moon was older. Sir Wallis Budge concluded that many of the ancient Egyptian sun gods began their mythological lives as lunar deities, as was mentioned earlier. If that is true, the moon may in fact be the oldest deity commemorated and made manifest by humans. Samuel Noah Kramer, renowned Sumerian scholar, offers an insightful and straightforward way of explaining the Sumerian belief in a deity, which dates to approximately 2500 B.C.E. The Sumerians came to understand the sense of immortal beings by observation and extension; if humans kept their own world moving forward by their own actions, then likewise superhuman creatures must have kept the universe functioning. If the deities were not immortal, or if they did not attend to the cosmic workings, then chaos and destruction resulted. Of course, natural chaos and destruction did occur. In this way of thinking, floods, earthquakes, or even eclipses of the moon were viewed as signals from the gods that something was wrong, that they were displeased or even angry. As for simple observation, though the path of the sun could be followed with the naked-eye method used by the ancients, it could not be observed for long, as the moon can be. And while the sun would appear to have a sameness to its appearance in the sky, the moon was forever mutable and mysterious.

One of the most interesting possibilities of ancient lunar worship of a feminine form comes from Arabia, part of a culture that could be described as a contemporary patriarchal warrior society. The name of the goddess, also honored as the moon, was Al-Uzza. To this day Ka'aba, the name of her shrine at Mecca, contains a black stone, still treated with reverence, that was

honored as the moon. This stone has been described as a meteorite, which would make even a stronger case for the presence of lunar worship, to honor the presence of a piece of the Great Mother that fell from the sky. A cleft in the stone makes scholars believe it was associated with the feminine aspect. It is even now attended by male priests who dress as women and are known as the Beni-Shaybah, the "Sons of the Old Woman." Old Woman is one of the moon's many nicknames. Briffault comments that Arab women once believed the moon was the parent of all humans.

There is plenty of evidence of moon worship among the Hebrews. Scripture passages in the Book of Kings refer to the worship of Astarte and Ashtoreth, names for the moon, as well as to moon worship specifically. The city name Ashtaroth-Karnaim means "Ashtaroth of two horns," a name for the crescent moon. The *Encyclopedia of Religion* reports that a figure representing the moon lived on Mt. Sinai, which means "the Mountain of the Moon," a place that had a long previous association with lunar worship before Moses climbed the slopes to receive the law there.

Worship of the moon may be at the root of the religious belief of all Semitic peoples. Moses Maimonides claimed that Adam, the first man, worshipped the moon. Sun gods did exist among Semitic peoples, but they were not accorded as high a place of honor as the moon. The moon was the source of life and growth, while the sun brought death, not at all an odd notion in desert country scorched by the killing force of the sun. The mythical ancestor of the Hebrews was called Abraham (or Abram) of Ur. The ancient city of Ur was dedicated to the moon god Sin, who was discussed in Chapter Three. Abraham migrated from Ur to Harran, a second major center of moon worship. Briffault mentions that in the later struggle and change in the culture, the women resisted giving up their devotion to the Queen of Heaven, another name for the moon, but that patriarchal reformers caused the change from moon worship to sun worship, along with a move of the culture toward settled agriculture.

Ancient Persians worshipped the god Ormuzd in the form of light. Though this included the light of both the sun and the moon, they had a special prayer: "We sacrifice unto the new moon, the holy and master of holiness: we sacrifice unto the full moon, the holy and master of holiness." In India the moon was central to Vedic belief. According to the Rig Veda the moon, again much more important than the sun, creates and rules the world. The Parava, rulers of India, considered the moon to be the ancestress from whom they took their name. An Indian goddess known as Parasavati was pictured as a small, white-skinned woman with a crescent on her brow. She was known as the "Mistress of All." The god Shiva, often pictured with a crescent moon on his forehead, represented the moon in its waxing and waning phases.

In Japan, shrines of the moon god were located at Ise and Kadono. It has been said of Hawaii that there are as many myths about the moon and sun as there are islands. Anne Kent Rush mentions that on the Tahitian island of Moora, where Queen Pomare Vahine IV ruled from 1827 to 1877 in a matriarchy, a moon temple (marae) still remains.

In China, Confucianism recognized the female side of nature in Shang-ti and the male principle in the first father, Shang-te. Buddhists

Chinese goddess of prosperity and fertility.

called the moon Sasi or Sakchi in reference to the hare who made of itself a sacrificial meal for the hungry Buddha. The wife of the god Indra adopted this as her own name. In the Chinese system of knowledge, the two main principles at work in all of life are Yin and Yang. Yin represents the moon principle—feminine, moist, cool, and receptive. Yang represents the sun—masculine, dry, hot, and active. These principles shaped Chinese court protocol and governed dress, architecture, and cuisine. To this day, in the principle of placement and design known as feng-shui, "moon doorways" or arches exist to thwart harmful energies. Bridges are curved like the moon. In fashion the expressions of "moon eyebrows," and the "moon faces" of concubines were once well known.

Moving toward Europe once again, possible ancient lunar sites at Kintraw, Clava, and Callanish in northern Scotland were examined by archaeologists Alexander and Archie Thom, and by Aubrey Burl. Though their exact nature, whether observational or ritual, is still uncertain, it has been recorded by folklorists that old stone circles in the Orkneys were called "Temples of the Moon" and that elements of lunar worship (such as bowing to or greeting the new moon) persisted in the Scottish Highlands well into the twentieth century.

In both Christian and non-Christian countries throughout human history, lunar worship has prevailed. The ancient Hebrew fathers like Job forbade moon worship. So too the Christian Church issued warnings and edicts against it, indicating its persistence throughout history. St. Eligius declared that the sun and the moon were not to be called lords. Further ecclesiastical rules were directed against the use of moon cycles and worship of the moon goddess well into the Middle Ages wherever the Church held sway. In the fourth century, a group of women called Collyridians worshipped the Virgin Mary as a goddess and tried to propitiate her anger and plead for her mercy. In much the same way, she is prayed to today, although her fiercer aspects have been softened or transmuted to sorrow—her epithet as Our Lady of Sorrows or Our Lady of the Seven Sorrows is frequent even today.

NAMES OF MOON GODDESSES

Aataentsic (Algonquin, Iroquois)
Anath (Ugaritic)
Anu (Celtic)
Aphrodite Eurynome (Greece)
Arianrhod (Wales)
Artemis (Greece)
Ashtaroth (Phoenicia)
Astarte (Phoenicia)
Auchimalgen (Chile)
Black Anath
The Black Virgin
Britomartis (Celtic)
Brizo of Delos (Greece)
Ceridwen (Wales)
Coatlicue (Mexico)
Coyolxauhqui (Mexico)
Cybele (Phrygia)
Cynthia (Greece)
Diana (Rome)
Doris (Greece)
Durga (India)
Dyktinna (Greece)
Europa (Greece)
Etsanatlehi (Navajo)
Freija (Germany)
Frigga (Germany)
Hathor (Egypt)
Hekate (Greece)
Hera (Greece)
Hina (Hawaii, Tahiti)
Io (Greece)
Ishtar (Babylonia)
Isis (Egypt)
Juno Lucina (Rome)
Luna (Rome)
Mictlancihuatl (Mexico)
Mona (Celtic, Teutonic)
Morgana (Celtic)
Nuah (Babylonia)
Nyame (Ghana)

Pasiphae (Greece)
Pe (Africa)
Persephone (Greece)
Phoebe (Greece)
Sarasvati (India)
Sedna (Eskimo)
Selene (Greece)
Seshat (Egypt)
Shing Moon (China)

NAMES OF MOON GODS

Alako (Gypsy)
Anaitis (Iran)
Aningahk (Eskimo)
Apollo (Greece)
Bahloo (New South Wales)
Cata-quilla (Peru)
Chandra/Chandras (India)
Dionysus (Greece)
Endymion (Greece)
Haiatlila'qs (Tsimshian)
Hur (Sumeria, Babylonia)
Khons/Khonsu (Egypt)
Kun (Finland)
Mani (Scandinavian)
Maui, son of the moon (Polynesia)
Metzli (Mexico)
Myesyats (Yugoslavia)
Nanna/Sin (Babylonia, Sumeria)
Nantu (Ecuador)
Osiris (Egypt)
Ptah (Egypt)
Qat (Melanesia)
Roong (Haida, Canada)
Sin (Assyro-Babylonia)
Somas (Greece)
Tangarora (Samoa)
Tecciztecatl (Mexico)
Thoth/et (Egypt)
Tsuki-yomi (Japan)
Wiyot and Waklaut (California Indians)
Wotan (Germany)

Because such observances are private and personal, older practices stemming from lunar worship may have been slightly subverted to accommodate the transition to Christianity. It would be interesting to know for certain to what extent they continue today. Teaching children to wish on the moon and stars is probably such a leftover. A return to such observance rather than a true persistence of such practice can be found at the Findhorn Community in Scotland, a contemporary community guided by spiritual beliefs that have evolved with a deliberate and conscious effort to live a more natural life. Lunar observances are marked and celebrated at Findhorn, and the moon, along with the other natural cycles, is the focus of meditation and consideration in daily living.

Lunar worship has been well documented in Greece and Rome. English antiquarian Edward Clarke found that as late as 1801, Demeter was still worshipped at Eleusis; he found the villagers there still draping her statue with flowers. In a search for the lessons of mythology for contemporary lives, modern women are making the journey to Eleusis, as Greek women have always done, in the name of one religion or another.

Older lunar worship is often characterized by its relationship to fire, believed to be like the light of the moon (and in solar worship like the light of the sun). Briffault mentions a Roman temple dedicated to "Luna noctiluca" in which a dedication fire burned in much the same way the perpetual fire burned at Brigid's fire temple in Kildare, Ireland. It was officially put out by soldiers during the reign of King Henry VIII in the 1500s, when the Roman Catholic churches, monasteries, and abbeys were destroyed. The cold dug-out ruin of St. Brigid's temple can be visited today, in the shadow of the Christian cathedral in Kildare. Behind the solitary figure of the Christian Saint Brigid exists a triad of ancient Celtic goddesses who were also moon goddesses. In another close connection, the moon was the chief deity among the Basques and the Celtiberians, Celts who found their way into northwestern Spain. The Celts knew her as the Mother-moon goddess Galla. Many of the Celtic tribes took their names from their goddesses. In Galla's case, the region that came to be known as Gaul bore hers.

In the New World, at ancient ceremonial sites in Cuzco, Peru, priestesses had charge of the worship of lunar deities, and priests guided the worship of the solar gods. And on the Island of the Moon in Lake Titicaca, a priestess assumed the role of the moon while a priest took that of the sun for ceremonies.

In Peru, the moon goddess was called Mama-Quilla. She was recognized by her silver disk and human features. A temple dedicated to her in Cuzco was destroyed by the Incas. Among the Quiche Maya of Guatemala were women called Mama-Cuna who guarded the sacred fire which was lit at summer solstice. Moon worship among the Quiches was connected to respect for feminine nature—pottery was a woman's art, and each piece was invested with the spirit of the special connection between women and nature, as it is still. Anne Kent Rush found that some aspects of the peyote cult seem to show traces of an ancient ritual associated with the moon: the crescent-shaped altar is called a moon; ashes from the fire are made into a crescent shape at midnight; and a woman, Peyote Woman, rules the ritual.

The two deities of Peru were known as Pachamac ("earth animator"), the sun, and his wife, the moon. Attached to the Temple of the Sun at Cuzco is a temple to the moon, considered to be the mother of the Incas. John Hemming mentions another sacred site at Macchu Picchu, a shrine known as the Cave of the Moon.

Woodcut by Albrecht Dürer showing the Virgin and child behind the crescent moon.

Briffault also states that a people known as the Xaltoca honored the moon as the most important deity; likewise, in southern Chile the moon had precedence over the sun, as with Caribbean peoples in the Antilles. Whereas the descendants of largely European immigrants in twentieth-century North America may view the moon as a benevolent object or even as a hunk of lifeless rock, the Aztec people of Mexico connected spiritual belief with all nature. The moon figures prominently in their beliefs. Theirs was a pantheon not to be lured but feared and placated. Their gods were vengeful and just, not merciful and kind. A good example of this different view of the deities, and of the Mother-moon goddess in particular, comes from Aztec mythology.

The Aztec moon goddess had two aspects, as do many of the moon goddesses in older cultures. Though she brought harvests and fruitfulness, she was also responsible for the cold, the damp, sickness, and even death. Harley refers to Metzli as a female deity, although Metzli is described elsewhere as a male moon god. There is no need to quibble over Metzli's gender, however, as Briffault and others have mentioned the pattern in older cultures of alternating genders among gods and goddesses. This is particularly true of Aztec deities. In story form, the tale of Metzli tells of the setting of the moon and the rising of the sun. As Harley told it, when the world was still in chaos and darkness, nothing but a human sacrifice could bring forth the sun. Metzli brought forth a sick creature named Nanahautl, and persuaded him to leap into a sacrificial fire. Metzli followed, and from that fire, the sun rose and Metzli, the moon, declined, or set.

According to Briffault, the Great Mother in Mexico was also the Moon Mother. He describes a pre-Conquest statue of her that was painted white above the mouth and black below, a perfect representation of the moon as it waxes and wanes, similar to images found in many other cultures.

The pre-eminent moon goddess of the Aztecs was Coyolxauhqui, daughter of Coatlicue, the mother of the stars and the sun. The carved head of Coyolxauhqui, in the National Museum of Anthropology in Mexico City,

depicts a perfect moon goddess—round-faced, her eyes closed, her headdress full of the beautiful scallop shapes that also decorate her cheeks and have been described as tears and the ball-shaped tufts of down referred to in her story. Her name translates as "Golden Bells." There is something deep and mysterious about her depiction in sculpture. She commands respect; she looks as if she could have just emerged from the moon. And like the moon, she is never pictured as a whole body, which is in keeping with her story.

As with any goddess who has traversed so many years and generations, there are different versions of her life and death. As one story goes, Coatlicue ("She of the Serpent Skirt") was sweeping up in front of the temple on Serpent Mountain where she lived when suddenly a feather dropped out of the air and nestled itself into her bosom. As a result, Coatlicue found herself pregnant. When Coatlicue's many other children, who were all the stars, learned that their mother had become pregnant they became enraged at the disgrace and plotted to kill her. Here the versions differ: in one, Coyolxauhqui leads her outraged siblings forward, urging them to matricide; in the other, she runs to the temple to warn her mother of the approaching murderous band. Her reputation, even today, adheres to the first version. Meanwhile, the warrior child in Coatlicue's womb speaks to her, telling her not to be afraid, that he will protect her. As the four hundred children swarm up the hill to their mother's temple, Coatlicue gives birth to Huitzilopochtli ("Hummingbird on the Left"), the Aztec god of war and sacrifice. Like so many other culture heroes, he was born fully clad and armed for battle. He first slew Coyolxauhqui by cutting off her head and dismembering her, and then the rest of his sisters and brothers. The mythical story of Coyolxauhqui's demise was confirmed when in 1978 at the Templo Mayor in the center of Mexico City, a ten-ton ceremonial stone was unearthed that showed the dismembered goddess. Significantly, this stone lay at the base of a pyramid marked with serpents (symbolizing Serpent Mountain); the temple of the sun god Huitzilopochtli was atop the pyramid.

◐ *Triads*

One of the earliest representations of the Mother-moon goddess is as a triad of deities. Chapter Three discussed the Greek threesome of Persephone the maiden, Demeter the mother, and Hekate the crone, who were known as the Moirai and portrayed the three most obvious changes in the moon: new, waxing, and waning. Other moon goddesses from the Greek pantheon who alternated as members of this triad include Selene, recognized as the full moon and actually a member of the Titans who preceded the gods of Olympus, and Aphrodite, the goddess of love who later came to represent the Bright Moon or full moon. Hekate, it seems, has always been associated with the power of the dark moon. Still later, in the kind of change that is not uncommon in any culture, Artemis represented the crescent moon, Selene the full moon, and Hekate the waning moon. In the Minoan culture on Crete, three doves symbolized the moon goddess, who also wore a necklace graced by twelve lunar discs, which may have represented a lunar count.

Many lunar deities, when tracked to their mythical origins, were at one time triads. Besides the triad of the Moirai, other examples are the Celtic Brigid, the Scandinavian Norns, the German Valkyries, the Sirens, the Hesperides, the Charities, the Gorgons, the Horai (all from Greek tradition) who were related to the seasons and to cycles of growth and decay, and the Erinyes, perhaps better known as the Greek Furies. Some of these triads survive in legend and story as the three Weird Sisters from Macbeth that Shakespeare made famous, or the three fairy godmothers assigned to watch over children from birth, as in the story of Sleeping Beauty. Briffault found that among the native people of New Britain three lunar deities were known as the "White Woman" and her two sons. There are many other instances of a moon goddess with twins, as well as a single son who dies and is reborn. Some triads are worth examining more closely. The great goddess of Arabia had three aspects, acclaimed as three holy virgins who brought good and back luck. They invite obvious comparison to the Greek Moirai

and the Norns of northern Europe. They were also known as Allah's daughters, and as such probably represent the three aspects of the moon. We have already mentioned Al-Uzza, the black mother stone still revered at Mecca; her sister Mamat represents Time, and their sibling Al-Ilat represents Fate.

In Rome, the moon goddess Diana was also known as Diana Triformis (three forms). Because of her association with animals, she was represented by the heads of a horse, a dog, and a bear, her most frequent companions. In addition, she was portrayed as Luna the Moon in heaven, Diana on Earth, and Hekate below in the dark underworld. Though classical writers described one of Diana's sanctuaries on the Aventine in Rome, her most famous temple was located at Lake Nemi. This was the place that held such fascination for Sir James Frazer, author of *The Golden Bough*. From the worship activities that he concluded took place at Nemi, he formed the basis of his ideas about kingship and its relation to the moon goddess. Built in a deeply wooded area inside a grove of trees, it was most often visited by women. A lake nearby was once known as Diana's Mirror. The conclusion that it was a site dedicated to fertility has been drawn from the artifacts found there—phalluses and female genital organs carved from wood or stone, as well as statues of pregnant women and women holding children on their laps. In addition to being a huntress and protector of both wild and domestic animals, Diana was also a goddess of fertility and childbirth. Similarly, the Roman Juno-Lucina aided pregnant women during confinement. Diana's Greek counterpart, Artemis, was a huntress who also looked after women who were in danger.

Triads still have great power over the religious thinking of humans. Many people have listened in amazement to the story of Saint Patrick explaining the Trinity, the theology of three gods in one God, to the residents of fifth-century Ireland. Since the Celtic deities almost always had three aspects, it was a matter of simple transference for converts, not the cosmic leap in understanding it has often been made out to be. A prime example of this triad was the pre-Christian Brigid mentioned above, who in

Turn-of-the-century print depicting a moon maiden with a water creature. (From the collection of Steve Wilson)

her different aspects was a special protector of women, the arts, and of blacksmiths, whose "magic power" enabled them to bend metal. Another figure known to both Celtic and Teutonic peoples was Mona, who represented the mother goddess, the month, and the moon. There are dozens of others. Among the Huron tribe, the three aspects of the spirit woman Aataentsic listed by both Harley and Briffault were water, sorcery, and destiny, familiar lunar associations. In a move that reflects how deeply rooted the belief in triads persisted from older times, Pope Urban VIII ordered three-headed gods to be removed from churches and in 1628 had them burned.

As cultures developed, quite often the three aspects that lunar triads represented came to be differentiated, considered separately with qualities of their own. What had been three in one became three separate deities. Perhaps Christianity may have met a deep-seated urge to restore the concept of three-in-one that had been a part of human spiritual life for so long. Much of the contemporary scholarship on the history of women discusses the differentiation of the female deities at length, often using Greece as an example. Individual "great" lunar goddesses have emerged from different cultures and civilizations. Ishtar was mentioned previously; like so many goddesses and gods, she had multiple names, reflecting the lingering nature of her many aspects. Jastrow gathered some of them: Nana, Innina, Irnini, Ninni, Nina, Inanna, Ninmakh, and the Lady of Arbela. She was a member of the second astronomical triad of Sumerian deities, which included the moon and sun gods, Sin and Shamash. In her different aspects, and as she was worshipped in different cities, she was a goddess of both love and war, though primarily the mother goddess of fertility and all life. Though in time she became affiliated with the moon, she was once associated with the planet Venus, and as such was often called the "daughter of the moon." Like many other planetary bodies, the movements of Venus through the sky were a source of divination for the Babylonians. One invocation beseeches her:

I pray to thee, mistress of mistresses, goddess of godesses,
Ishtar, queen of all habitations, guide of mankind.

Her center of worship was Uruk. Jastrow gives the name of her temple as the "heavenly house" and describes her symbols as an eight-rayed star and a sixteen-rayed star. The story of Ishtar's (also Inanna's) descent into the underworld, one of the greatest Mesopotamian myths, foreshadowed the later Greek story of Demeter and Persephone. In ancient Syria, Anath was the most important moon goddess and was, like Ishtar, a goddess of love and war. She was called the "Lady of Heaven" and "Mistress of All the Gods."

In Carthage, Tanit (or Tanith) was a goddess of the heavens and the moon. She was later compared to both Demeter and Dido. Spence gives her nickname as "the countenance of Baal" and her symbol as the crescent moon. A temple was raised to her in Carthage and in it hung a veil believed to bring good luck. Eliade gives the name of the Iranian moon goddess as Ardivisur Anahita. In Phrygia, Aphrodite was known as Aphrodite Eurynome. In this manifestation, she was depicted by a wooden statue of a mermaid. Her sacred plants and creatures included the murex, myrtle tree, palm tree, dove, tunny, sturgeon, scallop, and periwinkle.

Rush further elaborates that her sacred colors were green, blue, and scarlet.

In Egypt, of course, the most famous moon goddess was Isis, whose name means "moisture." Another was Hathor, the Celestial or Heavenly Cow (Holy Cow!?). Less well known is Seshat, an Egyptian moon goddess of learning and temple building whose symbol was a star on a pole, with inverted horns on top. The Roman goddess Luna was the daughter of Hyperion and sister of the sun. The Roman poet Livy mentions a temple to her on the Aventine. Tacitus also mentions a temple to the moon. The German moon goddess was named Freija. Her possession of a golden necklace may indicate that she was a sun goddess in an earlier mythology. Another moon goddess was Frigga, whose symbol was the unmistakable crescent.

There are many interesting and curious moon goddesses to be found among the Celts. In arguing that King Arthur was a mythical and not a historical figure, Briffault refers to a passage from Nennius, a popular historian like Geoffrey of Monmouth, that describes the Celtic goddess Anu as sister to King Arthur, and goes on to say that at Arthur's death the moon was the chief mourner. Since Anu has been identified as a lunar goddess, perhaps this is what the reference means. He also describes Morgana as a Celtic moon goddess; she was also known as the "Lady of the Lake" and the patroness of springs and wells, in addition to being addressed as "The White Lady."

Though the name of Ceridwen may not be as famous as that of Morgana (or Morgan La Fey), some refer to her as the best known of the Welsh goddesses. Ceridwen's symbols are by now familiar: one is the cow, and another is the crescent moon, which serves as her barge. Darkness was embodied by the evil Avagddu, also known as Black Wings. In Welsh mythology, as in many other mythologies, the gods and goddesses assumed the characteristics of natural events. Ceridwen's task was to protect her shining crescent barge against Avagddu's darkness. In an analogy that recalls the Babylonian explanation of the powers at work during eclipse, the Druids believed that on the shortest day of the year the sun battled with Black Wings but was mortally wounded. The sun's soul escaped into Ceridwen's barge and was eventually reborn, although Black Wings reigned temporarily. When the sun god attempted to punish Black Wings for all the trouble he had caused, Black Wings hid under the earth. Like Hekate, only Ceridwen, all-seeing in her journeys across the sky, knows where he is. She tells. In retaliation, Black Wings constantly pursues Ceridwen and the sun god across the sky.

With few exceptions, what has been discussed so far deals with what was, what has been. Are there contemporary examples of lunar worship? If so, where do they exist? Who practices them? The answer to the first question is clearly yes. The most prominent continuation of lunar worship, granted that it has undergone a transformation from older times until now, continues in the veneration of the Virgin Mary, the mother of Jesus Christ. Even during the early stages of the development of Christianity, the epithets and honor once associated to the Great Mother–moon goddess were transferred to the Virgin. She is clearly associated with the moon in terms of her qualities, and bears many of the same names as previous goddesses of the moon, epithets established from within the church as well as without: Star of the Sea, Queen of Heaven, The Moon of the Church, The Spiritual Moon, the Perfect and Eternal Moon. As noted by Katzeff, during the Middle Ages, the moon was worshipped openly by ordinary Christians in the person of the Virgin. More recently, Marina Warner's study of the history of the worship of the Virgin Mary, in *Alone of All Her Sex: The Myth and Cult of the Virgin Mary*, traces the origins of the Virgin to worship of the Great Mother goddess.

Crescent moon symbols used as halos for the Virgin Mary.

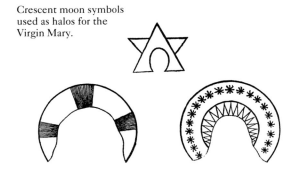

Briffault claims that after courtly love had been purged and punished by the Church, sentiments of love were often sublimated and directed to the Virgin, who he also found to have close and obvious connections to the moon. He offers as one example the words of an Italian poet, Guido Guinicelli: "The lady who in my heart awakened love seems like unto the orb that measures time and sheds her splendor in the sky of love."

Nearly all of the Great Mother–moon goddess's dark, fearsome, and devouring qualities have been eliminated from the Virgin. She is kind, gentle, forgiving, shedding her beatific light on all who embrace her. The closest she gets to anger is sorrow. Her dark side exists now primarily in the figures of the approximately four hundred Black Virgins documented by Ean Begg and discussed in Chapter Five. Even here her association with darkness is more that of nature than it is of the dark side as it comes to be equated with negative energy, destruction, anger, and death, clearly aspects that older lunar goddesses had and showed. Ishtar represented love and war. Isis searched for life and death. Coatlicue brought forth Huitzilopochtli, the god who required human blood to feed the sun, and like the Indian goddess Kali, devoured life as well.

Other more overt forms of lunar worship or lunar reverence can be found in New Age religions, many of which derive from or are a return to older forms of Eastern religions. In some instances the practice is one of pure unadulterated moon worship. In others, the reverence approaches the mythological, in attempt to honor the spirit many think the moon represents. Many Native American peoples are continuing their own traditional practices, many of which contain lunar elements, just as they have done all along in many cases, only again in more open ways. Some, though rightfully cautious in the effort, are willing to share the wisdom and knowledge of traditional practices, many of which have been scorned and even outlawed by those outside the Native American traditions.

The contemporary practice of Wicca has active elements of lunar worship, best chronicled by Margot Adler in *Drawing Down the Moon*, a comprehensive text to which little could be added. More conscientious efforts at conservation and preservation of planetary and interplanetary resources have also led many people to a new and different awareness of the moon that could certainly assume philosophical if not quite religious dimensions. Though it would be impossible to try and state categorically what the status is of lunar "worship" in these times, it is quite clear that the awareness of the environment, perhaps triggered by the Apollo lunar missions, has certainly made for more conscientious consideration of Luna, earth's sister and closest neighbor.

◑ *Moon Gods*

Though the focus of this chapter has been on the Great Mother goddess and forms she assumes as a lunar goddess, male lunar deities should also be mentioned. As the feature on page 138 listing their names shows, they have been found all over the world. Whether or not they were the first representations of the moon is still open for discussion, but it is clear that the moon is not always female.

When investigating the history of the well-known Egyptian sun god Amen-Ra, Briffault made an interesting discovery. The god's name has been translated as "The Obscure" or "The Hidden One," odd names for a bright deity whose light penetrates the world. These same nicknames are well-known epithets for the moon. Pointing to a connection between the two cultures, Briffault notes that the Greeks knew this god as Ammon and associated him with a much older deity named Min, who was called, "the Fiery Bull" and the "Lord of the New Moon." As aspects of the changing moon, Persephone and Hekate were described as the maiden and the crone. Amen was likewise portrayed as a child and an old man as he aged, an indication of his lunar heritage.

With more information provided by Briffault, some conclusions can be drawn about the god Horus' affiliation with the moon. Like the Mexican moon goddess Coyolxauhqui, only his face is often pictured, typical for many lunar deities. One of his names means "Face," while another was "The Lord of Transformations."

Cloaked in mythical metaphor, the story of Horus emerges. A common name for the moon was the "Left Eye of Horus." The mythical explanation for this is that Set, the god of shadow (specifically the shadow cast over the moon as it wanes and appears to swallow it) devoured the right eye of Horus. Eventually Set also devoured the left eye. During that time Horus was called "Dark Horus" or "Blind." The temple of Horus at Panoplis was known as the "Temple of the Moon."

The god Osiris, companion of Isis, also has a lunar history. One meaning of his name is "Lord of the Moon." Another is "The Mighty One." He was also called "The Great Hare." The moon itself was called "The House of Osiris." Many statues representing this god were titled "The Moon." None have been found that connect him with the sun. In the mythic battle with the shadow god Set, Osiris was dismembered and cut into fourteen pieces, the number of days of the waning moon (one source says twenty-six pieces, which would also be close to the lunar month). Special funeral rites to Osiris were celebrated during the last nine days of the waning moon.

Ptah is another Egyptian moon god, sometimes described as the father of Ra, sometimes indistinct from Ra. He was known as the creator of the egg of the moon, and sometimes as the egg of the moon itself. As cultural traditions change, what was once the creation itself often later becomes the creator. Like Ra, Ptah has names and epithets that link him to the moon: The Lord of the Thirty Years, the Two-Faced God, and the God of Multitudinous Forms.

Though the astronomer Sir Norman Lockyer says that all forms of Thoth appear as an ibis, another source says he is often pictured as a baboon, and, in an action that is the opposite of its fellow creature the mercat (who greets the rising and setting sun) is recorded to have stood up and greeted the moon. The Egyptian year began on 1 Thoth, originally thought by Lockyer to be the autumnal equinox; later, the year began on the summer solstice as sun worship took precedence over lunar worship. As in Babylonian mythology, the sun god was the offspring of the moon god, a fact which makes a case for the greater age of lunar worship. Lock-

DANCE

*A*s Briffault pointed out, the word "dance" as applied to traditional cultures where worship or reverence for the moon existed didn't have the same modern meaning we give it. "To dance" in many languages is another way to say "pray." Sacred dance has long been a part of the spiritual and religious practices of human beings. In ancient Greece the performance that later became drama evolved from the enactment of religious ritual, including dance. The dancing associated with moon rites was a form or praying, of celebrating the spirit of the deity. There is even some suggestion that the Olympic games were originally not strictly for athletic prowess, but intended as a form of ritual performed to help the planets and stars in their path across the heavens. In Rome, one of the activities the goddess Luna watched over was the circus. Even the games of cricket and football may have their origins in the well-intentioned human effort to help restore the moon from its weakened state.

In *A Mantis Carol*, Laurens van der Post recalls how the African Bushmen have a dance for everything. They dance at the new moon and they dance at the full moon. When van der Post asked about the latter, he was told:

You see that the moon which is sitting there so nicely, feeling itself to be so full of light is about to wither and fade and die utterly away and will not renew itself in dying and return again to us with such a heart full of light unless we here, feeling ourselves to be dancing thus, make her feel utterly how much our hearts belong to her and need her light to know our way in the darkness of life on earth.

The movements of the moon across the sky suggest the motions of dance itself—the most natural of dances. The rising figure of the dancer lifts herself lightly and easily across the sky. Though she repeats the same movements again and again, they are the same and not quite the same. She rises and dances and disappears, growing brighter and more obvious as she goes. And then the dance declines, ending as she disappears in darkness.

yer believed he found evidence for the same sort of transition in Egypt. Egyptian moon gods were not the only lunar deities that existed in the world—far from it. Yet they do provide a model for the sort of male lunar deity found throughout many other cultures.

In addition to Briffault, Esther Harding is a good source of information about male lunar deities. She provides an interesting history of the sons of moon goddesses, many of whom prefigure Jesus. One of the characteristics of these sons is that they are born of "virgin" birth, virgin here in its older meaning of an independent figure, not without a male complement, but "one-in-herself." They are often the consort or lover of the moon goddess. They often die and are reborn in a cycle that reflects either a lunar cycle or an earth cycle. They are Tammuz, Dumuzi, Adonis, Osiris, Horus, and Jesus, to name a few. Certainly their mythological histories from a lunar perspective would be worth further investigation.

146

CHAPTER NOTES
Page numbers are in parentheses at the end of each citation.

The event described on page pp. 130–131 happened to the author.

Marshack, Alexander. *The Roots of Civilization: The Cognitive Beginnings of Man's First Art, Symbol and Notation.* McGraw-Hill. New York. 1972. (131)

Gimbutas, Marija. *The Goddesses and Gods of Old Europe.* University of California Press. Berkeley. 1982. (131, 132, 134)

———— *The Language of the Goddess.* Harper & Row. San Francisco. 1989. (131, 132, 134)

Harding, M. Esther. *Woman's Mysteries Ancient and Modern.* Harper & Row. New York. 1976. (132, 134, 146)

Piercy, Marge. *The Moon Is Always Female.* Alfred A. Knopf. New York. 1980. (132)

Harley, Rev. Timothy. *Moon Lore.* Swan Sonnenschein, Le Bas & Lowrey. London. 1885. Reissued by Singing Tree Press. Detroit. 1969. (134, 140, 142)

Gray, Louis Herbert. *The Mythology of All Races.* Marshall Jones. Boston. 1916. (134)

Rush, Anne Kent. *Moon, Moon.* Random House. New York. 1976. (134, 137, 139, 143)

Budge, E. A. Wallis. *The Egyptian Book of the Dead* (The Papyrus of Ani). Dover. New York. 1967. (136)

The Encyclopedia of Religion. Mircea Eliade, editor. Macmillan. New York. 1987. (136)

The Oxford Annotated Bible with the Apocrypha. Revised Standard Version. Herbert G. May and Bruce M. Metzger, editors. Oxford University Press. 1965. (136)

The Persian prayer is quoted in Harley. (136–137)

Historian Michael Woods mentioned Clarke's discovery in a recent television episode of "Travels" entitled "The Sacred Way," viewed during January 1991. (139)

The author visited the site of Brigid's fire temple in Kildare, Ireland, in June 1990. (139)

Hemming, John. *Monuments of the Incas.* University of New Mexico Press. Albuquerque. 1990. (139)

Frazer, Sir James. *The Golden Bough.* Macmillan. New York.. (139)

Jastrow, Morris. *The Civilization of Babylonia and Assyria.* J. B. Lippincott Company. Philadelphia. 1915. (143)

Spence, Lewis. *Myths & Legends of Babylonia & Assyria.* George G. Harrap & Company. London. 1916. (143)

Eliade, Mircea. "The Moon and Its Mystique" in *Patterns in Comparative Religion.* Sheed & Ward. London and New York. 1958. (143)

Warner, Marina. *Alone Of All Her Sex: The Myth and the Cult of the Virgin Mary.* Knopf. New York. 1976. (144)

Adler, Margot. *Drawing Down the Moon.* Beacon Press. Boston. 1986. (144)

Lockyer, Norman. *The Dawn of Astronomy.* M.I.T. Press. Cambridge. 1964 (repr. 1894) (145)

Van der Post, Laurens. *A Mantis Carol.* Island Press. Washington, D.C. 1975. (feature) (146)

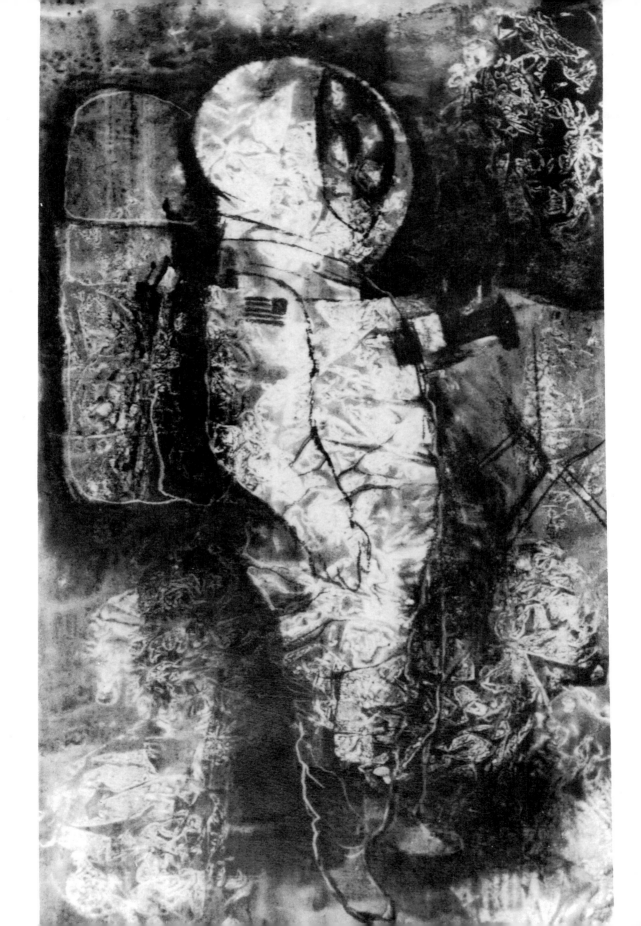

FROM MAN IN THE MOON TO MAN ON THE MOON

✳

Is Our Romance With Luna Dead?

"What was most significant about the lunar voyage was not that men set foot on the moon but that they set eye upon the earth."
–Reader's Digest
1980

Opposite page: "On the Moon" by Mitchell Jamieson. (Courtesy of NASA)

Bootprint on the lunar surface.

IT IS NOT MUCH to look at in simple black and white, an accordion-like wrinkle on a stark landscape. But it marks a step into another dimension, another way of thinking about and viewing the universe, and possibly another level of human evolution. It is the footprint of a man's boot on the surface of the moon. Unlike the oversize footprints of Buddha honored at a shrine in India, these are minuscule when seen from above at even a slight distance. Although the man who made them claimed neither holiness nor saintliness, in one way they resemble the "footprints" of saints and the holy people of legend still revered on isolated hillsides in Ireland: due to lack of atmosphere on the moon, this footprint may also endure for centuries.

The man who left the first marks is a man of science, a man of the future. Yet his footprint is still celebrated in words that are as easily recognizable as "Once upon a time," or "Fourscore and seven years ago," or "In the beginning was the Word." The words he spoke as he made that first footprint on the moon sounded more like an incantation than a scientific formula. On July 20, 1969, from the surface of the moon Neil Armstrong declared: "That's a small step for a man, one giant step for mankind." There was both humility and pride in the statement. Though his words were uttered at a time when little conscientiousness about inclusive language existed (i.e., humankind rather than mankind), he did mean all of us, all of humanity. (This quotation is an excerpt; for the full first words, see Chapter Notes.)

Did he come as a warrior, stepping onto the lunar surface, nearly 240,000 miles from home, to conquer it for God and country? With John Kennedy's declaration in May of 1961 that the United States was committed to putting a man on the moon by the end of the decade, the race was on. Yet the words and gestures upon finally landing were larger than one nation or culture could contain. The plaque that Armstrong and his fellow astronauts left behind declared:

Here men from the planet earth first set foot upon
*   the moon*
July 1969 A.D.
We came in peace for all mankind.

They planted the American flag, and the action was more one of reverence than of claiming land or territory (besides, treaties in existence at the time forbade any nation from claiming the moon for itself). The plaque and the flag remain on the moon to this day. So do a four-leaf clover, for good luck, and a falcon feather, used to test gravity but also left as a talisman of the things of earth (though some claim it is simply litter).

That first human footprint also remains, left behind in perfect silence on that still world of light and shadow, undisturbed. In that land of no atmosphere, no cloud, rain, storm, sand, wind, or lightning will erase it. Perhaps one day a meteor, like thousands that have created their own geological footprints during the 4.5 billion years of the moon's existence, will strike in that exact spot. Or perhaps someone else will also step down in that place and cover it over. But with space exploration moving beyond the reaches of the moon, that is unlikely for some time yet. As the footprint remains imprinted on the surface of the moon, so is it imprinted on our imaginations, where it remains a superlative—the first sign of human presence in a nonhuman world.

Western culture is fascinated with superlatives. Whatever is first, fastest, longest, and strongest is held in the highest regard. Whatever is last, slowest, shortest, or weakest are measured, too—they get less consideration, but they are marked and commemorated. This is an age that could easily be renamed for the Roman deity Trivia, once goddess of the dark of the moon and guardian of the crossroads (Hekate's counterpart), now the patroness of tidbits of history and information. Most Americans love the notion of the first footprint on the moon having been made by one of our own. Thanks to the television cameras, millions of people on earth were able to cross the vast stellar ocean, arrive on the moon, and see that footprint for themselves, that tiny human mark on the sister planet so otherwise devoid of human touch. In that footprint many human hopes and fears were confirmed or destroyed. It proved that the astronauts and their craft would not sink into the surface and disappear. It proved that the moon could sustain the human pres-

ence, that one slow step after another could be taken there, after the tens of thousands of years spent dreaming about walking there, traveling along in spirit journeys and flights of imagination to the moon and back. Whether Eskimo shaman or tribal Celt, Roman citizen or Japanese farmer, French writer or American astronaut, it seems that all of humanity has dreamed of going to the moon.

Among the Bushmen of South Africa, for instance, walking and the moon have a special connection. The creator god among them, the praying mantis known as !kaggen had a great affinity for the sky. As he walked along one night under the stars, he took off his shoe and threw it at the sky. This shoe became the moon, known as "!kaggen's shoe."

To the Western mind, so strongly influenced by the Judeo-Christian traditions from which have emerged a powerful father-God, from which the Age of Reason and the Enlightenment developed, where the powers of reason and logic have come to assume a power on a par with religious belief, the notion of a praying mantis as a deity seems odd. Viewing someone else's deity as odd bespeaks the danger of too much logic and too much reason. It reveals a tendency to take everything in the world literally and from only one point of view. By doing that, it is easy to lose the beautiful and magical language of myth, of legend, of story, of metaphor, to know more deeply and even more personally the meaning behind the words and the symbols.

Lately, though, this same Western culture has finally begun to look around and see what logic and reason, taken to their superlative and unquestioned extremes, have done to the elements that the ancient Celts used to swear their oaths by—the sky above them, the earth below them, and the sea around them. If the attempts to travel to the moon have been costly in the realms of both human and scientific life, in the long run perhaps they will be more valuable than might be imagined, for the journey to the moon offered us a new metaphor for life.

Catching that first glimpse of the small, lovely, marbled earth peeking over the moon's horizon, seeing that first footprint on the distant silver surface, caused us to think differently about ourselves. For the first time, the fragile planet could be observed from a way no one had seen before. The astronauts' journey allowed everyone on earth a chance to perceive themselves from the outside, from a distance— to see the fragile globe called home spinning in the universe's night. They told what it was like to leave home and go far enough away that, as astronaut James Irwin later noted, loneliness assumed a cosmic nature. From the distance, too, the damage that poor care and neglect had caused were also easy to see. The view caused great feelings of awe, pride, and humility.

Some people, of course, have never forgotten the earth. Traditional peoples who have kept closely connected, relying on her as a mother or a living partner, keeping in their minds and hearts and in the manner of their living, that they emerged from her body, have also kept the stories of the earth. Living in and on the earth —as opposed to above her, as more modern cultures do, building high-rises, ostensibly to house more people in less space, though they also physically distance people from earth— allowed a closer connection to the nature of earth and the nature of the universe. !kaggen has affection for the sky because he walks beneath it all the time. He lives and dies in its shadow or its light. When he throws his shoe up into the sky to create a moon, it is not just a fanciful gesture. It is a way of telling the story of creation, of how and why the moon was made. !kaggen's footprint moving across the sky as the moon is as graphic as Neil Armstrong's footprint upon it. !kaggen's gesture is a gift, some mark of himself and his people. To the human view below, it was the footprint of the god across the sky, the mark of the creator

visible to humans, a sign that other stronger powers guided the world. Armstrong's action creates a powerful irony: his is the footprint of the human upon the face of the god. Considered in that light, it is easy to understand why the people of Bali believed that walking on the moon violated its sanctity, and threatened to cut off diplomatic relations with the United States because of the Apollo 11 landing. How the worlds have changed. !kaggen's shoe has lasted through generations of storytellers whose words may date to the time when humans first began telling stories. Armstrong's footprint could last as many more.

On July 16, 1969, a journey was undertaken quite unlike any other venture on earth, though humans had dreamt of it for centuries. At 9:32 A.M. EDT Apollo 11 left Pad A from Launch Complex 39 at the Kennedy Space Center in Florida. Nearly a million first-hand observers watched as the rocket left the earth. Nearly one-fifth of the inhabitants of earth watched and listened on televisions and radios around the world. The lunar module, named the Eagle, landed four days later at 4:18 P.M. EDT at a location known as Tranquility Base, named for the nearby Mare Tranquilitatis, the Sea of Tranquility. At 10:56 P.M. EDT Neil Armstrong set foot on the surface of the moon, the first human being to do so. At 11:15 P.M. EDT Edwin "Buzz" Aldrin joined him. The two set up research equipment, planted an American flag, spoke with President Richard Nixon, and collected lunar rock and soil samples. They departed the moon at 1:54 P.M. EDT on July 21, 1969 and landed mid-Pacific three days later at 12:51 P.M. EDT on July 24. They were quarantined for three weeks after arriving back on earth, to make sure that they had not brought back with them any dangerous life forms.

It has been asked by more than one person, "Can you trust a nation that names its moon missions for the sun god?" Though largely ignored by all but a few at the time, the question has since arisen as to whether or not Americans really knew their mythology, considering that Apollo is best known as a sun god. The name for the Apollo missions was suggested by Abe Silverstein, director of NASA's Office of Space Flight Programs and approved by NASA

*W*hat's in a name? Plenty. This list of names given to the command modules and the lunar landing modules during the Apollo missions reflects history, mystery, and mythology in such choices as Columbia (Jules Verne named his capsule the Columbiad), the Odyssey of Greek myth, and Aquarius, in which age the journeys took place.

Apollo 11
Columbia (Command Module)
Eagle (Lunar Module)

Apollo 12
Yankee Clipper (Command Module)
Intrepid (Lunar Module)

Apollo 13
Odyssey (Command Module)
Aquarius (Lunar Module)

Apollo 14
Kitty Hawk (Command Module)
Antares (Lunar Module)

Apollo 15
Endeavour (Command Module)
Falcon (Lunar Module)

Apollo 16
Casper (Command Module)
Orion (Lunar Module)

Apollo 17
America (Command Module)
Challenger (Lunar Module)

The fact that twelve men from earth have walked on the moon can only invite comparison with the other magical figures of twelve: the twelve signs in the heavenly zodiac, and of course the twelve apostles. Here are the Lunar Twelve, in order of their appearance.

Neil Armstrong	*Edgar D. Mitchell*
Edwin Aldrin	*David R. Scott*
Charles Conrad, Jr.	*John W. Young*
Alan L. Bean	*Charles M. Duke, Jr.*
James A. Lovell, Jr.	*Eugene A. Cernan*
Fred W. Haise, Jr.	*Harrison H. Schmitt*
Alan B. Shephard, Jr.	

Administrator T. Keith Glennan in July 1960. Whatever their knowledge of mythology, the namers and approvers saw in Apollo his qualities of light and truth, the archer whose aim and reach was as precise as they wanted their own to be.

Yet the more veiled and mysterious nature of Luna lurked behind even this naming, since, as scholars and serious students of Greek mythology have pointed out, the god Apollo's earliest realms were those of prophecy, divination, and trance—all aspects of a lunar deity and an indication of Apollo's earlier life as a moon god. So, consciously or not, the naming of the Apollo missions may have struck at a deeper hidden mythological truth. At the same time it elevated not just American but world culture to new levels of scientific, historical, and psychological awareness.

◉ *Journeys to the Moon*

As for the journey of Apollo 11, it is a mistake to regard this mission as a one-in-itself kind of mythical-technical adventure. The Apollo 11 moon landing and moon walk were part of a much larger journey. The full Apollo program included ten missions, excluding the tragic fire in which the Apollo 1 crew lost their lives on the ground. Each mission was designed to test and prove the eventual success of a lunar landing, and to develop scientific experiments that would expand our knowledge about the earth, the moon, and the universe. Apollo 7 and 9 orbited the earth. Apollo 8 and 10 orbited the moon. The Apollo 13 landing, aborted because of an explosion on board, went to the moon and returned. Apollo 11, 12, 14, 15, 16, and 17 landed and returned. According to various sources, the full cost of the Apollo program ranged between $20 and $80 billion. During the Apollo missions, more than 33,000 photographs were taken. Twelve astronauts have walked on the moon, a number that has had its own kind of symbolism since the beginning of time.

Was this really the first true journey to the moon? Some people did not think so. Describing what they thought to be another kind of "moon hoax" (the last one had been in 1853), skeptics challenged the reality of the Apollo 11 landing, insisting that the entire drama had been staged in television studios.

While the Apollo astronauts may have been the first humans to actually visit and walk on the moon, they were certainly not the first ones to attempt to travel there—humans have always found many different ways to travel. The literary record is full of the fascination with pilgrimages to the moon. Perhaps two of the most famous are *From the Earth to the Moon* and *Around the Moon*, both by Jules Verne. Among the earliest is a work known as the *Voyage to the Globe of the Moon* by Lucian, a Greek satirist of the second century. According to science fiction critic Roger Green, Lucian's first journey shows an understanding of the moon as a heavenly body distinct from the earth, and not simply as the symbolic chariot of the goddess Selene traveling across the sky. Lucian might have had a model for his interplanetary travel guide, a work called *Of the Wonderful Things Beyond Thule* by Antonius Diogenes. The work no longer survives, but knowledge of it indicates that its author also wrote of a journey to the moon. Lucian's main character, named Menippus, undertakes his journey by learning from the mistakes of Icarus, whose artificial wings were held together by wax and melted in the heat of the sun. Instead, Menippus took one wing from an eagle and another from a vulture. He described a view of earth that, except for the use of the language of the time, could have come from the NASA chronicles: ". . . at first, me thought I saw a very little kind of earth, far less than the Moon; and thereupon stooping down, could not yet find where such Mountains were, or such a Sea. . . . At the last, the glittering of the Ocean by the Sun beams shining upon it, made me conjecture it was the Earth I saw. . . ."

Lucian wrote a second moon travel story, which was more of a romance than the first and was written in the form of a dialogue, a literary form popular at the time. The second story has an element that later appeared in the Domingo Gonsales (the pseudonym of Francis Godwin) voyage and in *The Adventures of Baron Von Munchausen*, namely that the original journey in a ship is interrupted by a whirlwind which carries the ship to the moon.

The Man in the Moone by Dr. Francis Godwin, published under the pseudonym Domingo Gonsales, was first published in 1638. It was followed by Cyrano de Bergerac's contribution, *Worlds of the Sun and Moon*, first published in 1657, in which Cyrano listed seven ways to travel to the moon. Aphra Behn's contribution, *The Emperor of the Moon: A Farce* appeared in 1687. In addition to writing of castaways on earth islands, Daniel Defoe also penned *The Consolidator, or Memoires of Sundry Transactions from the World in the Moon* (1705). A title with a more familiar ring to it was *The Adventures of Baron von Munchausen* (1785) by Rudolph E. Raspe. It included, among other earthly expeditions, a visit to the moon. It might be familiar because the story was the basis of a recent movie, "The Adventures of Baron von Munchausen," starring some of the former Monty Python comedy team members. The American writer Edgar Allan Poe, best known for his Gothic horror tales, also took one of his characters on a moon journey via balloon in *The Unparalleled Adventures of One Hans Pfaall*.

In another kind of record, some people believe that the cave paintings of early tribal cultures may reflect a desire to travel to the moon. It is fairly well known by scholars that among Siberian shamans a ritual trip to the moon was taken through the medium of trance. Siberian tribes felt a special kinship to the moon; the shaman traveled to the moon to intercede on behalf of the people, to ask for a good hunt, for prosperity, for luck. A spirit figure called a *tunghak* dwelt in the moon, and was believed to be responsible for the appearance of the animals and the success of the hunt. The figure of the tunghak, most often depicted as a male but sometimes also as a female, appears on a number of masks used for the shaman's ritual passage.

A practice related to trance is meditation, the internal journey long recognized by ancient cultures and particularly used in many Eastern religions and philosophical systems. Its origin is

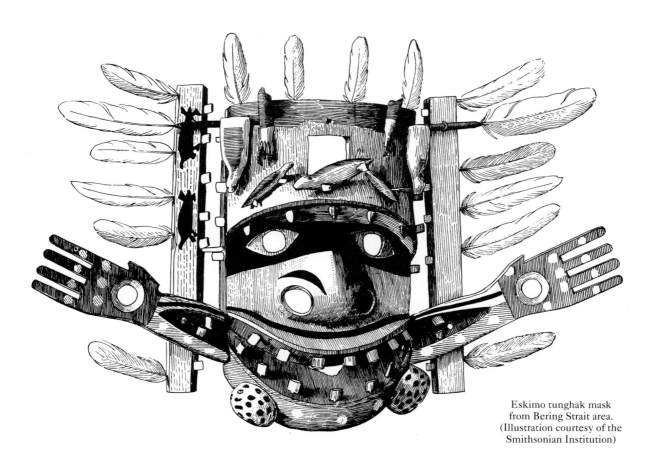

Eskimo tunghak mask
from Bering Strait area.
(Illustration courtesy of the
Smithsonian Institution)

LUNAR TRIVIA

*I*n zero gravity, the human body tends to stretch. Astronaut Charlie Duke grew about an inch and a half during the Apollo 16 flight.

● There is no up or down in space.

● The top speed record set by a Lunar rover on the moon was 11 m.p.h. (Apollo 16, Duke and Young).

● The largest moon rock brought back by the Apollo 16 mission, weighing 213 lbs. and nicknamed "Big Muley," was made of melted breccia caused by a meteor hitting the lunar surface.

● The Apollo 16 mission collected soil that had never been exposed to sunlight.

● In honor of the twenty-fifth anniversary of the Air Force, Charlie Duke left a special medallion on the moon. There were only two struck. The other is on display at Wright-Patterson Air Force Base in Ohio.

● Charlie Duke left a picture of his family, including his wife, two sons, and the family dog Booster, on the moon. The family signed the photo and included thumbprints. Booster left a pawprint.

● Technology from the Apollo space program has benefitted the development of satellites, medical technology, information management, manufacturing techniques. About 400,000 people were employed during Apollo's tenure.

● While orbiting the moon, Apollo 8 crew members read from the book of Genesis. The Apollo 11 crew chose Psalm number 8.

● Neil Armstrong carried pieces of the cloth wing and the propeller of the Wright Brothers' airplane on the Apollo 11 mission.

● An Apollo 1 patch was left on the moon by the Apollo 11 crew in remembrance of Gus Grissom, Ed White, and Roger Chaffee. Memorial medals were also left behind for Soviet cosmonauts Yuri Gugarin and Vladimir Komarov, along with a message on disc made by 73 world leaders.

● The Apollo 15 crew left another memorial plaque on the moon, one that contained the names of astronauts and cosmonauts who had died.

● The longest long-distance phone call was made between President Nixon and the Apollo 11 astronauts.

● In a poll conducted at the time, it was said that 15 percent of the American people believed the moonwalk by Apollo 11 astronauts to be a hoax.

quite old. Mircea Eliade quoted an Indian meditation related to the moon: "Conceiving in his own heart the moon's orb as developed from the primal sound . . . evolved from the letter 'A,' let him visualize therein a beautiful blue lotus, within its filaments the moon's unspotted orb, and thereon the yellow seed-syllable Tam . . ." That the moon and the moon journey are still a source of focus for meditation is obvious, as even a quick scan of the section on meditative records, tapes, or discs in most contemporary music stores reveals.

◎ *Moon Rocks*

To return to the Apollo 11 moon landing, the world held its breath as the Eagle touched down. Even at that remote point, the scientists and engineers still were not certain, in spite of lunar probes that preceded the landing, whether the lunar module would sink into the surface. In spite of the technical and scientific knowledge, no one was sure what life forms might be found on the moon. Although there did not seem to be any little green men or women, as the three-week quarantine endured by the returning voyagers at the Lunar Receiving Laboratory at the Johnson Space Center in Houston indicated, there was concern that microbial life forms might exist on the moon that might be harmful to human or other earth life. No life forms were found: no one-eyed creatures with pointy heads, no carnivorous Lunarians, no Selenites with an appetite for either frightening or destroying humans and their spaceships; not even any bacterial or virus-like sprites that might wreak havoc on earth. Likewise, there were no rabbits, no trees, and no beautiful maidens. There were no elephants, no toads or frogs or dogs, no coyotes or wolves, no seven evil spirits. There were no works of art and no mysterious cities made of crystal or other strange stones.

Though the surface was described at one time as like that of a beach after the tide has gone out, and from the lunar module it looked as if it could be wet, there was no water to be found.

The stones that were there, however, seemed strange enough. They proved to be of utter fascination to the space program and to the watchers back on earth. What were they made of?

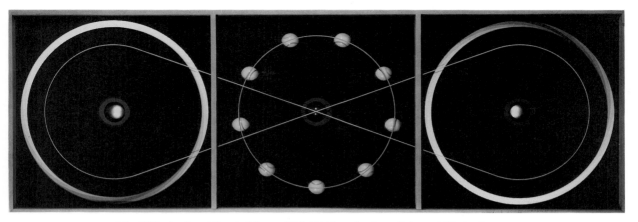

John Willenbecher, *Allegorical System: Night* (1965), collection of John and Kimiko Powers.

How old were they? Were they dangerous? Did they contain life forms? They have been the subject of great reverence here on earth, assuming a kind of talismanic magic about them, even now, as revealed in a special feature report to the *Denver Post* in June 1991 entitled "Outta This World." Among the other wonders of moon rocks, the author compiled a list of twenty-nine museums in North America that display moon rocks in their collections.

Stones have long served as special symbols for humans, and have long been associated with the moon. As mentioned in Chapter Seven, the shrine known as Ka'aba at Mecca contains a black stone named after the moon goddess Al-Uazza. Believed to actually be a meteorite, the long history of honor accorded this stone reminds us of the link humans have found between the moon and stones from the earliest times. Esther Harding described how the first lunar deities, moon goddesses, were revered in the form of sacred stones.

The spirit of the moon god Sin was once said to inhabit the stone of the moon. Among other Semitic peoples, Briffault found that every god in the pantheon was represented by a stone and could be called upon by setting up a stone. Traditional tribes of Australia and British Columbia performed a rite in which rock crystals, symbols of the moon, were swallowed. This was similar to the practice of eating moon-palm bark and partaking of a special moon drink by other tribal groups in Polynesia, as noted by Briffault, significant because it represented taking in the power and essence of the moon. Likewise, he

found that on an island in the Torres Straits near Australia, two sacred stones represented the moon. In the Banks Islands, "Round Head," the mother of the moon-god Qat, was represented as a stone. In a place called Lepers' Island, the sacred stones all belonged to the Polynesian moon-god Tagaro.

One stone in particular that has had a special link to the moon, now perhaps slightly displaced by the actual moon rocks, is a feldspar known as moonstone. The Hindus believed that it was made of condensed moon rays, so shimmering and translucent a quality does moonstone have. Apparently Pope Leo X (1475–1521) owned a moonstone, which popular legend of the time claimed waxed and waned with the phases of the real moon. Another popular belief claimed that moonstones are good for a simple way of foretelling the future: the prescription is to hold one in your mouth, although the formula does not elaborate on what to do next. The moonstone is supposed to aid romance, as it is said to bring out tenderness in lovers. It brings its own kind of luck and health, and was said to cure epilepsy, a disease thought to be caused by the moon. It is thought to help decrease nervousness and have a cooling effect on a hot temperament. If that is not enough, it can also help trees bear fruit. One contemporary jeweler does not recommend it for rings because it is too soft and shatters easily, but it does make a nice shimmering pendant.

To say that this sort of veneration is dead can be easily disputed, considering the kind of reverent affection many people worldwide came to have for the lunar samples. These samples quickly entered the world vocabulary as "moon rocks," those actual pieces of Luna herself. Incorporated into the exhibit of the National Air and Space Museum which opened in Washington, D.C. in 1976 was a display of moon rocks which could be touched. By 1983 they had become worn and felt nearly as soft as soapstone. Part of the United States exhibit for the World Fair held in Osaka, Japan, in 1970 included samples of moon rocks. According to *Science*

Scientists and Technicians window at the Washington National Cathedral.

Rodney Windfield, artist; Alex Martin, photographer. Photograph courtesy of the Washington National Cathedral and Alex Martin

News magazine, people waited in line for as long as twelve hours just to get a glimpse of these treasures. One Japanese woman, reflecting her country's long and ancient reverence for the moon, had traveled hundreds of miles just to "be in the presence of the moon." One of the contemporary gestures of reverence extended to the moon rocks is inclusion in a house of worship: a moon rock is poised at the center of a stained glass window depicting space travel in the National Cathedral in Washington, D.C.

What are moon rocks like? Samples collected by the Apollo astronauts have been analyzed and described as basalt and dumite, an olivine from within the crust of the moon, believed to be approximately 4.5 billion (4500 million) years old. The rocks were found solidified in breccias, older rocks that have been melded together, that are 4.25 to 3.9 billion years old. Scientists report that moon rocks are three-fifths as heavy as earth rocks. According to astronaut James Irwin, even though the surface of the moon does not vary much in color, the moon rocks he helped collect had different colored crystals in them: black, white, green, yellow, and red. Microscopic examinations and crosscut sections of moon rocks reveal rich colors that look like modern abstract art.

To continue on the subject of moon rocks for a moment, all of the rock samples returned to earth were fascinating because of what they taught us about the moon and our own planet as well. Of particular interest was one called the Genesis Rock, which has been analyzed and dated at 4.15 billion years old, older than anything on earth. The Genesis Rock was important because by its discovery and examination many scientific theories, which incidentally often sound more fanciful than anything mythology could conjure, stood or fell. For example, a nineteenth-century man, Baron A. d'Espiard de Cologne, believed that layers of the moon had fallen off and landed on earth. Crazy? Well, not entirely, considering the report from astronomer-philosopher Chet Raymo, who says that moon rocks have been falling to earth for some time. When asteroids strike the moon, pieces of lunar material, though perhaps not in huge layers, are shot into space. Some land on earth, many in

Antarctica, where geologists have found and gathered them. Donald K. Wilson, in *Our Mysterious Spaceship Moon* (1975), theorized that the moon was built by extraterrestrial visitors. In spite of Apollo observations to the contrary, aliens are at work building all sorts of things on the moon, according to George H. Leonard, writing in *Someone Else is on Our Moon* (1976).

Though the lunar missions discovered that the color of the moon ranged from white to grey to yellowish-beige, color has long been an important part of the moon's mystique. As one astronomer has perceptively described it, we are probably lucky to have made such strides in astronomy and space science, since even with the advantage of powerful telescopes and other equipment, viewing the cosmos through the earth's atmosphere is like watching from underwater. The atmospheric conditions on earth have caused us to see color on the moon with both naked-eye and mechanical observation. The colors most obviously and most often associated with the moon are black, white, silver, and blue. These colors can be seen easily from earth in different conditions, and describe the phases of the moon. The Apollo astronauts found that the contrast of white and black on the moon was intense as it was nowhere else. Without an atmosphere, there is nothing to break the light waves into other colors. Thus, there is no variation in either the shadows or the light. And the sky overhead is constantly dark.

The color silver and the metallic element have both been linked to the moon from earliest times. The artists of Ephesus made silver shrines for Artemis, and only silver was used in relation to moon worship in Peru. Silver has always been described as a cool, calming metal, viewed in comparison with a "cool" moon (which, with a midnight temperature of −250° Fahrenheit, was a good comparison). Contemporary jewelry still reflects this association between silver and a lunar theme.

An interesting scientific phenomenon that has to do with the color of planetary bodies is known as albedo, which is the ratio of light a planetary body like the moon reflects to the amount of light it receives. Anne Kent Rush described a project undertaken by amateur

astronomers in the 1960s called "Operation Moonblink." These dedicated lunar observers watched the surface of the moon for changes of color that have been observed from time to time, and were thought perhaps to indicate volcanic activity of the moon's core. The scientific name for "moonblink" is Transient Lunar Phenomena (TLP) or Lunar Transient Phenomena (LTP). Amateur as well as professional observers still pay attention to any color changes on the moon's surface—in fact both the Association of Lunar and Planetary Observers and the Lunar Section of the British Astronomical Association have networks of observers for LTP/TLP. Though it would seem that powerful telescopes are needed to observe this kind of change on the lunar surface, a ques-

Harry Alden Grout, founder of the Denver Adult Astronomical Society, with telescope he rebuilt and mounted, ca. 1927.

Photograph courtesy of John K. Grout

THE MOON AS A SYMBOL

CRESCENT

- **Amulets:** Across all cultures, across all times, the crescent moon has been used as an amulet for either protection or adornment. It still figures prominently in contemporary jewelry design. The moon priestesses of Dahomey in West Africa wore a badge made of a single white shell and two black beads. In Greece the Minoan moon goddess wore a necklace with twelve lunar disks.

- **Italy:** In the south, women can be found wearing crescent shaped pendants in honor of the "Moon Mother," whose help they seek during labor. An old tradition found among Roman women was to insert silver crescents into one's shoes, as a measure to insure fertility.

- **United States** *(South):* African-Americans wore an amulet called a "birth head" that included beads and a lunar crescent, worn to help ease the pain of childbirth.

- **Cities:** During the siege of Byzantium, Alexander the Great instructed workmen to dig out the walls of the city. The work was "uncovered" by the crescent moon and the plan failed. The Byzantines erected a statue to Diana, and the crescent moon became a state symbol. Another story tells how the sultan Othman had a vision in which he saw the state like a waxing crescent moon. The crescent is still a symbol in Turkey.

- **Flags:** The flags of fourteen nations use a moon symbol:
  Algeria
  Brazil: The white band represents the path of the moon across the sky.
  Comoros: A crescent, with four stars.
  Iran
  Korea: The symbol of yin and yang; red half for the sun, blue half for the moon.
  Laos
  Lesotho
  Libya
  Malaysia
  Maldives
  Mauritania
  Mongolia: The sun and moon are the mythical father and mother of the Mongols.
  Nepal: The only flag that is not a rectangle, it consists of two triangular penants, now sewn together; the moon symbol stands for the king's family.
  Pakistan: A crescent symbolizes progress.
  Singapore: The new moon symbolizes a new country.
  Tunisia: An anonymous Spanish friar reported seeing a Tunisian flag in the 1400s which was white and contained a black crescent moon and star. This motif may be as old as Phoenician culture or it may have been adapted from other flags on the north coast of Africa.
  Turkey: The crescent and moon is a familiar symbol of Islam. The crescent with a star was a symbol for the old cities of Byzantium (now Istanbul) and Harran (special city of the moon god Sin). Around 1900 B.C.E., it was used as a symbol for Egypt.
  United States: The flag of South Carolina has a moon in its field.

- **Gems:** Pearls are symbolic of the moon because of their color, their association with the sea, and the changes that cause them to grow. Emeralds symbolize the waxing moon; cat's-eye stones represent the waning moon.

- **India:** The god Shiva wears the crest of the moon on his forehead. He is often associated with Soma, who is known as "the crest of the moon."

- **Islam:** The crescent motif, known as Hilal, is prominent in Muslim art. The crescent is the symbol of Islam, in which a star, representing Venus, and thus the close connection between Venus and the moon, is enclosed.

- **Japan:** The crescent moon and full moon were often used in Japanese family crests.

- **Music:** In the history of Chinese music, no note or tone is without its special relationship to the universe. The note E flat or D sharp is the moon's own sound.

- **Native American** *(Oglalla Sioux):* The Oglalla Sioux holy man Black Elk reported that a rawhide crescent had to be made for the Sun Dance. It represented the moon, and thus a person as well as all things that wax and wane, live and die.

  The crescent and star motif is found consistently throughout North America among Native Americans; it appears in rock art, headdresses, costumes, pottery, etc. There are some who believe that a particular motif in pottery found among several southwestern tribes may actually be a way of recording the supernova explosion of 1054.

- **Outhouse:** The familiar sign of the crescent moon on outhouses had a special significance. Originally it marked those who could afford two outhouses, and designated the privy reserved for the women. It later became general practice to carve the crescent on all outhouses.

- **Red Crescent:** Equivalent to the familiar Red Cross, the Red Crescent is a symbol of emergency medical relief in Eastern countries.

- **Richard I:** The badge of King Richard I of England bore a crescent moon on it.

- **Shrines:** The crescent moon was often found as a symbol at religious shrines from ancient worship sites to modern ones. A crescent moon design was found in the sanctuary at Mycenae.

- **Turkey:** The crescent moon is used in the Turkish flag, along with a star named "Ai Tarek," which could represent Venus, Saturn, or the Pleiades.

DESIGNS

Athene: The full moon can be found on Athene's shield. Her priestesses had lunar halos.

Israel: The moon is found as a symbol for Israel in Talmudic literature and in Hebrew tradition.

Lightning: Lightning represents light the way the moon does, and is also associated with water.

Native American: The Apache leader Cochise had the face of the moon on his shields.

Pearl: Its association to the ocean is obvious, but more than that the pearl is produced secretly and mysteriously inside the dark recesses of the oyster. It grows as the waxing moon grows. Its soft lustrous color resembles that of the moon. As an amulet, it would have once been like wearing a part of the moon itself, not just a pretty ornament.

INSECTS

Africa: In the Congo, a symbol of both the moon and its constant renewal could be found in the beetle. This association is similar to the Egyptian symbol of the scarab beetle, also linked to the moon. It deposits its eggs in a ball of dung that lies buried in the earth for twenty-eight days, the approximate time of the lunar month. The scarab is symbolized by Khephera, a beetle whose wings are stretched out in the shape of a lunar crescent.

OBJECTS

General: The cup, cauldron, ship, coffin, comb, fan, mirror—anything that reflects or can change shape or appearance has often been linked to the moon.

Babylonia: Symbols of the three most important Babylonian gods were inscribed on "boundary stones" that marked property agreements. Among them was the crescent of the moon god Sin.

Greece: Greek coins indicate an association of the olive with the moon; olive trees were associated with the moon from early times.

WALKING ON THE MOON

Belief existed in Kenya that floods would trouble the earth if humans walked on the moon.

tion from the realm of folklore can be asked of science: in describing the change of color of the cassia trees that grew on the moon, from white to red, could the ancient Chinese and Japanese, who watched the moon carefully, have been describing "moonblink"? Or other atmospheric phenomena? The TLP observers have reported the same rusty red color that the Chinese observers described.

The color of the moon has also had a considerable link to weather prediction. Though modern meteorologists more frequently provide the rising and setting time of the moon on nightly television weather reports (the "Weather Channel" now includes phases of the moon), as well as information about such events as lunar eclipses, the full moon, and a blue moon or two, it is still possible to find people who predict weather according to the moon's appearance. Perhaps you know someone who does this—a family member, a friend, or a neighbor; perhaps you do it yourself. These practices are quite old, and can still be found in daily (or nightly) use by gardeners, farmers, hunters, fishers, and others who for one reason or another need to pay attention to natural events. Like those today, the older beliefs varied from place to place and climate to climate, and were often contradictory. For example, a proverb translated from Latin says: "Red moon doth blow; white moon neither rain nor snow." A similar proverb found among the Zuni adds:

The moon, her face if red be,
Of water speaks she.

Yet another saying of uncertain origin says that "a pale moon doth rain," not a red one. The poet Virgil, an acclaimed naturalist who was thought to know a great deal about the Celts, had definite beliefs about the red moon. "If on her cheeks you see the maiden's blush," he wrote, "the ruddy moon foreshows that winds will rush." A nautical proverb having more to do with the wind than with color claims that "the moon swallows the wind." In Chile, the red moon symbolized death. In China, a too-red or too-pale moon was an ill omen in general.

In Wales, the color of the moon could likewise predict the turn of the weather, as William Cynwal, a sixteenth-century Welsh poet, recorded:

Observe, ye swain, where'er ye stand,
The pale-blue moon will drench the land;
Cynthia red portends much wind;
When fair, the weather fair you'll find.

According to Trevelyan, the Welsh also believed that a full red moon would be followed by a wind storm, but if a moon was red when it rose, it was a sign of hot weather.

Theories about the moon have always existed. Whether about its creation or its formation, both the scientific community and the ordinary person have offered their suggestions for discussion, and, just as often, been subject to ridicule. Though it is sometimes difficult to separate a serious scientific theory from a fanciful one, they are all most interesting in their own right. Johannes Kepler believed the craters of the moon could have been built by intelligent life. The controversial cosmogonist Immanuel Velikovsy thought the moon had been captured by the earth's gravitational pull. In *Mystery of the Ancients* (1974), the authors described how the Maya spent some time on the moon.

Noted astronomer Patrick Moore reported a suggestion by a man named P. Norcott that, in order to reduce the earthquakes caused by tidal effects for which the moon is responsible, the moon should be cut in half and used to buffer the earth on either side. More recently, in April 1991 the *Wall Street Journal* featured a front-page article about one of the theories of Alexander Abian, a mathematics professor at Iowa State University. One of his solutions for the bad weather he believes the moon causes on earth has a science-fiction quality about it: blow the moon up. When contacted, however, Abian stated that he was quoted out of context, and that this idea was simply one of several hypothetical possibilities.

Though the Apollo space program served to further the knowledge about the moon, particularly its composition and age, like any scientific effort it engendered as many questions as it answered. There are still many contemporary theories about the creation and formation of the

"First Look" by Mitchell Jamieson. (Courtesy of NASA)

```
I have not yet b            egun to relate y
ou dumb moon ston           es asleep in your
future dust and wh          at could be said o
f your stubborn sle         ep silent little wo
rlds that one should        listen dream contemp
late your dusty destr       uction and yet I awai
t that which will be said of the cold passion
ate moment that precedes all rupture the noth
ing yet ex    pressed of the softn    ess of you
r name and    carelessness of yo      ur form an
d the mean    inglessness of y        our dark t
exture you    ▌MOONSTONES▐            or simplex
stones pie      ces of falle          n moon sto
len and wh       ich remain           to be expl
ained touc        hed deco            mposed sil
ently in t         he lig             ht since o
ne must in          vent              you create
your silen           ce               now before
one can th                            ink you sp
eak you to                            awake your
dust out o                            f its dumb
moon exist                            ence now t
hat you ha                            ve reached
the terres                            tial space
```

```
          oooooo
        o        o
        o        o
        o        o
        o        o
        o        o
        o        o
          oooooo

          oooooo
        o        o
        o        o
        o        o
        o        o
        o        o
        o        o
          oooooo

        n          n
        nn         n
        n n        n
        n   n      n
        n     n    n
        n       n n
        n         nn
```

"Lune Concrete"
by Raymond Federman

164

moon. In what sounds as much like a mythological discussion as a scientific one, geologist and NASA scientist Farouk El-Baz, in an essay celebrating the tenth anniversary of Apollo 11, summarized the current theories by describing the moon as: the earth's wife, having been captured by the earth's orbit in much the way comets have been; the earth's daughter, having been created directly from the earth (and unintentionally giving a whole new possibility to the reading of the myth of Athena, springing full-blown from the head of her father Zeus); and finally as the earth's sister, having been created at the same time from the same material as the earth. If it is not surprising to find a male scientist describing the moon in clear gender-defined, some might even argue sexist, terms, it is certainly interesting to consider his scientific description in the light of lunar mythology and legend. The sister-theory seems consistent scientifically, and mythologically, to some extent. In astronomical terms, because of the closeness of time in which they were both created, and due to the similar composition of materials of each, the earth and the moon are considered to be a double planet system rather than a planet and its satellite. And, considering that earth is well known in a feminine form as "Mother Earth," and that the moon is slightly older, it makes sense that they would be considered sisters.

There have been many other scientific theories about the moon, including a belief that it might be hollow. The philosopher Gurdjieff proposed a Luna theory, one that in the age of James Lovelock's Gaia Theory, does not seem at all far-fetched, though slightly more sinister. He espoused that the moon was a living creature, an unborn planet that drew its psychic nourishment, vampire-fashion, from earth and from humans. Grant mentions one theory regarding the size of the moon and held by the Flat Earth Society, still in existence in England, namely that the moon is only about thirty-two miles across. Perhaps they got the idea from George Bernard Shaw, who believed that the moon was only thirty-seven miles from earth.

As for creation theories, mythology has had to work hard to keep up with science in that regard. Several lunar creation myths were discussed in the first chapter. The summary of the relationship theories of Dr. El-Baz given above could use some slight expansion. One of the most prevalent theories, enduring until the time of the moon landing, was put forth by Sir George Darwin in 1880. He believed that the moon had been torn from the earth's side in a kind of Caesarian birth, and that the moon was created from the floor of the Pacific Ocean. Examination of the Genesis Rock disproved this theory, since the lunar samples were older than that part of the earth. Another no less seemingly fantastic idea came from Hans Bellamy, who proposed the "World Ice Theory." Bellamy's theory was developed primarily to explain the deluge; he believed that it was caused by a distant relative of the current moon, which he believed to be just one of many. According to Bellamy, the ancestor moon descended perilously close to the earth, causing a huge tide at the equator, eventually shattering and sending enough ice to earth to cause the Ice Age.

Are these theories settled or put to rest yet? No. Though the enormous discoveries of the Apollo missions have provided the knowledge that the moon and the earth are more likely "sisters," having been created at nearly the same time, science in this way is sometimes no more precise than mythology, legends, folklore, or customs. Science may even have much to gain by a more serious examination of these myths, legends, and stories from folklore and customs.

For example, one moon myth from ancient Japan recently found its way into the history of modern space flight. One version of the myth was collected by F. Hadland Davis. This myth reveals the identity of a moon goddess who came to earth, and tells of a special feathered robe that has come to symbolize twentieth-century space efforts. In some ways the story resembles that of the Chinese moon goddess Chang-Ho mentioned in Chapter Two. (China and Japan share many common mythological elements about the moon.) Davis' story tells of the Lady Kaguya, who was found by an ordinary bamboo cutter busy at his day's work. A tiny gleaming sprite at first, it took only a short time for Kaguya to develop into a full-grown, lovely, ethereal maiden.

Bamboo against the moon.

Because of her great shining beauty, as intense as that of the moon itself, five young men sought to marry her. She set each of them a task: bring me the begging bowl of the Buddha she told one; I want a tree-branch that bears jewels, she commanded another; from the third she sought a robe made from the fur of a flame-proof rat; from the fourth, a jewel in the head of a dragon; and she implored the fifth to bring her a special cowrie shell. None of her suitors was equal to his task; they even tried to trick her by duplicating the objects she requested. But she was the moon maiden—she had special ways of shining her knowing light on hidden things, and would not be deceived. Even the power of a great Mikado (or ruler) of whom she was fond could not win her. She began to spend her time gazing homeward at the moon. As she did, she grew full of grief. No one could comfort her, not even her loving step-father, the bamboo cutter. When he asked her what was wrong, she told him what he had suspected all along. She was not of the earth, but of the moon. During the eighth month (still the time of moon festival celebrations in contemporary China, Japan, and other Asian countries), she told him her own people, the moonfolk, would come to take her back home. Nothing could stop them, not the Mikado's power, not

even her own grief, or her father's. The moon-folk arrived as predicted, bringing with them the special elixir of life which they offered to her, to cleanse her of the heaviness of earthly life before her return home. They also carried with them a beautiful magical feathered robe for her to wear in her ascent to the moon. She was sad to leave the father who had been so kind to her, yet she recognized that the time for her visit to earth was ended. Time had come for her to return to her own people. She returned to the moon. In her honor a ceremony was later offered from the slopes of Mount Fuji.

The feathered robe, white and shining as the moon and known as Hagoromo, shows up again in Japanese mythology. A fisherman finds it hanging on the branch of a tree, and claims it for his own, in spite of the appearance of an extraordinary maiden who tells him that it belongs to her. When she requests its return, at first he refuses. Later he promises to return it if she will dance for him. She agrees, but insists on wearing the robe. She dances and sings about her faraway homeland, the moon, and describes its beautiful palace where thirty lords rule, a poetic description of the calendar: fifteen dressed in shining white as the moon grows full, fifteen in deepest black as the moon declines.

The latest mention of the feathered robe Hagoromo came not centuries ago as we might expect, but only a short time ago, in January 1990. During that month the nation of Japan launched a satellite named Hiten into orbit. Its primary job is to collect micrometeoroid dust for study on earth, to determine how much of the material moves through space and how fast, and what effects it might have. Its secondary task was to release a smaller satellite into orbit during March 1990. That smaller satellite is called Hagoromo, the Feathered Robe. Hagoromo's task is simple: it is a gift from the Japanese people to Luna, thus providing the moon with its own moon. The Feathered Robe has taken flight once again. Hagoromo, the Moon's moon, symbolizes a blend of science and mythology.

By using the symbol of the feathered robe that the moon goddess wore in her return to her lunar home, the Japanese people have expressed a reverence for the moon that might seem to have existed only in the past. Yet while doing the research and writing of this book it was easy to see that the symbolism and reverence for the moon is still alive everywhere in cultures throughout the world. There are many who brand such attention and respect as superstition. Certainly that element is present. Humans have always been superstitious. Even the Apollo astronauts carried their good luck charms to and from the moon, and even left some there. In reading and studying and talking to people from all walks of life, in different parts of the country and even the world, we find that the moon is still a part of human culture and belief.

Lovers still haunt the pathways that the full moon follows. A young couple give their child the nickname "Luna" in honor of the blue moon during which she was conceived. A local newspaper reporter wonders in print if the blue moon had anything to do with the hometown college team's unexpected win. A neighbor remembers how, when she was young, her first-generation Italian mother insisted on cutting her hair only at new moon. One man's grandfather not only still gardens by the phases of the moon, but directed his farming operation by it as well. Another man prunes his trees faithfully at the full moon in February. Pregnant women he knows avoid full moonlight, or protect themselves with a silver amulet if they cannot. A psychic turns over the Moon Card in her Tarot deck and interprets its qualities for her client. Eager astronomers, amateur as well as professional, hope eagerly for a chance to sight the new moon at less than the current record of approximately thirteen and one-half hours old. Scholars investigate ancient sites thought to be solar, to see if in fact they were lunar. A woman collects moon decorations. Another one keeps albums full of Man-in-the-Moon postcards. Merchants still feature "Moonlight Madness" sales.

Special parties are organized around lunar eclipses and full moons. The modern practitioners of Wicca set and celebrate rituals by the moon. Laurens van der Post documented the mood changes his captors went through as the moon changed, and learned how to protect his men from the cruelty of the dark side in a Japanese POW camp during World War II,

when beatings and mistreatment of prisoners increased at the dark of the moon (or new moon). A town in Indiana holds a special celebration at the time of the Hunter's Moon in October. Women whose menstrual cycles are not regulated artificially know the power of the moon's pull; at least one husband who believes nothing else about the moon believes this. So do people who live on the coasts of all the countries in the world. This may seem like a laundry list of only anecdotal information, but these items would seem to indicate that in spite of the Apollo missions to the moon and back, in spite of what is known scientifically and factually about the moon, the world's romance with Luna is not dead. A piece of artwork is no less beautiful, no less moving or enchanting, for knowing that it is made of wood, canvas, oils, and pigments. Is the moon then less beautiful, less mysterious and mythical for knowing that it is made of rock that is 4.6 billion years old?

If active awareness of the moon is not a part of everyday life—and certainly it is not, judging by the sheer numbers of people who cannot even describe the moon's phase on a given day—it still remains an important symbol in human existence. A symbol, whether from mythology, legend, folklore, or simple story, is one thing that represents another: a character, an event, a place, even a quality that may give some deeper instruction than the immediate description may reveal. The symbol does not necessarily have to be a moral lesson, but it has the ability to inform on more than one level. Thus a story with three women characters, one a maiden, one a mother, and one an old woman, becomes a moon tale. A monster eating the moon and spitting it out tells the story of an eclipse. The footprint of a god's shoe becomes the track of the moon across the sky. A symbol takes one step back behind the obvious. It may instruct, enlighten, motivate, or simply exist on some deeper level in the awareness of life.

The moon became a special symbol for John F. Kennedy, and subsequently for the American people. He believed that America in the 1960s needed a new and different symbol. For Kennedy, the Apollo missions and the idea of sending an American to the moon and bringing him back safely (for it was clear at that point that the voyager would be a man) was a symbol as much as it was a scientific goal.

In retrospect, in 1977 English writer Anthony R. Michaelis listed the Apollo program among the top ten human technological feats. In 1969 the United States was still engaged in the Cold War with the Soviet Union. The lagging technological and scientific ability of the United States had been clearly demonstrated by the surprise launch of the Soviet Sputnik in 1957. The nation needed a boost to renew its confidence. Wouldn't it be strange, in a most curious sort of way, if Kennedy's declaration in 1961 about committing the country's resources to a moon landing by the end of the decade—and its fulfillment—were to become what he is most remembered for?

Even if that were to happen, his decision was clearly political, and not one born from the romance of the astro-knight-explorer. Veteran moon voyage observer Richard Lewis critically discussed what he called "the Kennedy effect" in 1968, claiming that the focus on the Apollo lunar missions would determine the direction of the space program until the end of the century. He did not view this possibility in a positive light, but believed it "mutilated" the rest of the program, creating what we might call today a "frozen paradigm." Other writers and observers, in addition to the realities of accomplishments and spinoffs generated by the Apollo missions, have disproved Lewis' statement. Very little of the technology developed for Apollo was useful for other programs, per se. While that lack of usefulness can be considered wasteful on one hand, it has been useful if it led to the development of other technology in other areas—medicine and industry, to name only two.

One unexpected and unintended result of that effect appears to be an awareness increasing every day about the fragility and vulnerability of the life of planet earth and all the life it contains. It remains to be seen whether or not the environmental movement is just one of the many world "causes," or whether it will continue to spread and deepen of its own accord. If consciousness and conscientiousness about the environment continue to take root, it will be a movement that will mean a change in attitude

toward culture, history, and even life itself. Some say that is happening now. If it continues to occur on a larger scale, it will be necessary to look back to those moments spent hovering far above the earth on the still mythical, still mysterious Luna, which allowed the view from above and outside ourselves that paradoxically began the internal search to "act locally, think globally" for the answers to life on earth. Those views will be momentous in the psychological and spiritual development of human beings, as momentous as the recognition in early human history of the moon as a symbol of a deity, of life, death, regeneration; as significant as the time taken to carve what may be the earliest lunar notations on stone and bone.

◐ *What's Next?*

Predictions about the human encounter with the moon have existed since people started writing about the moon. In the 1950s and 1960s, with a lunar landing imminent, predictions flourished. One noted technical writer foresaw that a lunar base would be established by 1990, and that the moon would be a source for mining and for manufacturing processes that require vacuum packing or a sterile environment.

Eminent astronomer Patrick Moore, writing in 1976, was more accurate. He predicted that the United States would begin plans to establish a lunar base, and that new expeditions would take place after 1989 or 1990. During 1990 the U.S. House of Representatives cut funding that would have helped establish such a base for the combined Moon-Mars exploration effort. A ninety-day study was developed which involved NASA and several agencies working together to gather ideas from both the scientific community and the general public about how to proceed with a lunar base or an international space station. Groups involved included the National Space Council, the American Institute of Aeronautics and Astronautics, The Rand Corporation, and the Aerospace Industries Association. Former Apollo astronaut Thomas P. Stafford, who is also a retired Lieutenant General in the Air Force, heads the Lunar/Mars Synthesis Group. Release of the results was imminent as of March 1991.

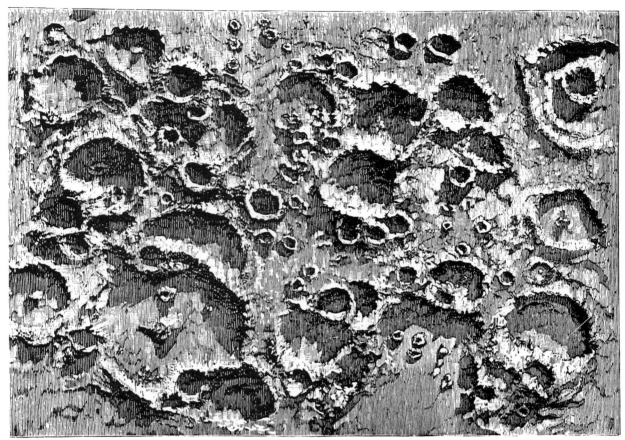

Lunar terrain.

As for the mining and manufacturing, at least one American company has an eye out for glass production from lunar surface material that would surpass the current process. Such an idea is bound to elicit a response from members of the environmental movement. After the Exxon Valdez incident and other similar ecologic disasters, environmental groups and the public may not be in a mood to consider mining the moon a worthy cause. And, on a side note that is both ironic and full of humor straight from the "dark side," it seems the savings and loan scandal tried to reach for the moon, too. The October 1990 issue of *Harper's Magazine* quoted from a 1984 application to the government to establish an S&L on the moon, to serve the economic needs of lunar base employees. The man who proposed it was facing fourteen counts of fraud at the time the *Harper's* article was published.

The next steps toward the moon and the rest of the solar system will be challenging and exciting. The exploration so far has provided many benefits. We know more about our origins and our place in the solar system. Some of the advances in computer technology can be traced to the Apollo missions. Advances in flameproof clothing have helped to protect firefighters, children, and hospital patients. The development of new materials has found a commercial application. New devices for handicapped people have been created. Like any human endeavor, there are many positive steps forward—and just as many reservations. The lunar missions allowed us to find new solutions to old problems, and come face to face with new ones. Yet again, our eyes will turn toward the moon in a new and different way.

Moon Music

Come to the Moon
East of the Moon, West of the Stars
East of the Sun and West of the Moon
Everyone's Gone to the Moon
Fly Me to the Moon
In the Valley of the Moon
Islands of the Moon (Clannad)
It's Only a Paper Moon
The Moon is Walking (Ladysmith Black
    Mambazo)
Moon Rock (Dory Previn)
The Moon Was Yellow
Moonbeams
Moonraker
The Moonshine Steer
Moonwalker (Michael Jackson)
Mountains Beyond the Moon
Once in a Blue Moon
Pale Moon
Racing with the Moon
Reaching for the Moon
Ridin' on the Moon
The Rising of the Moon
Rocket Man (Elton John)
Roll on, Silver Moon
Silver Moon
Sister Moon
Stardust on the Moon
Telstar
Walking on the Moon (Sting)
Young Moon (Malvina Reynolds)

Here is a list of contemporary albums that are available on either cassette tape or compact disc. Check your favorite music store for more information.

Abacus Moon
Apollo, by Brian Eno
Between Two Worlds, by Patrick O'Hearn
Conferring with the Moon, by William
    Ackerman
Desert Moon Song, by Dean Evenson
Down to the Moon, by Andreas Vollenweider
Eclipse, by Hamza el Din
Full Moon Story, by Kitaro
Half Moon Bay, by William Aura
Into the Night, by Exchange
Moon at Dawn, by Tamako Sunazaki
Moon Pastels
Moon Run, by Trapezoid
Moon Water, by Hime Kami
Moonwind, by Wave Star
Moving Moments, by Luna
Sea of Tranquility, by Phil Coulter
Song of Isis, by Anne Williams (recorded in the
    temples of Egypt)
The Standing Stones of Callanish, by Jon Mark
Tear of the Moon, by Coyote Oldman

CHAPTER NOTES
Page numbers are in parentheses at the end of each citation.

The complete wording when Armstrong set foot on the moon was: "O.K. I'm going to step off the LM now. That's a small step for a man, a giant leap for mankind. The surface is fine and powdery. I can kick it up loosely with my toe. The dust adheres in fine layers like powdered charcoal." (150)

Laurens van der Post tells the story of !kaggen's shoe in *A Mantis Carol* (Island Press: Washington, D.C., 1975). (151)

Much of the Apollo 11 landing information is contained in NASA documents. Another good source was John M. Mansfield's *Man on the Moon* (Stein and Day: New York, 1969). (150–154)

Some of the most interesting information about the Apollo program can be found in the anniversary publication edited by Richard P. Hallion and Tom D. Crouch (*Apollo: Ten Years Since Tranquility Base*. National Air and Space Museum. Smithsonian Institution: Washington, D.C., 1979). (153–154)

Green, Roger Lancelyn. *Into Other Worlds: Space-Flight in Fiction, from Lucian to Lewis*. Arno Press. New York. 1975. (154)

The shaman's journey is discussed in William Fitzhugh and Aron Crowell's *Crossroads of Continents: Cultures of Siberia and Alaska* (Smithsonian Institution: Washington, D.C., 1988). (155)

Eliade, Mircea. "The Moon and Its Mystique" in *Patterns in Comparative Religion*. Sheed & Ward. London and New York. 1958. (156)

Lovett, Richard A. "Outta this World." *Denver Post*. June 2, 1991. (157).

Information on Apollo trivia can be found in *History of NASA* by E. John and Nancy DeWaard (Exeter Books: New York, 1984). (156)

Harding, Esther M. *Woman's Mysteries Ancient and Modern*. New York. Harper & Row. 1976. (157)

Briffault, Robert. *The Mothers*. Abrdg. Gordon Rattray Taylor. George Allen & Unwin Ltd. London. 1927. (157)

Eberhart, Jonathan. "From Earth to the Moon with Love." *Science News* 137:138-9+. March 3, 1990. (158)

Rush, Anne Kent. *Moon, Moon*. Random House. New York. 1976. (159)

Trevelyan, Marie. *Folk-lore and Folk-stories of Wales*. Norwood Editions. Darby, Pennsylvania. 1973. (162)

Raymo, Chet. *The Soul of the Night*. Prentice-Hall. Englewood Cliffs, New Jersey. 1985. (158)

Valente, Judith. "Hate Winter? Here's a Scientist's Answer: Blow Up the Moon." *Wall Street Journal*. April 22, 1991. p. 1. (162)

Grant, John. *A Directory of Discarded Ideas*. Ashgrove Press. Sevenoaks, Kent. 1981. (162)

El-Baz, Farouk. "Apollo and the Scientific Harvest," in *Apollo: Ten Years Since Tranquility Base*. Richard P. Hallion and Tom D. Crouch, editors. National Air and Space Museum. Smithsonian Institution. Washington, D.C. 1979. (165)

$\mathcal{V}$ITAL STATISTICS

- The moon is fourteen times smaller than the earth. Earthlight seen from the moon is fourteen times brighter than moonlight seen from the earth.

- The moon only has one-sixth the gravity of earth. If you weigh 160 pounds on earth, you'd weigh 10 pounds on the moon. The force of gravity on earth is 280,000 times stronger than the gravitational pull of the earth on the moon, but the moon has a powerful effect on the tides, even more than that of the sun.

- The mountains of the moon rise as high as 25,000 feet. The depth of some of the craters can extend to 10,000 feet below the crater walls.

- Astronomically speaking, the earth and moon are not a planet and its satellite, but a binary or double planet system. This is because they are so close together and because of the effect of the sun on both. And, as the Apollo missions revealed, they were created relatively close together in time.

E P I L O G U E

*D*uring the preparation of this book for publication, it became more and more obvious that moonlore is still a part of contemporary life. Everywhere I began to turn, it seemed, someone had a story to tell, a custom, or even a family tradition that concerned the moon. The focus of *Luna: Myth and Mystery* was to consider a broad perspective of the past in examining how people in different times throughout history have viewed the moon through myths, legends, folklore, poetry, customs, and, to some extent, their artwork. Wherever it was possible, contemporary beliefs and information were included to emphasize the change and "updating" of past practices and beliefs. The past inevitably leads to the present, whether the subject is rocket science or moonlore. I believe there is easily enough contemporary information to substantiate another book. If readers are interested in sharing information about such lore—whether it be in the realms of gardening, good luck, turning away bad luck, special celebrations (including special foods), special collections or memorabilia, special events, sayings, beliefs, stories, myths, or family customs associated with the moon, please write to me at the address below.

Kathleen Cain
c/o Johnson Books
1880 South 57th Court
Boulder, Colorado 80301

THE MOON

Age: 4.6+ billion years

Atmosphere: None

Brightness: reflects approximately 7–10% of sunlight that strikes it

Color: Yellowish; ink-black shadows

Composition: aluminum, anorthosites, basalts, calcium, ilmenite, olivine, plagioclases, pyroxenes, spinels, titanium

Crust (thickness): 36–62 miles (60–100 km)

Day: 14 earth days long

Density: 208.52 pounds/cubic foot (3.34 grams/cc)

Diameter: 2,160 mi. (3,378 km)

Distance from earth: approximately 238,857 miles; farthest 251,983 miles (405, 508 km.); nearest 225, 755 miles (363,300 km)

Eclipse: Approx. 1 hour, 45 minutes

Gravity: 1/6 that of earth; on the moon, a 160-pound person would weigh 10 pounds

Heat flow: 1/3 that of earth

Highest point: Mt. Huygens, +25,000 ft. (5.5 km) above the surface

Lowest point: 10,000 feet (3 km) below the surface

Magnetic field: Currently none

Mass: 1/80 that of earth

Month: (sidereal—sighted by fixed star) 27.3 days

Month: (synodical—phases) 29.53 earth days

Moonbeams: Light reaches earth in approximately 1.2 seconds

Night: 14 earth days long

Oldest rocks: 4–4.3 billion years old

Orbit: elliptical, angled at 5 degrees; approximately 30 times diameter of earth away; 27 days, 7 hours, 43 minutes, 17.6 seconds

Radius (mean): 1,080 miles (1,738 km)

Seasons: None

Surface area: 11,700,000 square miles (30,300,000 km); compare with Africa

Temperature at lunar noon: 212 degrees F (127C)

Temperature at lunar midnight: –250 degrees F. (–153C)

Tidal pull: causes tide to rise 1 yard

Velocity of day-night border at equator: 10 mph

Volume: 1/50 that of earth

Year: 354.36 days (354 days, 8 hours, 48 minutes, 36 seconds)

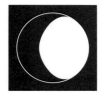 # BIBLIOGRAPHY

Adler, Margot. *Drawing Down the Moon*. Beacon Press. Boston. 1986.

Apollo Expeditions to the Moon. Ed. Edgar M. Cortright. Scientific and Technical Information Office. NASA. Government Printing Office. Washington, D. C. 1975.

Aveni, Anthony F. *Empires of Time*. Basic Books, Inc. New York. 1989.

———. *Skywatchers of Ancient Mexico*. University of Texas Press. Austin and London. 1980.

Baring-Gould. J. S. *Curious Myths of the Middle Ages*. Rivington's. London. 1888.

Beckwith, Martha. *Hawaiian Mythology*. University of Hawaii Press. Honolulu. 1970.

Begg, Ean. *The Cult of the Black Virgin*. Arkana. London. 1985.

Bellamy, Hans Schindler. *Moons, Myths and Man: A Reinterpretation*. University Microfilms International. Ann Arbor, Michigan. 1959.

Bierhorst, John. *The Mythology of South America*. William Morrow and Company, Inc. New York. 1988.

Branston, Brian. *The Lost Gods of England*. Oxford University Press. New York. 1974.

Brecher, Kenneth and Michael Feirtag. *Astronomy of the Ancients*. MIT Press. Cambridge, Massachusetts and London. 1979.

Brennan, Martin. *The Stars and the Stones/Ancient Astronomy in Ireland*. Thames and Hudson. London. 1983.

Briffault, Robert. *The Mothers*. Abrdg. Gordon Rattray Taylor. George Allen & Unwin Ltd. London. 1927.

Buckland, Ray. *Gypsy Dream Reading*. Llewellyn Publications. St. Paul., Minnesota. 1990.

Budge, E. A. Wallis. *The Egyptian Book of the Dead (The Papyrus of Ani)*. Dover. New York, 1967.

Bullchild, Percy. *The Sun Came Down/The History of the World as My Blackfeet Elders Told It*. Harper and Row. San Francisco. 1985.

Burriss, Eli Edward. *Taboo, Magic, Spirits*. Greenwood Press. Connecticut. repr. 1972 (1931).

Bushnaq, Inea. *Arab Folk Tales*. Pantheon Books. New York. 1986.

Carmichael, Alexander. *Celtic Invocations*. Vineyard Books. Noroton, Connecticut: 1972 (o.p.)

Carpenter, Frances. *Tales of a Chinese Grandmother*. Doubleday, Doran & Company. New York. 1937.

Carter, Dorothy Sharp. *The Enchanted Orchard*. Harcourt, Brace Jovanovich. New York. 1972.

Cavendish, Richard, ed. *Man, Myth & Magic/An Illustrated Encyclopedia of the Supernatural*. Marshall Cavendish Corporation. New York. 1970.

Cornell, James. *The First Stargazers: An Introduction to the Origins of Astronomy*. Charles Scribner's Sons. New York. 1961.

Cunliffe, Barry. *The Celtic World*. New York. McGraw-Hill. 1979.

Curtin, Jeremiah. *Creation Myths of Primitive America*. Little, Brown, and Company. Boston. 1903.

Davis, F. Hadland. *Myths and Legends of Japan*. Farrar & Rinehart. New York. n.d.

Dennys, N. B. *Folk-Lore of China*. Benjamin Blom, Inc. New York. 1972.

DeWaard, E. John and Nancy. *History of NASA*, Exeter Books. New York. 1984.

Dictionary of Superstitions. Eds. Ione Opie and Moira Tatem. Oxford University Press. Oxford. 1989.

Eberhard, Wolfram. *Studies in Chinese Folklore and Related Essays*. Indiana University. Bloomington. 1970.

Eberhart, Jonathan. "From Earth to the Moon with Love." *Science News* 137:138-9+. March 3, 1990.

Eliade, Mircea. "The Moon and Its Mystique" in *Patterns in Comparative Religion*. Sheed & Ward. London and New York. 1958.

The Encyclopedia of Religion. Ed. Mircea Eliade. MacMillan. New York. 1987.

Eyewitness to Space/Paintings and Drawings Related to the Apollo Mission to the Moon. Harry N. Abrams. New York. 1971.

Fitzhugh, Wm. and Aron Crowell. *Crossroads of Continents/Cultures of Siberia and Alaska*. Smithsonian Institution. Washington, D.C. 1988.

Fox, Robin Lane. *V. Sackville-West/The Illustrated Garden Book/A New Anthology*. Atheneum. New York. 1986.

Frazer, Sir James G. *The Golden Bough*. New York. Macmillan. 1922.

Frobenius, Leo. *African Genesis*. Stackpole Sons. New York. 1937.

Funk & Wagnalls Standard Dictionary of Folklore, Mythology & Legend. Ed. Maria Leach. Funk & Wagnalls. New York. 1972. FRCC:

Gadd, C. J. *History and Monuments of Ur*. Arno Press. New York. 1980.

Gimbutas, Marija. *The Goddesses and Gods of Old Europe*. University of California Press. Berkeley. 1982.

The Language of the Goddess. Harper & Row. San Francisco. 1989.

Graham, Francis. "A Hypothetical Ancient Telescope." *Selenology* (n.d.).

Grant, John. *A Directory of Discarded Ideas*. Ashgrove Press. Sevenoaks, Kent. 1981.

Graves, Robert. *The White Goddess*. Farrar, Straus and Giroux. New York. 1948.

Gray, Louis Herbert. *The Mythology of All Races*. Marshall Jones. Boston. 1916.

Green, Roger Lancelyn. *Into Other Worlds/Space-Flight in Fiction, from Lucian to Lewis*. Arno Press. New York. 1975.

Gyles, Anna Benson and Chole Sayer. *Of Gods and Men/The Heritage of Ancient Mexico*. Harper & Row. New York. 1980

Hadingham, Evan. *Early Man and the Cosmos*. Walker and Company. New York. 1984.

Hallion, Richard P. and Tom D. Crouch, eds. *Apollo/Ten Years Since Tranquility Base*. National Air and Space Museum. Smithsonian Institution. Washington, D.C. 1979.

Harding, M. Esther. *Woman's Mysteries Ancient and Modern*. New York. Harper & Row. 1976.

Hardwick, Charles. *Traditions, Superstitions, and Folk-Lore*. Arno Press. New York. 1980.

Harley, Rev. Timothy. *Moon Lore*. Swan Sonnenschein, Le Bas & Lowrey. London. 1885. Reissued by Singing Tree Press. Detroit. 1969.

Hemming, John. *Monuments of the Incas*. University of New Mexico Press. Albuquerque. 1990.

Herr, Rebecca. Interview regarding the timekeeping methods of the Maya. November 11, 1990.

Hesiod. Works and Days. Ed. by T. A. Sinclair. London. 1932.

Hillhouse, Laurens. *Man in Essence*. Hillhouse Publications. Los Altos, California. 1990.

Iglehart, Hallie. *Womanspirit: A Guide to Women's Wisdom*. New York. Harper & Row. 1983.

Illustrated Festivals of Japan. Japan Travel Bureau, Inc. 1985.

Inwards, Richard. *Weather Lore*. Rider and Company. London. 1950.

Irwin, James with William A. Emerson, Jr.. *To Rule the Night*. Ballantine Books. New York. 1973.

Jablow, Alta and Carl Withers. *The Man in the Moon/Sky Tales from Many Lands*. Holt, Rinehart and Winston. New York. 1969.

Jacobsen, Thorkild. *The Treasures of Darkness/A History of Mesopotamian Religion*. Yale University Press. New Haven. 1976.

Jastrow, Morris. *The Civilization of Babylonia and Assyria*. J. B. Lippincott Company. Philadelphia. 1915.

Katzeff, Paul. *Full Moons*. Citadel Press. Secaucus, New Jersey. 1981.

Kramer, Samuel Noah. *The Sumerians: Their History, Culture, and Character*. University of Chicago Press. Chicago. 1963.

Lattimore, Deborah Nourse. *Why There is No Arguing in Heaven*. Harper & Row. New York.

Leach, Maria. *The Beginning/Creation Myths around the World*. Funk & Wagnalls. New York. 1956.

Leland, Charles Godfrey. *Gypsy Sorcery and Fortune Telling*. University Books. New Hyde Park, New York. 1962.

Lewis, Tim. "Moonshine Bucks." *Nebraska Game & Fish*. 1987 (11):50-53. December 1987.

Lieber, Arnold L. *The Lunar Effect*. Anchor Press/Doubleday. Garden City, New York: 1978.

Lockyer, Norman. *The Dawn of Astronomy*. M.I.T. Press. Cambridge. 1964 (repr. 1894)

Long, Kim. *The Moon Book*. Johnson Books. Boulder. 1988.

Maas, Selve. *The Moon Painters and Other Estonian Folk Tales*. Viking Press. New York. 1971.

MacDonagh, Steve. *A Visitor's Guide to the Dingle Peninsula*. Brandon Press. Ireland. 1985.

Mackenzie, Donald A. *Myths of Babylonia and Assyria*. Bresham Publishing Company. London, 193?

MacKinnon, Douglas and Joseph Baldanza. *Footprints/The Twelve Men Who Walked on the Moon Reflect on Their Flights, Their Lives, and the Future*. Acropolis Books, Ltd. Washington, D. C. 1989.

McLean, Adam. *A Treatise on Angel Magic*. Phanes Press. Grand Rapids, Michigan. 1990.

Mansfield, John M. *Man on the Moon*. Stein and Day. New York. 1969.

Marie de France. *The Lais of Marie de France*. Trs. Robert Hanning & Joan Ferrante. Labyrinth Press. Durham, NC. 1978.

Marshack, Alexander. *The Roots of Civilization/ The Cognitive Beginnings of Man's First Art, Symbol and Notation*. McGraw-Hill. New York. 1972.

Masursky, Harold and Mary Strobell. "Memorials on the Moon." *Sky and Telescope*. 77 (3): 165. March 1989.

Mathews, John Joseph. *Talking to the Moon*. University of Oklahoma Press. Norman, Oklahoma. 1945.

Monaghan, Patricia. *The Book of Goddesses and Heroines*. E. P. Dutton. New York. 1981.

Montagu, Ashley and Edward Darling. *The Ignorance of Certainty*. Harper & Row. New York. 1970.

"The Moon and Murder." *Sky & Telescope*. 70:28. July 1985.

Moore, Patrick. Moon *Flight Atlas*. Rand McNally & Company. 1969.

The Next Fifty Years in Space. Taplinger Publishing Company. New York. 1976.

Morgan, Harry T. *Chinese Symbols and Superstitions*. P.D. and Ione Perkins. California. 1942. (republished by Gale Research Company. Book Tower, Detroit. 1972).

Neuenswander, Helen. "Vestiges of Early Maya Time Concepts in a Contemporary Maya (Cubulco Achi) Community: Implications for Epigraphy." Paper originally presented at 77th. Annual Meeting. American Anthropological Association, Los Angeles, California, November 14-18, 1978.

Tour of New Grange tumulus grave in County Meath, Ireland tape-recorded September 28, 1984 by the author.

Newall, Venetia. *An Egg at Easter: A Folklore Study*. Indiania University Presss. Bloomington. 1971.

Nilsson, Martin P. *Greek Folk Religion*. Harper & Brothers. New York. 1940.

O'Kelly, Michael J. *Early Ireland/An Introduction to Irish Prehistory*. Cambridge University Press. Cambridge. 1989.

The Oxford Annotated Bible with the Apocrypha. Revised Standard Version. Eds. Herbert G. May and Bruce M. Metzger. Oxford University Press. 1965.

Oxford English Dictionary. Oxford University Press. Oxford. 1988.

Pagels, Elaine. *The Gnostic Gospels*. Ballantine Books. New York. 1979.

Phillips, Robert. *Moonstruck/An Anthology of Lunar Poetry*. Vanguard Press. New York. 1974.

Piercy, Marge. *The Moon Is Always Female*. Alfred A. Knopf. New York. 1980.

Piggott, Juliet. *Japanese Mythology*. Paul Hamlyn. London. 1969.

Pugh, Ellen. *More Tales from the Welsh Hills*. Dodd, Mead & Company. New York. 1971.

Raymo, Chet. *The Soul of the Night*. Prentice-Hall. Englewood Cliffs, N. J. 1985.

Rush, Anne Kent. *Moon, Moon*. Random House. New York. 1976.

Sahagun, Fray Bernardino. *A History of Ancient Mexico*. The Rio Grande Pr. Glorieta, New Mexico. 1976.

Simon, Seymour. *The Moon*. Four Winds Press. New York. 1984.

Sjoo, Monica and Barbara Mor. *The Great Cosmic Mother/Rediscovering the Religion of the Earth*. Harper & Row. San Francisco. 1987.

Smith, George. *The Chaldean Account of Genesis*. new ed. rev. & corrected by A. H. Sayce. Scribner's. New York. 1880.

Spence, Lewis. *Myths & Legends of Babylonia & Assyria*. George G. Harrap & Company. London. 1916.

Stewart, Mary. *The Moon-Spinners*. M. S. Mill and William Morrow. New York. 1963.

Tedlock, Dennis, tr.. *Popol Vuh*. Simon and Schuster. New York. 1985.

Thom, Alexander. *Megalithic Lunar Observatories*. Clarendon Press. Oxford. 1971.

Thompson, J. Eric S. *Maya Hieroglyphic Writing*. University of Oklahoma Press. Norman. 1971.

Thompson, Stith. *Motif-Index of Folk Literature*. Indiana University Press. Bloomington. 1955-58.

Traven, B. *The Creation of the Sun and the Moon*. Hill and Wang. New York. 1968.

A Treasury of New England Folklore. Ed. B. A. Botkin. Crown Publications. New York. 1949.

Trevelyan, Marie. *Folk-lore and Folk-stories of Wales*. Norwood Editions. Darby, Pennsylvania. 1973.

Trigg, Elwood B. *Gypsy Demons and Divinities*. Citadel Press. Seacaucus, New Jersey. 1973.

Turnbull, Ian. "The Sun and Moon Are the Same Size." *One Earth*. (8 (3):16-18 Autumn 1988).

van der Post, Laurens. *A Mantis Carol*. Island Press. Washington, D. C. 1975.

The Night of the New Moon. Hogarth Press. London. 1970.

Verne, Jules. *From the Earth to the Moon and Round the Moon*. Dodd, Mead & Company. New York. 1962.

Walton, Evangeline. *The Prince of Annwn/The First Branch of the Mabinogion*. Ballantine Books. New York. 1974.

Webster, Hutton. *Rest Days/The Christian Sunday, the Jewish Sabbath and Their Historical and Anthropological Prototypes*. The Macmillan Company. New York. 1916. (republished by Gale Research Company. Detroit. 1968).

Willetts, R. F. *Cretan Cults and Festivals*. Greenwood Press. Connecticut. 1962.

Winter, Jeanette. *The Girl and the Moon Man*. Pantheon Books. New York. 1984.

Wolkstein, Diane and Samuel Noah Kramer. *Inanna Queen of Heaven and Earth*. Harper & Row. New York. 1983.

Word Origins and Their Romantic Stories. Funk & Wagnalls. New York. 1950.

Wylie, Francis E. *Tides and the Pull of the Moon*. The Stephen Green Press. Brattleboro, Vermont: 1979.

FURTHER READING

The current edition of *Books in Print* lists nearly two pages of titles beginning with the word "moon," proof that Luna is still a popular topic for literature of all kinds, including fiction, nonfiction, and poetry. This essay includes only selected titles. If you cannot find these books and publications through new or used bookstores, ask about interlibrary loan at your local library.

The moon has long figured in mystery, fantasy, science fiction, and what is currently called speculative fiction. One can hardly talk about the moon and science fiction without mentioning Jules Verne's *From the Earth to the Moon* and *Around the Moon*. These titles are still in print and available for purchase. And though the staff might have to drag this volume from the basement if you ask about it at the library, it's a worthwhile re-read. After the reality of the Apollo missions, it won't be the book you remember as a kid. Kids should still be able to find some wonder in it, too.

A later work by the well-known science fiction writer Robert Heinlein is *The Moon is a Harsh Mistress* (Ace Books, 1987). In this novel Heinlein envisioned the moon as a prison colony. Like Verne before him and others like Arthur C. Clarke who were his contemporaries, Heinlein also prefigured the Apollo missions.

The Moonstone by Wilkie Collins has endured over the years. Still available in several current editions, this story about a stolen gemstone has been described as both the first detective novel and the first novel with a detective in it. The English writer Mary Stewart has a mystery contribution entitled *Moon-spinners* (M. S. Mill and William Morrow, 1963). Set on a Greek island, this tale of mystery, murder, and intrigue was the source of a Disney movie starring an adolescent Haley Mills.

In *The Moon & Sixpence* (Penguin, 1977) Somerset Maugham's classic story told the story of the artist's life, based on the life of painter Paul Gauguin.

Other fantasy and mystery stories with a lunar theme reflect the belief held by some peoples of an ominous or even evil presence in the moon. "The Moon Pool" by A. Merritt, published in *The Ancient Mysteries Reader* (Doubleday and Company, Inc., 1975) tells a creepy story of the first order. First pub-

lished in 1918, the story was later developed into a novel, *The Conquest of the Moon Pool*, in which a scientist disturbs the lunar mysteries of a tribal people.

Similarly, Clark Ashton Smith's "An Offering to the Moon," also published in *The Ancient Mysteries Reader* tells how the ancient memory of a man drawn to search for the legendary continent of Mu pulls him into lunar worship of the past.

Going in a slightly different direction, "The Woman Who Loved the Moon," by Elizabeth A. Lynn, won a 1980 World Fantasy Award. Published in *The Woman Who Loved the Moon and Other Stories* (Berkley Books, 1981), this eerie short story tells of a woman warrior who falls under the spell of the moon, depicted as a powerful old woman.

The moon has been a favorite topic of those interested in the occult. A contribution from the master of the occult himself, Aleister Crowley, is *Moonchild* (Weiser, 1970) first published in 1917.

A blend of the mystical, the occult, and the fantastic is *The Mind Parasites* (Oneiric Press, 1967). Framed in a science fiction novel, phenomenologist and "existential realist" Colin Wilson tells a mostly gripping tale about the influence of a malevolent moon. The mystic and philosopher-teacher Gurdjieff had a theory that the moon took psychic energy from humans. Wilson explores such an idea, invoking archaeology, history, depth psychology, mysticism, and intrigue as helpmates. Not a book to read late at night alone at the dark of the moon!

For readers interested in a more scientific approach, many volumes present themselves. Kim Long's *The Moon Book: The Meaning of the Methodical Movements of the Magnificent, Mysterious Moon & Other Interesting Facts* (Johnson Books, 1988) is a favorite. This strictly no-nonsense guide to the moon is perfect for the student, the amateur astronomer you'd love to encourage, and for your own ordinary questions about the moon. Seymour Simon's *Moon* (Macmillan, 1984) is great way to introduce kids to the mysteries and science of the moon. Helpful for grown-ups, too, especially when it comes to explaining those tricky questions like "How come we only see one side of the moon's face?" For adults interested in the moon, most anything by astronomer Patrick Moore will fit the bill.

There are plenty of kids' books about the moon, from some of the basic Mother Goose nursery rhymes to the fairy tales of Hans Christian Andersen and the Grimm Brothers. A favorite that never seems to age even though it's growing older is Margaret Wise Brown's *Goodnight Moon* (Harper, 1947). Since reprinted, this may be the quintessential children's moon book. Still popular with young children whose parents once enjoyed it as a bedtime tale, the delightful and simple movement of moon and time continues to teach, entertain, and soothe.

In *The Nightgown of the Sullen Moon* (Harcourt, Brace, Jovanovich, 1983), poet Nancy Willard, explains an old story (the dark of the moon) to children for new times. Diane Wolkstein, the woman who retold the ancient story of the moon goddess Inanna for contemporary readers, also retells a beautiful children's story about a moon goddess who comes to the aid of a lonely farmer in *White Wave* (Thomas Y. Crowell, 1979). Not for children only!

For adult readers seriously interested in the mythology of the moon, the October 1983 issue of *Parabola* magazine (Vol. VIII, No. 4) will be of interest (back copies can be ordered). This issue was prepared for the mythically inclined, in *Parabola*'s inimitable style—always pushing the edge of the imagination, always esoteric, thoughtful, meditative—and always a bit "out there" without going over the edge. Don't miss "She Who Has No Light of Her Own."

Much contemporary scholarship on women has a special focus on the moon. Many titles have been mentioned throughout *Luna*, but one of special interest is Nor Hall's *The Moon & the Virgin: Reflections on the Archetypal Feminine* (Harper & Row, 1981). This could easily be the working woman's guide to the archetypal feminine—for women doing their own internal work, that is. It serves as a sourcebook to return to again and again. Other writers whose lunar reflections will interest readers include Starhawk, Hallie Austin Iglehart, Marija

Gimbutas, Elaine Pagels, Luisah Teish, and Charlene Spretnak, and a host of others.

And finally, though the moon has been the subject of more poetry than could probably fill several volumes, those poems are mostly scattered. A few small presses and magazines have published special lunar issues or lunar features, but one anthology specifically devoted to the moon is *Moonstruck: an Anthology of Lunar Poetry* (Vanguard Press, 1974. o.p.), edited by Robert Phillips. From Anonymous to Ann Sexton, from William Blake to Denise Levertov, this collection waxes and wanes like the moon itself, from the sparse to the lush in poems about our lovely orb. Marge Piercy's *The Moon is Always Female* (Knopf, 1980) will interest readers for whom the political and the poetic are inseparable. The title poem is a cry against violence toward women, taken up by one of America's leading poets. Nancy Willard's *Household Tales of Moon and Water* (Harcourt, Brace, Jovanovich, 1975) is a collection of poems, each of which contains a shimmering transformation. Like the moon itself, from the old, Willard creates the new; from the ordinary, the extraordinary. A final selection is *The Ink Dark Moon/Love Poems* by Ono no Komachie and Izumi Shikibu, Women of the Ancient Court of Japan, translated by Jane Hirshfield with Mariko Aratani. (Vintage Books, 1990). Possibly the loveliest collection of translations of Japanese women court poets to surface in years. The passion in these poems moves through the centuries undiminished.

These are only a few books that have some aspect of the moon as a theme. Interested readers will no doubt turn up dozens, even hundreds of others. Exploring books with a lunar theme could easily accommodate a lifetime's work! If your favorite author or publication has not been mentioned here, please do not take offense. Instead, write to me at Johnson Books and let me know what those favorites are! See also the "Publications" section of the Moon Products appendix.

G R O U P S

There are many groups and organizations—too many to list here—that encourage study of the solar system. Here are a few who have special activities related to the moon.

Amateur Astronomers, Inc.
George Chaplenko, Corresponding Secretary
Union County College
1033 Springfield Avenue
Cranford, NJ 07016
908-709-7520

Founded in 1949, AAI promotes interest in astronomy by way of educational activities, including courses, lectures, monthly star parties, and college scholarships. 400 members. Different aspects include: observation, education, research, sales, computer services, and library. Publishes monthly newsletter "Asterism" September-May. Access to the Sperry Observatory. 1991 lecture series included "Mapping the Moon." Offers weekly taped phone service, 908-276-STAR, for sky information. Membership open to anyone age 14 or older.

American Lunar Society
Francis Graham, Editor and President
P.O. Box 209
East Pittsburgh, PA 15112
412-829-2627

Founded in 1982 as the Pennsylvania Selenological Society, ALS is a small national organization interested in the study of and issues surrounding the moon: astronomy, exploration, resource exploitation, lunar mythology, history of lunar astronomy, and the moon in science fiction. Membership open to all. Publishes quarterly journal *Selenology*. Has volunteer projects: Transient Lunar Phenomena Network; Lunar Dome Survey (joint project with A.L.P.O.); Lunar Occultation Timings; Lunar Photometry and Eclipses. A lunar probe study underway with the Tripoli Rocketry Association; forming study groups for lunar colony problems and proposals. Annual business meeting.

Association of Lunar and Planetary Observers (A.L.P.O.)
John E. Westfall, Ph.D.
Executive Director
P.O. Box 16131
San Francisco, CA 94116
Harry D. Jamieson
A.L.P.O. Membership Secretary
P.O. Box 142
Heber Springs, AR 72543

Founded in 1947, ALPO welcomes amateur and professional astronomers. Goals are to stimulate, coordinate, and promote study of the sun, moon, planets, asteroids, meteors, and comets. Annual summer conference. Publishes a quarterly journal, "The Strolling Astronomer" and annual solar system ephemeris ($6.00). The Lunar Section is involved with "Luna Incognita" mapping project; Lunar Transient Phenomena observation; Lunar Selected Areas Program that systematically monitors variations of certain areas on the moon; observation of lunar eclipses; and the Lunar Dome Survey which examines lunar photographic atlases and charts.

International Astronomical Union (IAU)
(Union Astronomique Internationale)
c/o Dr. D. McNally
IAU General Secretary
98 bis, boulevard Arago
75014 Paris, France
33 (1) 43258358

The IAU's Working Group on Planetary System Nomenclature is responsible for naming objects in the Solar System, as well as conspicuous features of each. Deliberations of the Working Group can be found in IAU Transactions (A and B), available in the libraries of major astronomical observatories.

International Lunar Society (ILS)
Dr. James Q. Gant, Jr., Executive Secretary
4349 Klingle Street, N.W.
Washington, D.C. 20016
202-363-0744

Founded in 1955, ILS studies astronomical and astro-geological aspects of the moon. Conducts mapping, optical radar studies of the lunar surface. Statistics, biographical archives, research and evaluation of lunar phenomena. Quarterly publication, Lunar Newsletter.

International Occultation Timing Association
Craig and Terri McManus, Secretary-Treasurer
1177 Collins Avenue
Topeka, KS 66604-1524

This non-profit scientific research group of amateur and professional astronomers predict and observe "grazes" (eclipses or occultations) of stars by the moon. This helps accurately measure the profile of the lunar mountains. Data used by astronomers throughout the world.

AAAS/American Astronomical Society
Historical Astronomy division
Center for Archaeoastronomy
University of Maryland
P.O. Box X

In the Temple of the Moon

MOON PRODUCTS

 Artwork

Kirsten Gallery
5320 Roosevelt Way N.E.
Seattle, WA 98105
(206) 522-2011, 523-9216
Nicholas Kirsten Honshin, manager
Richard Kirsten-Daiensai, artist

This father and son team of artists draw on several mystical and esoteric traditions in their prints and drawings, but reveal a primarily Zen Buddhist approach (Richard is an ordained Zen Buddhist priest). The moon features in much of the work, and the Oracle Prints and Card series depicts it specifically: e.g., "Essence of Iris. Essence of Moon, Becoming One"; "In the Temple of the Moon"; "Offering to the Renewal of the Spring Moon"; and "Night Voyager with Guiding Moon." Widely distributed in bookshops and finer card stores. Lovely, joyful, evocative, meditative work.

The Moon Dance Gallery
233 Canyon Road
Santa Fe, NM 87501
(505)-982-3421
Luis and Linda Quintana Ouran, owners

To the owners of the Moon Dance Gallery, the moon as an artistic symbol offers a chance to reconnect with the earth, with the animals, with ourselves. Committed to local efforts, they feature the work of about 20 artists, including Native American artisans and the work of southwestern artist Diana Bryer. They describe the focus of the gallery as: mythological, ecological, shamanistic, and ceremonial. Linda Quintana Ouran encourages you to "walk in and have an experience."

 Calendars

Ancient Hawaiian Moon Calendar
Prince Kuhio Hawaiian Civic Club
P.O. Box 7132
Honolulu, HI 96821

This fascinating and attractive calendar preserves Hawaiian lunar calendar traditions and explains hunting and fishing practices developed according to the moon's phases. It lists the twenty-eight Hawaiian names of the phases of the moon, the names of the months, and offers practical advice for farming and fishing. ($6.00)

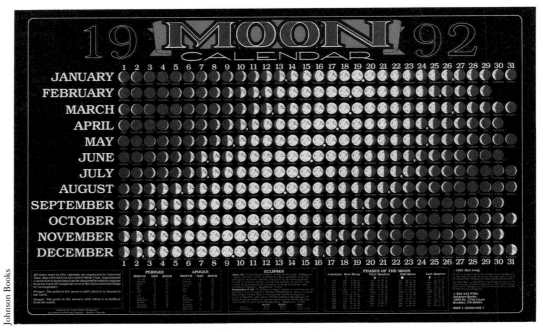

1992 Moon Calendar by Kim Long

"Month of Coll/Hazel" from the 1990 Lunar Calendar: Dedicated to the Goddess in Her Many Guises, Nancy FW Passmore, editor; leaf-rubbing by Joan Anderson.

The Celtic Calendar (annual)
c/o Celtic League
2973 Valentine Avenue
Bronx, NY 10458

Though not strictly a lunar calendar, this annual timetable, extends from November 1 (the beginning of the ancient Celtic new year at Samhain) to October 31. In art and narrative it honors the feasts, festivals, and prominent persons among the Celts, who did follow a lunar calendar. Stunning black and white line drawings (which are fun to color) illustrate each month and recall the heroines and heroes of Celtic myth. Approximate list price $6.00. New calendars available June 1. Back years available.

The Lunar Calendar
Luna Press
P.O. Box 511 Kenmore Station
Boston, MA 02215
(612) 427-9846

This lavishly illustrated calendar offers a delightful change in perception about the moon and the calendar. Instead of linear grids, thirteen lunations appear in spirals that mark one new moon to the next. It follows Robert Graves' interpretation of the Celtic tree alphabet for each time period. An added bonus is top-flight poetry, a bibliography, and a resource guide. You won't be able to throw it away at the end of the year! ($12.95)

"the lunarian" moon calendar
Cylla Bonneau
5375 Roswell Road
Atlanta, GA
1-800-741-2242

In another unique approach to design, "the lunarian" calendar descends gracefully and vertically along a wall space. At a glance, the twelve months of the year, denoted by the moon's phases for each day, appear. ($9.95)

Moon Calendar
Johnson Books
1880 South 57th Court
Boulder, CO 80301
(303) 443-1576

Illustrator and writer Kim Long designed this calendar in a moment of creative distraction, putting together several small moons he'd been using for pages in an almanac. The linear grid shows the phases of the moon for each day of the year and creates an artwork of its own, a breathtaking perception of Luna. It is a stunning annual wall poster (31½″ x 20½″). ($9.95)

Moon Calendar
Sharkstreams
1734 Fillmore St.
San Francisco, CA 94115

This gorgeous collection of color photographs includes the moon at different phases and from different scenic locations—the seaside, the mountainside, the plains. The picture for each month will set you dreaming and the black and white line drawings depicting the phases at the bottom of each page will keep you on track. ($10.00)

◖ *Catalogs*

The GAIA Bookstore & Catalogue Company
Mail Order and Bookstore
1400 Shattuck Avenue at Rose
Berkeley, CA 94709

"The spiritual dimension of life offers the greatest untapped reservoir of power and strength, clarity and imagination for facing the planetary challenges which surround us." In addition to a wide array of books on ecology, the spiritual life, and myth and ritual, choose from among the spirit moon rattles, moonstones, crescent moon earrings, and specially crafted pendants of the goddess drawing down the moon as a way to connect or reconnect with lunar wisdom.

Magickal Childe
35 W. 19th Street
New York, NY 10011

While not strictly a lunar lover's guide, this potpourri of (nearly overwhelming in its quantity) includes books on moonlore and lunar cycles, jewelry with a lunar theme, tarot cards, horoscopes, and almost any possible source on the sacred and the profane. Includes calendars, cure-alls, curse-alls, herbals, and much, much more!

◖ *Lunar Globes*

Replogle Globes, Inc.
2801-T S. 25th Avenue
Broadview, IL 60153-4589
312-343-0900

◖ *Miscellaneous*

Moon Magick Incense
P.O. Box 395
Littleton, CO 80120

◖ *Moon Stamps*

The U.S. Postal Service issued two commemorative stamps in honor of the lunar missions: a $2.40 stamp of the Apollo landing shows astronauts Armstrong and Aldrin raising a U. S. flag on the moon; and a 10¢ stamp features the Apollo-Soyuz mission. A T-shirt is also available of the lunar landing. Inquire at your local post office.

◖ *Moon Stickers*

There is no end of choices in stickers, and many of them contain moons. Hallmark has several that appeal to young children. One of the more interesting ones is a full moon, glow-in-the-dark variety which contains basic information about the moon and the Apollo landing on the back. Novelty gift stores and planetariums are great places to find them. Sold by California Pacific Designs/Box 2660/Alameda, CA 94501.

◐ *Moonlight Garden*

White Swan offers the makings of a moon garden in a can. Retails for around $18.00 and contains the perfect combination of seeds for a "white" or "moonlight" garden: Cosmos (Moonlight); Centaurea (Imperialis); Baby's Breath (Covent Garden); White Love in a Mist, Iberis (Empress); Sweet Rocket; Nicotiana (Grandiflora); Echinacea (White Swan); Moonflower, Satin Flower, Cleome (White Queen); Nemophila, Stock (Yellow Goddess); Dusky Yellow Wallflower; Night Scented Stock; Pink Evening Primrose; Cosmos (Pinkie); Dimorphoteca (Polar Star); Alyssum (Carpet of Snow); Alyssum (Oriental Night); Digitalis (Yellow Bells); Aquilegia (Crystal Star); Scabiosa (Silver Moon). Inquire at your favorite nursery or contact: White Swan Ltd./8030 SW Nimbus Avenue/Beaverton, OR 97005/1-800-233-7926 or (503) 641-4477. FAX (503) 641-4620.

Photograph courtesy of White Swan Ltd.

"Moonlight Garden" flower seed.

◑ *Perfume*

Luna. There may be no smell on the moon, but this fragrance makes up for it. If you think romance and the moon are dead, you've got another sniff coming. Lingers, and then it's gone. Half-moon orb for around $11.00. Prince Matchabelli, Inc. Greenwich, CT 06830.

◑ *Publications*

Llewellyn's Moon Sign Book and Lunar Planting Guide (annual)
Llewllyn Publications
P.O. Box 6483-458
St. Paul, MN 55164-0383

For anyone who wants to explore a little bit more about lunar rhythms, this annual publication should find a place on the shelf right beside the *Old Farmers Almanac*. Includes sections on how to plan more than 100 activities by the moon, including when to hunt, fish, get a haircut, or plant peas! Plenty of down-to-earth gardening and conservation advice as well. ($4.95)

Making a White Garden
Joan Clifton
Grove Weidenfeld
841 Broadway
New York, NY 10003-4793

Inspired by the original white garden of English writer Vita Sackville-West at Sissinghurst Castle in Kent, this book is written for the serious gardener who wants to do more than toss a handful of white varieties out in the garden. The orientation is to gardening conditions in Britain, but that should only encourage serious gardeners toward adapting plans and ideas for local situations. The contents are as thoughtfully laid out as a good garden plan, considering first the esthetics of a white garden, then moving on to considerations about where, when. how, and what to plant. Whether it's a small corner or a couple of acres, a conservatory or a patio, there are plenty of suggestions. Illustrated, includes plans, planting ideas, and a thorough reference guide to the plants themselves. A great gift (even for yourself). ($19.95)

Old Farmers Almanac
Dublin, NH 03444

You can't love the moon and not love the *Old Farmer's Almanac*. An American original since 1792, this faithful, humble friend is good company for lunar planting, hunting, fishing, tidekeeping, and other natural chores. Now featuring a special Western edition (many of us west of the Mississippi waited a long time for this). Available at grocery store and bookstores everywhere. Under $3.00; priceless for the sensible information it contains.

Sky & Telescope
P.O. Box 9111
Belmont, MA 02178-9111

Monthly magazine. Regular features and articles on the moon, including both research and lore. $2.95 newsstand price. $24.00 yr. subscription.

The Wildflower Press
P.O. Box 4757
Albuquerque, NM 87196-4757
Jeanne Shannon, Editor/Publisher

The moon figures prominently in these poetry chapbooks, poemcards and broadsides, all available from The Wildflower Press. *Moon of Changing Seasons*, a chapbook by Jeanne Shannon, published 1986; 24 pages, $6.95 postpaid. *Queen Anne's Lace*, a collection of poetry by Mary Rising Higgins, Karen McKinnon, Alexis Rotella, and Jeanne Shannon, published 1991; 96 pages, $9.50 postpaid. Poemcards (postcards containing one poem each) by Jeanne Shannon: "Along the Clinch River at Dungannon, Virginia," "Autumn," "Bach on an Autumn Evening, A Forest in New Mexico," "Cat," "July Nights," "Moon of Popping Trees," "Tell Me How the Stars Looked in That Country." Cards are 50¢ each.

Yellow Moon Press
Robert Smyth
P.O. Box 1316
Cambridge, MA 02238
617-628-7894

Now beginning its second decade, Yellow Moon Press specializes in publishing material from the oral tradition as it relates to storytelling, poetry, and music. It also distributes a wide selection of storytelling books and tapes from across the United States. A new release is an 80-minute audio cassette entitled *Gluskabe* by Joe Bruchac, an Adirondack native of Abenaki ancestry. Bruchac relates the stories, once told only from September to May, of Gluskabe's adventures with the Creator, the Wind Eagle, Skunk and the Day Eagle, Grandmother Woodchuck and the baby who is the only creature more powerful than Gluskabe. ($9.95)

 Toys

Museum of Fine Arts, Boston
Catalog Sales Department
P.O. Box 1044
Boston, MA 02120

Just two of the many listings in this catalog include a "Hey Diddle" puzzle for tots based on art prints from the 1800s, and bibs with a nursery rhyme theme, complete with that old familiar bovine going for the record leap over the lunar orb.

 Watches

Lunar watches vary in beauty, style, originality, and price. Take your pick from one based on a grandfather clock in the Museum of Fine Arts in Boston (see Toys for address).

$\mathcal{T}$HE EARTH

Age: 4.5 billion years
Atmosphere: carbon dioxide, nitrogen, oxygen, water vapor
Composition: aluminum, iron, silicon
Circumference (equatorial): 24,901.55 miles (40,075.16 km)
Crust (thickness): 20 miles thick
Day: 24 hours
Density (average): 344.7 pounds/cubic foot (5.52 gr/cc)
Diameter: 7,910 miles (12, 740 km)
Highest point: 29, 028 feet (8.8 km)— Mt. Everest
Highest temperature: 136.4F.
Lowest point: 8,326 feet below sea level
Lowest temperature: –128.6F.
Magnetic field: yes
Night: 12 hours
Oldest known rocks: 3.5 billion years
Orbit: elliptical, angled at 23½ degrees; around sun every 365.25 days
Radius: 3,963 miles at equator
Seasons: one to four
Surface area: 197 million square miles (510 million sq. km)
Velocity of day-night border at equator: 1000 mph

GLOSSARY

Albedo: From the Latin, meaning "whiteness"; the amount of light a celestial body reflects.

Astronomical Unit *(AU):* A distance used in outer space, equal to a little more than 92 million miles, the distance from the earth to the sun.

Bloody moon: The eclipse at full moon causes a reddish tinge around the edges of the moon that was once considered an ill omen by many cultures.

Blue moon: Now more commonly the name of the second full moon that appears within the same month, a phenomenon which occurs once every 2.72 years, but previously a full moon seen through the bluish smoke or haze of a forest fire or volcanic eruption.

Bumpdown: The Russian equivalent of a splashdown, since Russian space vehicles landed on earth instead of water.

Calendar Moon *(also Ecclesiastical Moon):* An imaginary moon used to establish the date of Easter. *(see also Mean Moon)*

Earthshine: Light reflected from the earth onto the moon; seen most clearly during the first quarter when the whole disc is visible and more poetically described as "the old holding the new moon in her arms."

Embolismic year: A lunar year of thirteen months.

Hippogypians: A name given to the horses that the Greek satirist Lucian saw on his early journey to the moon.

Honeymoon: The editors of The Oxford English Dictionary unearthed the first written reference to this word in 1564. It was used to refer to the initial time period just after marriage, when couples were full of sweetness toward one another. The analogy carried farther, as affection in marriage was often seen to wax full and sweet and then decline, as the moon itself does.

Interlunium: The time between moons *(dark of the moon).*

Liar's Moon: Name for a moon that appears through a misty, cloudy, hard-to-see-through sky.

Lunar caustic: A name for fused silver nitrate.

Lunares: A name given to those thought to be under the influence of the moon. *(see also Moon Man)*

Lunatic: A slang word for a mentally unstable person; from the Latin lunaticus, or "moon struck."

Lunette: Crescent-shaped objects or spaces; also the name for the glass boat once used in Druidic ceremonies.

Lunioloatry: Worship of the moon. *(see also Selenolatry)*

Lurain: The landscape of the moon (as terrain is the landscape of the earth). *(see also Moonscape)*

Mascons: Units of measure for the massive concentration of heavy material beneath the moon's surface, caused by the uneven gravity.

Mean Moon: Not a surly moon, but an astronomy term that refers to an imaginary moon travelling in a perfect elliptical orbit and completing its orbit in the same time that the real moon does.

Mezzaluna: A metal cooking implement used for chopping, shaped like a half moon and held in place by two wooden handles.

Mister Moonshine: A name sometimes given to the bridegroom among Southern Slavs.

Moon cakes: Special cakes filled with fruit and nuts made at certain times of the year for celebrations in honor of the moon; an ancient Chinese tradition still current, and one noted in Biblical times.

Moon calf: In England and other countries, it was once believed that the moon could impregnate women. The result was a misshapen fetus called a "moon calf." Moles were also once called moon-calves; Pliny described them as the offspring of women who had not had sexual intercourse.

Moon dogs *(sailor's term):* the lunar counterpart to sun dogs, visible when ice particles reflect moonlight in the atmosphere. *(see also Moonbow)*

Moon-glade: The trail of moonlight seen on water.

Moon guitar: Among Chinese musical instruments, another name for the guitar, as its round shape was thought to resemble the moon.

Moon-letters: Special runes that could be read only with the light of the moon behind them, and only during the phase of the moon in which they were written; created by the J.R.R. Tolkien and described in *The Hobbit.*

Moon Man: The figure of a man often found in almanacs that illustrated which signs of the zodiac influenced which parts of the human body. *(see also Lunares)*

Moon Rocks: The name given to rock samples brought back from the moon by the Apollo astronauts. They are exhibited at various places, including the National Air and Space Museum in Washington, D.C. A stained glass window depicting outer space at the National Cathedral in Washington, D.C. contains a moon rock at its center.

Moonblink: Temporary blindness caused by sleeping in the light of the full moon.

Moonblood: Another word for menstruation.

Moonbow: Also known as a lunar rainbow and a moon dog, caused by the reflection of light from ice particles in the atmosphere. *(see also Moon dogs)*

Mooncussers: In seventeenth-century England, the name given to thieves who waited on corners, pretending to help late-night travelers find their way on moonless nights. In New England on moonless nights, lanterns held up to light the way were sometimes mistaken for ships that other ships tried to follow, only to run aground. Looters who took advantage of the misfortune were called mooncussers. Still later, the name was applied to residents of Cape Cod, in a general way.

Moondown: The lunar equivalent of sundown.

Mooned: Formerly an expression used in Brittany to denote women who had been impregnated by the moon *(see also Moon Calf)* because they had exposed the lower halves of their bodies to moonlight. A fine example of how definitions change, since in the current vernacular this means to deliberately expose one's backsides as a way to shock or insult others.

Mooneye: A fish, formally known as Hyodonter gisus, informally called a lake or a river herring.

Moonquake: Tremors that occur below the lunar surface, thought to be triggered by activity within the lunar core; Apollo 11 astronauts placed moonquake monitors on the moon when they landed, later turned off due to lack of funding.

Moonscape: A name for the lunar surface. *(see also Lurain)*

Moonscaping: A new term used by nurseries, greenhouses, and seed companies to refer to the creation of a moonlight garden composed of plants that either bloom or can be seen at night and whose scents fill the night air.

Moonsee: Buckminster Fuller's term for the rising of the moon.

Moonshine: Illegal liquor made in secret under cover of night by moonshiners.

Moonstroke, moonstruck: Once meant to be pierced by the moon goddess Luna in the positive sense of being blessed or charmed; has now come to mean lovestruck, or even the harmful effect of the moon's rays on human beings or the suffering caused by those effects.

Moonraker: In nautical terms, a sail set above the sky sail, also known as a moonsail; an older meaning is a simpleton, possibly from the story of the man who tried to "rake" the moon's reflection out of the water.

Noctidiurnal cycle: The method of measuring time not from day to day, but from night to night; still evident in the Jewish Sabbath, which begins at sundown, or in the Christian Christmas Eve. Celtic peoples measured time beginning at night.

Operation Moonblink: The activities of a group of amateur astronomers observing any changes in color on the surface of the moon.

Paraselenae: "Mock moons" which are really ice crystals that appear as patches of colored light and give the appearance of more than one moon in the sky.

Selenites: The name Jules Verne gave to possible inhabitants of the moon.

Selenium: A nonmetallic chemical element that resembles sulfur and tellurium; its chemical resistance varies with exposure to light.

Selenography: In astronomy, mapping the moon's surface.

Selenolatry: Worship of the moon, after the Greek moon goddess Selene. *(see also Lunioloatry)*

Selenology: Astronomical study of the physical characteristics of the moon.

Shoot the Moon: An impossible task.

Synodic month: Also known as the lunar month; measured from new moon to new moon or full moon to full moon. Due to a "wobble" in the moon's orbit, the time can vary by as much as thirteen hours, though its mean value is 29 days, 12 hours, 44 minutes and 3 seconds.

Terminator: The dividing line between the lit and unlit sides of the moon.

Transient Lunar Phenomena: the observation of possible activity below the surface of the moon, such as a reddish mist above a crater; aka Lunar Transient Phenomena (LTP). *(see also Operation Moonblink)*

GYPSIES

*T*hough the Gypsies have a myth that tells of incest between the brother and sister, Sun and Moon, they also have another myth about the early time of the universe. The Sun King married a woman with golden hair. His brother the Moon King married a woman with silver hair. Between them all they had many children, so many in fact that the Sun King decided they would have to eat some of them to survive. When the Sun King did this, his wife was so horrified she died instantly. When the Moon King saw what happened, afraid his wife would die, too, he refused. When the Sun King found this out, he was furious and began to chase his brother and the remaining children around the world. He still chases them today, the moon and the stars, through the skies. The Gypsies had a reverence for the moon, because of his compassion for his wife and children. They also believed the moon brought special help to children and pregnant women.

The Gypsies had a third belief about the moon, one that sounds as if it might have been influenced by Christian and other traditions. In ancient times, God sent his son to Earth to live among the Gypsies and give them the word and the law of God. Eventually this son ascended into heaven as the moon. His name was Alako. This same Alako was a savior figure similar to Jesus and King Arthur, who came among the people and helped them in their time of need, one who would return again when the people needed him. He fought with the forces of evil, which can be seen when the moon is eclipsed, and he always emerged triumphant. Scholars tell us that Scandinavian Gypsies may have worshipped Alako in the form of small idols that have been found which show him bearing a sword in one hand and a quill in the other. Worshippers gathered during full moon to honor him. Newlyweds and children baptized during the previous year were his special wards. His power was said to be strongest during new moon. Though moon worship does not seem to be prevalent among contemporary Gypsies, a nickname for Gypsies in sixteenth-century England was "moonmen," in reference to their many night-time activities.

Among the Gypsies was also a cult devoted to the Black Virgin, known to them as Sara Kali, the Black Woman. The Black Virgin represents the dark of the moon.

INDEX